GRUMMAN F-14 TOMCAT

All models 1970–2006

COVER IMAGE: Grumman F-14A Tomcat.
(Mike Badrocke)

Dedication

This book is dedicated to the memory of Cdr Neil 'Waylon' Jennings, who lost his two-year battle with cancer on 14 February 2017. A highly skilled pilot with more than 900 carrier landings to his name, 'Waylon' completed combat deployments in both the F-14A (with VF-1 and VF-213) and the F/A-18A/C (with VFA-97 and VFA-147) and served as an adversary instructor with the Naval Fighter Weapons School, flying the A-4F and F-16N. He was one of the few Naval Aviators that the author has met who was not a fan of the Tomcat. This might have had something to do with the fact that the aircraft tried to kill him on two separate occasions. Nevertheless, 'Waylon' had a grudging respect for the 'Big Fighter'.

First published in May 2018
Reprinted in November 2018, December 2022 and August 2023

A catalogue record for this book is available from the British Library.

ISBN 978 1 78521 100 3

Library of Congress control no. 2017933529

Published by Haynes Group Limited,
Sparkford, Yeovil, Somerset BA22 7JJ, UK.
Tel: 01963 440635
Int. tel: +44 1963 440635
Website: www.haynes.com

Haynes North America Inc.,
2801 Townsgate Road, Suite 340, Thousand Oaks, CA 91361, USA.

Printed in Malaysia.

Senior Commissioning Editor: Jonathan Falconer
Copy editor: Michelle Tilling
Proof reader: Penny Housden
Indexer: Peter Nicholson
Page design: James Robertson

Acknowledgements

Although I am the author of this book, as always when producing a volume such as this one I have relied heavily on my myriad contacts – military and civilian – for both information and photographs to help tell the story of a Naval Aviation icon. As per usual, such a request has opened up the floodgates in respect to photographs, and it has been a real job to pare the selection down from several thousand images to the 300 seen in this book – many appearing in print for the first time. I would, therefore, like to thank Mark Aldrich at the Tailhook Association, Julia L. Blum at the Cradle of Aviation Museum, David F. Brown, Ted Carlson, Richard Cooper, Danny Coremans, Takashi Hashimoto, Erik Hildebrandt, Jennifer Jennings, Craig Kaston, Gert Kromhout, Tim Lent, Rick Llinares, Cdr Peter Mersky, US Navy Reserve (Ret.), Frank Mormillo, Paul Newman, Tyler Rogoway from *The Warzone*, Angelo Romano and Cdr Scott Timmester, US Navy, for the supply of photographs and documentation.

I have also received invaluable assistance with the text from the following individuals (many of them also supplied photographs), all of whom have vast knowledge of the Tomcat – Cdr Dave Baranek, US Navy (Ret.), Bill Barto, Cdr Pete Clayton, US Navy (Ret.), Capt Pat Cleary, US Navy (Ret.), Tom Cooper, Cdr Doug Denneny, US Navy (Ret.), AD1 (AW) Dan Dixon, US Navy (Ret.), Cdr Neil Jennings, US Navy (Ret.), Cdr William Lind, US Navy (Ret.), Lt Cdr Rick Morgan, US Navy (Ret.), Lt Cdr Paul Nickell, US Navy (Ret.), Lt Cdr Dave Parsons, US Navy (Ret.), Lindsay Peacock, Cdr Ted Ricciardella, US Navy, Cdr John Saccomando, US Navy, Lt Cdr Jon Schreiber, US Navy (Ret.), Capt Randy Stearns, US Navy (Ret.), William Stevens and Cdr Tom Twomey, US Navy (Ret.).

Finally, a hearty thank you to my editor, Jonathan Falconer, for his patience and understanding.

Tony Holmes
Sevenoaks, Kent
February 2018

GRUMMAN
F-14 TOMCAT

All models 1970–2006

Owners' Workshop Manual

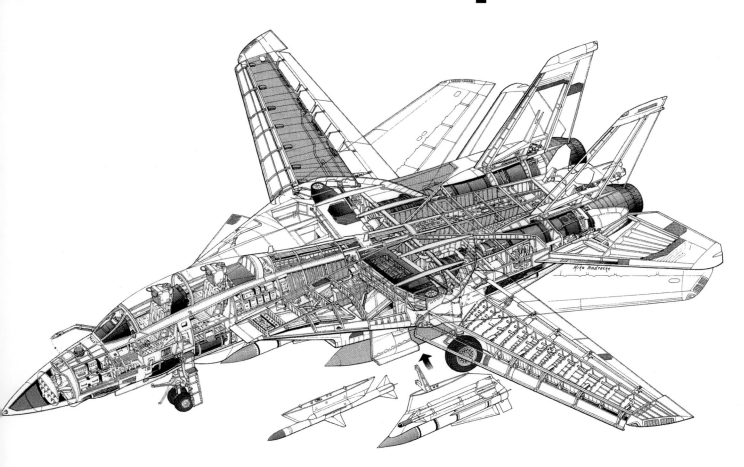

Insights into operating and maintaining the US Navy's legendary
variable-geometry carrier-based air superiority fighter

Tony Holmes

Contents

BELOW Missile-toting F-14A 'Lance 205' (BuNo 161293) tops off its tanks from a KC-135 tanker configured for probe and drogue refuelling in August 1990. *(US Navy)*

OPPOSITE With their centreline bomb pallets devoid of Laser Guided Bombs (LGBs), three VF-154 F-14As (led by 'Nite 101' BuNo 161276) overfly USS *Kitty Hawk* (CV-63) at dusk with their tailhooks extended prior to 'pitching out' of formation and entering the recovery pattern. Naval Aviators take great pride in tight formation flying when within visual distance of their carrier. *(US Navy)*

Introduction

BELOW Among the very first F-14 Tomcats the author saw, in late August 1981, were these three jets from VF-213 'Black Lions'. Part of CVW-11, VF-213 was embarked in USS *America* (CV-66) at the time, the carrier commencing its one and only visit to Fremantle, Western Australia, on 25 August following a 68-day stint on GONZO station. *(Bob Lawson via Tailhook)*

Thanks to the exploits of Lt Pete Mitchell and Lt Nick Bradshaw, better known as 'Maverick' and 'Goose' respectively, the mighty Grumman F-14 Tomcat is arguably the most famous American jet fighter of them all. Sure, the F-4 Phantom II was built in far greater numbers and saw considerably more combat, while the F-15 Eagle has achieved unrivalled success as an interceptor and, more recently, as a precision bomber in Strike Eagle form. However, the 'Big Fighter', as the Tomcat is known to those who either flew or maintained it, is an instantly recognisable icon of Naval Aviation from the Cold War period. The jet's profile was done no harm by having a starring role in Tony Scott's 1986 motion picture *Top Gun*, either.

I was fortunate enough to see myriad F-14s on a pretty regular basis throughout the 1980s, despite living almost 10,000 miles from Naval Air Station (NAS) Miramar, in San Diego – the closest US Navy fighter base to my hometown of Fremantle, Western Australia. Following the revolution in Iran in 1979, the US Navy increased its operational tempo in the region with the establishment of the Gulf of Oman Naval Zone of Operations (GONZO). Typically, a carrier battle group would be on station in this area at all times, with vessels from the Pacific and Atlantic fleets taking it in turns to spend weeks on end patrolling the warm waters of the Persian Gulf while on GONZO station. Once their commitment to operations in the Middle East had been completed, the carrier and its supporting ships would head home, often calling in to the port of Fremantle for a week-

LEFT *America* leads its battle group south through the Suez Canal on 6 May 1981, having left its homeport of Naval Station Norfolk, Virginia, three weeks earlier on a then unique Mediterranean/Indian Ocean deployment. Upon entering the Gulf of Suez, CV-66 became the first US Navy carrier to transit through the canal since USS *Intrepid* (CVS-11) had done so in June 1967. *(US Navy)*

long spell of rest and recreation (R&R).

Between July 1981 and September 1987, 12 Tomcat units visited Fremantle on board a handful of carriers during R&R visits, with some squadrons being seen on multiple occasions during this six-year period. I was also able to conduct three at-sea embarkations in 1986–87, spending several days at a time on board USS *Enterprise* (CVN-65), USS *Carl Vinson* (CVN-70) and USS *Ranger* (CV-61) documenting 'blue water' operations in the Indian Ocean and northern Pacific for my very first book, *Seventh Fleet Supercarriers* (Osprey Publishing, 1987). These were the first of more than 25 visits I would make to US Navy carriers under way across the globe over the next two decades.

Observing the carefully choreographed 'chaos' that is a fully functioning flight deck at first hand never fails to impress. During my brief spells at sea witnessing 'blue water' ops, the aircraft that always commanded the most attention when it entered the recovery pattern with a ripping 5g high-speed break overhead, or accelerated down the waist or bow catapults, shrouded in steam and trailing 15ft of flame from its afterburners, was the mighty Tomcat.

Among the first F-14s I saw up close were the jets of VF-213 'Black Lions' (and sister squadron VF-114 'Aardvarks') embarked in USS *America* (CV-66) as part of CVW-11 in August 1981. Five years later, when I was flown out to

CVN-65 from Perth during the 'Big E's' world cruise, the carrier was now CVW-11's floating home. I duly witnessed VF-213 (and VF-114) conducting cyclic operations following months

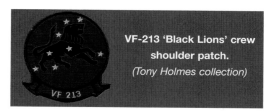

VF-213 'Black Lions' crew shoulder patch. *(Tony Holmes collection)*

USS *Enterprise* (CVN-65) ship's patch. *(Tony Holmes collection)*

CVW-11 crew patch. *(Tony Holmes collection)*

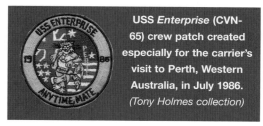

USS *Enterprise* (CVN-65) crew patch created especially for the carrier's visit to Perth, Western Australia, in July 1986. *(Tony Holmes collection)*

RIGHT F-14A BuNo 160920 was assigned to VF-213 when the unit next visited Western Australia in January 1983 on board the recently overhauled USS *Enterprise* (CVN-65). As with the squadron's previous deployment, VF-213 and the rest of CVW-11 had spent several months on GONZO station prior to heading home via Fremantle. *(Bob Lawson via Tailhook)*

on GONZO station. I next saw VF-213 at sea in January 1999, by which time the unit had transitioned to F-14Ds and the 'Black Lions' had become the sole remaining Tomcat squadron in CVW-11 following VF-114's disbandment six years earlier. The unit was busy flying Operation Southern Watch missions over Iraq

at the time of my visit to CVN-70 in the northern Arabian Gulf (NAG). Finally, seven years later, again in the NAG, I flew out to USS *Theodore Roosevelt* (CVN-71) to cover the final operational deployment of the Tomcat with the US Navy. CVW-8 was embarked in 'TR', and one of its two F-14 units was none other than VF-213. My connection with the 'Black Lions' and its Tomcats had lasted the best part of 25 years.

As impressive as the Tomcat was in its natural environment flying from a carrier, the aircraft relied on highly trained Naval Aviators and Radar Intercept Officers to get the best out of Grumman's final fighter when performing

BELOW CVN-65 motors along at close to 30kts during CVW-11 work-ups off the coast of southern California in late 1985. In January 1986 the vessel departed NAS Alameda on an eight-month world cruise. The author flew out to the ship several days before it reached Freemantle in July 1986 for the first of his many at-sea embarkations on board US Navy carriers. *(US Navy)*

its many operational roles. They were in turn supported by a veritable army of maintainers – typically more than 200 per fleet squadron – who were required to keep the F-14 operational in the harshest working environment of them all. Getting the opportunity to interview the men and, latterly, women who flew the 'Big Fighter' in both war and peace has been a highlight of my long career as an aviation photo-journalist. I have spoken with them at length both while under way in theatre, ashore at Naval Air Stations on both the east and west coasts of the USA and in their homes in California, Virginia, Nevada and Washington DC. Many more have communicated with me via e-mail or during telephone interviews over the years, and they have always been supportive of my publishing efforts.

For this particular book, I have striven to produce a 'manual' that includes the experiences of those who truly were the 'owners' of the F-14 during its front-line service. Thanks to the input of both air- and groundcrew, I hope that I have succeeded in my brief, thus giving the reader a rare insight into flying, fighting and fixing the mighty

VF-213 1998–99 WestPac cruise patch, highlighting the F-14D's combat debut (both as a precision bomber and a long-range interceptor) with the 'Black Lions'. *(Tony Holmes collection)*

VF-213 'Black Lions' crew shoulder patch. *(Tony Holmes collection)*

VF-213 'Black Lions' and VF-31 'Tomcatters' last Tomcat cruise patch. *(Tony Holmes collection)*

Tomcat – as well as providing a concise history of the jet's service with the US Navy and the Imperial Iranian Air Force/Islamic Republic of Iran Air Force. More than a decade after the 'Big Fighter's' retirement from fleet service, the F-14's demise is still lamented by those who flew it, as well as those like myself who idolised the aircraft.

BELOW 'Blacklion 213' – armed with a GBU-38 500lb JDAM and a GBU-12 500lb LGB on its centreline weapons pallets – is marshalled towards waist catapult one on board USS *Theodore Roosevelt* (CVN-71) as part of a wave of OEF III jets heading off on a night patrol over Iraq in January 2006 during the Tomcat's last operational deployment with the US Navy. *(Richard Cooper)*

Chapter One

The Tomcat story

Few aircraft of the Cold War era have attained such cult status and adoration among those who flew it, wanted to fly it or kept it flying as the mighty Grumman F-14 Tomcat. As big, bold and brash as the *Top Gun* film in which it played the starring role in 1986, the US Navy's ultimate fleet fighter epitomised what Naval Aviation was all about throughout the jet's three decades of service with its primary operator. Although acquired as a single-mission interceptor, the Tomcat had evolved into a multi-role precision strike bomber by the time it was retired by the fleet in 2006.

OPPOSITE His left arm raised to signal that 'Blacklion 105' (F-14D BuNo 161613) is successfully attached to *Theodore Roosevelt*'s waist catapult three, the hook-up 'Green Shirt' runs to the left of the jet followed closely by the plane director and his deputy. The Tomcat is now under the control of the catapult officer, better known as the Shooter, who oversees the entire launch sequence. *(US Navy)*

11

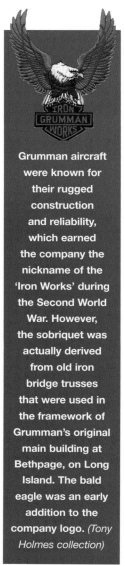

Grumman aircraft were known for their rugged construction and reliability, which earned the company the nickname of the 'Iron Works' during the Second World War. However, the sobriquet was actually derived from old iron bridge trusses that were used in the framework of Grumman's original main building at Bethpage, on Long Island. The bald eagle was an early addition to the company logo. *(Tony Holmes collection)*

Evolution

The Tomcat was the final creation of the Grumman Aircraft Corporation, which had been building fighters for the US Navy in its Bethpage, New York, factory since the early 1930s. Wildcats and Hellcats dominated carrier flight decks during the Second World War, Tigercats and Bearcats served with front-line units in the immediate post-war years, Panthers saw considerable combat during the Korean War and Cougars and Tigers were among the first Cold War fighter types to be embarked in the new supercarriers that were ushered into service from the late 1950s. All of these Grumman machines garnered for themselves a reputation for being effective fighters that proved their durability in the front-line, and often in combat.

As the ultimate product of the Grumman 'Iron Works', the F-14 would inherit all the qualities of its feline forebears. Like them, it would marry good performance with immense strength – a prerequisite if the aircraft was to withstand the violence of operations from a pitching carrier deck at sea. The Tomcat also possessed handling qualities that made it more than a match for all but the most agile of its opponents.

Known as the 'Big Fighter' in US Navy service, the F-14 lived up to this sobriquet by tipping the scales at 74,350lb when fully loaded – Grumman's first fleet fighter, the biplane FF-1 of 1933, weighed in at just 4,828lb. Of the

Tomcat's Cold War contemporaries, only the MiG-25 'Foxbat' was heavier, and pilots flying the fearsome Soviet interceptor enjoyed the luxury of operating them from vast runways in the USSR. When it comes to the unique environment of 'blue water ops', the Tomcat remains the largest fighter to have been regularly flown from a carrier.

Grumman had originally designed the F-14 to perform one mission, and one mission only – fleet defence. The US Navy's need for a long-endurance aircraft that was capable of launching several high-speed, long-range air-to-air missiles came about thanks to the rapid improvement of Soviet weapons technology in the late 1950s. Long-range cruise missiles launched from high-speed bombers at a stand-off distance of up to 200 nautical miles posed the greatest threat to the 'jewel' in the US Navy's surface fleet 'crown' – the supercarrier.

By the early 1960s Tupolev was churning out Tu-16, Tu-22 and Tu-95 bombers, all armed with Kh-series cruise missiles, at an alarming rate. The US Navy's F-4 Phantom II and F-8 Crusader, although both outstanding fighters against comparable Communist types such as the MiG-17 and MiG-21, lacked the radar performance and weaponry to adequately deal with Soviet bombers armed with cruise missiles. In order to defeat this ever-growing threat, a new type of interceptor was required. The US Navy needed a carrier-capable aircraft fitted with an incredibly powerful radar that could detect the bombers before they got to within missile-launching range of the fleet.

The interceptor's weapon system would be crucial to its effectiveness in this role, and the missile chosen, in 1958, was the Bendix XAAM-M-10 Eagle. Like the bombers it would be hunting, the Eagle was a big weapon. Appreciably larger than the much shorter-ranged air-to-air missiles carried by US Navy fighters at the time, the XAAM-N-10 was 16ft long and weighed 1,284lb. By comparison, American fleet fighters were then armed with 155lb AIM-9B Sidewinder and/or 452lb AIM-7E Sparrow missiles. The former had a range of 2 miles and the latter 28 miles. The AAM-N-10, however, was designed to intercept targets up to 127 miles away.

Development of the Eagle was eventually taken on by Hughes Aircraft from 1960, and

BELOW The portly XF10F-1 Jaguar was Grumman's first attempt at building a 'swing-wing' fighter. Initially based on the F9F Panther, the one-off prototype eventually emerged with a T-tail and variable-geometry wings. Grumman test pilot Corwin 'Corky' Meyer was the only pilot to fly the Jaguar, describing it as entertaining when aloft 'because there was so much wrong with it'. *(Grumman via David F. Brown)*

the company incorporated numerous aspects of the missile into its AIM-54 Phoenix (initially designated the AAM-N-11). This weapon emerged in the early 1960s as the most sophisticated, and most expensive, air-to-air missile in the world. At the same time the company developed the AN/AWG-9 advanced fire control system to help detect targets for the Phoenix. Starting out life as the APN-122(V), the AN/AWG-9 would have a track-while-scan capability that allowed it to simultaneously follow 24 targets and attack 6 of them. The latter – cruise missile-toting Soviet bombers – would be engaged at extreme range. Like the AIM-54, the AN/AWG-9 was a weighty system, boasting the largest circular aerial of planar-type ever carried by a fighter. It also had stunning performance figures, with a look-down target acquisition capability out to 150 miles.

The aircraft that the US Navy hoped would defend the fleet with XAAM-N-10s guided by the pulse Doppler AN/AWG-9 radar was the Douglas F6D-1 Missileer. Featuring an unswept, shoulder-mounted wing and non-afterburning engines that gave it a top speed of just Mach 0.8, the Missileer was the complete antithesis of the fast and highly agile F-14 Tomcat. Although the F6D-1 would have been well suited to the anti-bomber role (thanks to its combat load of up to eight Eagle missiles), it lacked any hope of defending itself in aerial combat against agile MiG fighters.

With the XAAM-N-10 suffering ongoing development problems, the Missileer was abandoned in December 1960. However, the AN/AWG-9 remained a viable project, with the Eagle being reborn as the AAM-N-11 Phoenix.

In 1961, in an effort to cut costs by avoiding duplication in the procurement of weapons systems, new Secretary of Defense Robert S. McNamara encouraged the development of a common USAF/US Navy fighter aircraft called the TFX (Tactical Fighter Experimental). Both services needed a platform that could carry a heavy weapons load at high speed over long distances. The USAF, however, was planning on arming its aircraft with bombs, not air-to-air missiles. The TFX subsequently evolved into the highly successful 'swing-wing' General Dynamics F-111A bomber, which would serve the USAF well for almost 30 years. The same

LEFT Defense Secretary Robert S. McNamara played a major part in the development of the F-14's predecessor, the F-111B. The latter, based on the USAF's ultimately successful F-111 'swing-wing' tactical bomber, was an abject failure. *(LBJ Library)*

could not be said about the near-identical airframe that was foisted upon the US Navy in the form of the Grumman F-111B, as highly experienced Naval Aviator and test pilot Rear Admiral Paul T. Gillcrist explained:

The Tomcat had a hell of a time getting itself born. It was the era of the McNamara Whiz Kids in the Pentagon, and they were fixated on a new fighter that could be flown in common by the Air Force and the Navy. That unfortunate bird was the TFX, which became the F-111. The F-111B was the Navy variant. Some wags called it 'the deviant'. The thing was so underpowered it couldn't generate the specified acceleration in mil [non-afterburner] power on approach to the ship. All the Navy tests were dismal, but the damn thing was on the track anyway.

A true American hero named Vice Admiral Tom Connolly [Deputy Chief of Naval Operations (Air Warfare)] shut the project down in a Senate hearing [on Capitol Hill]. Called upon by Armed Services Committee chairman Senator John Stennis, Connolly blunted reported, 'Mr Chairman, all the thrust in Christendom couldn't make a Navy fighter out of that airplane'. The deviant died at that moment, and the Tomcat was born. Vice Admiral Connolly knew his stand on the future of the F-111B was a career-ender, which it most certainly was. But he did what had to be done.

Like the Missileer before it, the F-111B had proven to be totally unsuited to the fighter mission, being too heavy owing to the

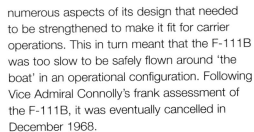

numerous aspects of its design that needed to be strengthened to make it fit for carrier operations. This in turn meant that the F-111B was too slow to be safely flown around 'the boat' in an operational configuration. Following Vice Admiral Connolly's frank assessment of the F-111B, it was eventually cancelled in December 1968.

In October of the previous year, having by then seen that the F-111B was 'falling well behind the power curve', Grumman proposed to the US Navy that it could quickly produce a new airframe that incorporated the missile armament (AIM-54A), avionics, AN/AWG-9 radar and twin engines (Pratt & Whitney TF30 turbofans) of the F-111B. Called the Model 303, this design also featured a variable-geometry 'swing-wing'. Grumman engineers had been secretly working on such a proposal since the mid-1960s,

ABOVE During July 1968, the US Navy conducted carrier suitability trials with the fifth F-111B prototype aboard USS *Coral Sea* (CVA-43) off the California coast. All flights were performed by Naval Aviators from the Naval Flight Test Center. *(Grumman via Tailhook)*

BELOW This full-scale mock-up, still under construction, of Grumman's Design 303E looks remarkably like the final Tomcat configuration settled on by the US Navy, bar the single tailfin and yet to be built outward-folding ventral fins. *(Cradle of Aviation Museum)*

BELOW LEFT The single fin mock-up was later modified to resemble the final Tomcat configuration, featuring twin fins and smaller, fixed, dorsal fins. Note the model's spurious BuNo, 00303 on the port tailfin, denoting Grumman's in-house designation for what would become the F-14. *(Grumman via Tailhook)*

BELOW A full-scale mock-up of the Design 303E cockpit was also meticulously constructed by Grumman engineers. The large artificial horizon that dominates the centre of the instrument panel would be replaced by a Vertical Display Indicator screen in production aircraft. *(Grumman via Tailhook)*

and the US Navy was keen to proceed with a replacement for the F-111B as expeditiously as possible. In July 1968 it issued a formal Request for Proposals to industry for a VFX (Heavier-than-air Fighter, Experimental). The US Navy's requirement stated that manufacturers should submit their designs for a two-seat, twin-engined aircraft that featured an advanced weapon control system, mixed missile armament consisting of AIM-54s, AIM-7s and AIM-9s and an integral Vulcan M61A1 20mm cannon.

Five companies, including Grumman, responded to the VFX competition, and on 14 January 1969 its Model 303E – effectively the brainchild of a single man, Mike Pelehach, who later became the company's vice president and F-14 Tomcat programme director – was selected as the winning design. Nevertheless, the actual production of the aeroplane almost went to a rival manufacturer, as veteran Grumman test pilot Corwin 'Corky' Meyer explains:

It's hard to believe, but the Navy almost handed the Tomcat project over to McDonnell Douglas. They thought their experience building thousands of F-4 Phantoms put them out front. We at Grumman hadn't done a proper sales job with our design. Some of our higher-ups had told us never to mention the F-111, since the Navy had such hatred for that programme and the way it was almost stuffed down their throats. But we had done excellent work as the prime F-111 subcontractor. We'd also put hundreds of successful test hours on the Navy variants. And the airplane was a swing-wing design that made the Phantom look like the Wright Flyer. It also had the same engines and radar as the first Tomcats. We finally got the real story across to the Navy, and the Tomcat went to Grumman.

Indeed, the company was awarded a contract for the construction of six research, development, test and evaluation (RDT&E) aircraft and 463 production examples for front-line service with both the US Navy and US Marine Corps.

The Tomcat was being acquired first and foremost as a fighter, as clearly stipulated in the VFX proposal issued by the US Navy. This fact was reiterated in 1969 by Capt L.S. 'Scotty' Lamoreaux, then F-14 Programme Project

ABOVE The first full-scale development (FSD) Tomcat, BuNo 157980, is seen here during the very early stages of its second flight on 30 December 1970. The aircraft spectacularly crashed on short finals to Grumman's Calverton facility shortly after this photograph was taken when it suffered a triple hydraulic failure. Both crew safely ejected, however. *(Grumman via Tailhook)*

Coordinator and, subsequently, a key figure in bringing the Tomcat into service before he retired in 1974 as the wing commander for all Pacific Fleet fighter squadrons at Naval Air Station (NAS) Miramar:

The time has come to provide our air wings with a fighter designed from scratch for air superiority. The F-14 is all fighter. Multimission capability has not been permitted to dilute the original concept, or degrade the performance required to out-fly and out-fight any aircraft encountered.

The service designation F-14 was bestowed upon the new fighter following Grumman's success in the VFX competition, and it was officially christened 'Tomcat' shortly thereafter.

BELOW Corwin 'Corky' Meyer was one of the most experienced aviators working for Grumman when the Tomcat commenced its flight test programme in the early 1970s. He had served as the project pilot for the F6F Hellcat, F7F Tigercat, F8F Bearcat, F9F Panther, XF10F-1 Jaguar and the F11F Tiger series. Meyer is seen here at the controls of the XTB3F-1 Guardian prototype in 1946. *(Cradle of Aviation Museum)*

The famous twin-tail Tomcat logo was created by Grumman's art department (specifically artists Jim Rodriguez and Tom Wood) following a request by Capt Norm Gandia, a former Blue Angels pilot and Director of Public Relations for Grumman in the early 1970s.
(via Peter Mersky)

How this name came to be chosen is the stuff of legend, as Corwin 'Corky' Meyer recalls:

During World War 2 the Grumman F7F was originally named for another outstanding night fighter, the tomcat. Some admiral cut that short with a note saying 'the name "Tomcat" denotes feline promiscuity and is not fitting and proper for a Navy fighter aircraft'. So that superb bird became the Tigercat as a follow-on to the Wildcat and Hellcat programmes. In 1969, Grumman again proposed the name Tomcat, and this time it passed muster. I suppose it didn't hurt that the three flags [admirals] at the top who headed up the competition [to select the new fleet fighter] were all named Tom.

In some circles the jet was even nicknamed 'Tom's Cat'.

Having wasted ten years on the stillborn Missileer and F-111B, the US Navy was anxious to make up for lost time with the F-14. It therefore stipulated in the contract entered into with Grumman that the first RDT&E aircraft would make its maiden flight on or before 31 January 1971. With the 'Iron Works' confident that it would be selected for the VFX programme, the company had already started the fabrication of minor components in December 1968. By May 1969 a full-scale mock-up had been assembled at Grumman's Bethpage facility that bore a striking resemblance to the finished fighter. The legend that would become the Tomcat was now nearing completion.

Design and testing

Production of all 712 Tomcats eventually built by Grumman was undertaken at the company's Calverton facility on Long Island. The aircraft's external appearance altered very little during the 22 years that F-14s rolled down the assembly line, its overall shape having been settled on by programme director Mike Pelehach and his team as early as January 1968. When interviewed by aviation historian Doug Richardson in the 1980s, Pelehach recalled:

When creating the most advanced air superiority fighter in history, our studies boiled down to eight specific design numbers: 303-60, 303A, 303B, 303C, 303D, 303E, 303F and 303G. We were close to the real thing with design 303-60, which had podded engines and a high variable-sweep wing like our eventual winning design, 303E. But it was more an assemblage of reasonable goals than a mature blend of aerodynamics, structures, electronics and airframe systems.

The VFX programme's conflicting demands of high speed, manoeuvrability and good handling at low speeds had meant that Grumman had little option but to use variable-geometry wings on its design. Pelehach explained:

A fixed-wing fighter design is at best a compromise, being optimised for one specific combination of speed and altitude. Operating away from this regime – the most likely circumstance for most of any individual sortie – its performance declines accordingly. We launched parallel investigations of three configurations when working on the company submission for the VFX programme. Refinement of the

BELOW Grumman test pilots Dennis Romano and 'Chuck' Sewell converse atop the 'pancake' section of Tomcat FSD BuNo 157981. A veteran of combat both in Korea and Vietnam, Sewell had joined Grumman in 1969 following 20 years as a fighter and test pilot with the US Marine Corps. He was killed in a take-off accident in a TBM Avenger on 4 August 1986.
(Grumman via Tailhook)

first configuration, 303A, resulted in 303B, which was evaluated against the other two layouts. Design 303C retained the high variable-geometry wing, but used a more conventional fuselage design with closely spaced, buried engines. It also introduced twin vertical tail surfaces [303A relied on a single vertical fin, with folding ventral fins on the outer surfaces of each aft engine bay – the ventral fins were fitted to provide good directional stability]. Design 303D moved the wings to a low position, buried the engines within the fuselage and also used twin vertical tails. Although of vaguely similar configuration to the F-4, 303D proved disappointing due to poor longitudinal stability and drag at subsonic speeds, as well as excessive fuel consumption. This design was dropped in April 1968.

Comparative analysis of the rival B and C versions clearly favoured the former. This offered better performance in areas such as fuel consumption and supersonic combat ceiling and an engine installation that would be easier to modify in the event of problems and simpler to rework at a later date in order to accommodate new engines. The B was therefore further refined in the late spring and early summer [of 1968], with the resulting 303E being defined by June.

According to Doug Richardson:

Back in the late 1960s the F-111 was not the only aircraft with powerplant and inlet problems. In designing the F-14, Grumman was determined to avoid the problems with inlets, engines, materials and base drag that had troubled the F-111. The first step was to avoid inlet problems which had affected the F-111, especially since the new fighter would use the same powerplant. 'We were looking for an inlet that was not curved – where there was very little distortion', Pelehach explained. The solution devised was a powerplant package – a nacelle in which a two-dimensional inlet led straight back to the engine. 'Okay, so we had a nacelle. Then we were looking for a body to hang a lot of stores from, and we were trying to get the wing pivot further outboard. So we put a

wing between the nacelles. How far apart we put the nacelles depended on the width that you need to carry two Phoenix [missiles] with proper clearance.'

The end result of this unique layout was a centrebody with an aerofoil-like cross section that formed more than half of the aircraft's

BELOW The second FSD Tomcat (BuNo 157981) arrives at the Calverton flight-test facility in 1971 after being transported from Grumman's Bethpage works. The aircraft lacks engines, fin tips and a radome. Note also the taller wing glove stiffeners and larger outboard fairings that extended aft to the trailing edges of the glove area. Both were reduced in height and size on later FSD aircraft. (Grumman via Tailhook)

high-strength titanium, the box was some 900lb lighter than the bolt-up steel structure used by the F-111. The box fitted to BuNo 157980 was recovered intact from the crash site, having buried itself 6ft under the ground.

Although the hydraulic line fix had been quick to implement, the loss of the first aircraft delayed further testing until 24 May 1971, when the second RDT&E jet made its first flight. Eventually, no fewer than 20 early-build aircraft would participate in the flight trials programme for the Tomcat, which was soon brought back on schedule. The No 2 jet performed low-speed handling and crucial stall/spin trials, No 3 conducted performance envelope expanding

flights with increasing loads and speeds, while Nos 4, 5 and 6 went to the Naval Missile Center at NAS Point Mugu, California, for operational test and evaluation. Here, they conducted weapons trials, with No 4 being the first F-14 to be fitted with a functioning AN/AWG-9/AIM-54 system. No 5 was lost during AIM-7 separation trials on 20 June 1973.

No 7 became Grumman's test aircraft for the F-14B, fitted with Pratt & Whitney F401-PW-400 turbofan engines, while No 8 was the first of several Tomcats delivered to the Naval Air Test Center (NATC) at NAS Patuxent River, Maryland. The follow-on RDT&E airframes were split between the NATC and Point Mugu's operational test and evaluation squadron, VX-4, with nine Tomcats having been assigned to various test programmes by December 1971. That same month Cdr George White became the first US Navy test pilot to fly the F-14.

Aircraft No 10 achieved the milestone of carrying out the first carrier launch and trap, aboard USS *Forrestal* (CVA-59), on 15 June 1972. The vessel was sailing 115 miles off the coast of Virginia at the time, the F-14 having been craned aboard in Norfolk two days earlier. By the 28th of that month the jet had completed its initial carrier operations following three catapult launches, two arrested landings, thirteen touch-and-goes and three intentional wave-offs. Two days later test pilot Bill Miller was killed in this aircraft when it crashed into Chesapeake Bay while he was practising for an airshow. Fellow test pilot Robert 'Bob' Smythe explained how the accident had occurred:

Bill Miller had been doing the F-14 carrier suitability trials at Pax [Patuxent] River in the spring and summer of 1972. During

BELOW FSD No 10 BuNo 157959 is carefully craned aboard USS *Forrestal* (CVA-59) while the vessel is alongside in Norfolk Navy Yard on 13 June 1972. The aircraft carried out the F-14's first launch and trap from the ship two days later off the coast of Virginia. *(Grumman via Tailhook)*

that segment of the aircraft's test and development programme, the manufacturer has to demonstrate that the airplane is structurally capable of performing to all the limits of arrestments and catapult launches required by the Navy. All this is done using the gear installed on the airfield at Pax River. The airplane never gets above 1,000ft and hardly ever retracts the gear or flaps. Also, there is little use for a back-seater, so we put an instrument package on the rear cockpit seat rails.

This particular airplane had a known problem with wing sweep because one of the interlocks that prevents wing sweep with the flaps down or spoilers up was hanging up. To sweep the wings the pilot had to fiddle with a circuit breaker and the flap handle at the same time – a two-handed job. Not a big problem, as Bill was quite familiar with the process.

Every 4th of July, Patuxent has a big Navy Relief airshow, with thousands attending. The Navy asks the contractors who have their latest aircraft there if they would participate in the airshow. They usually all say they will. Bill agreed to perform, and had planned a high-performance take-off, followed by a 90/270-degree reversal and return down the runway at 400 knots with the wings fully swept.

On 30 June 1972, Bill went out for a practice flight. The weather was said to be VFR [visual flight rules], with three miles or

better visibility. In actual fact it was much less out over Chesapeake Bay – a common summertime condition. Bill lined up on Runway 20, which is parallel to the bay. He advanced power to Zone Five afterburner and made his take-off run. He pulled up very steeply, retracted the gear, then rolled inverted, pulled the nose back down to the horizon and began his 90-degree left turn out over the bay. He noticed his gear did not show 'up and locked', so he had to recycle the gear. He then started fiddling with the circuit breaker and flap handle while starting his right 270-degree turn to line up with the runway.

At this point the nose fell slightly and he unwittingly started to descend from his 1,000ft altitude. There was no horizon and the water was flat calm. At the last minute he must have seen a sailboat (one saw him), went to full power and yanked the stick back. He hit the water at 350 knots and that was

LEFT FSD No 10 completes an early cat shot from CVA-59 during initial carrier operations for the F-14 in June 1972. By the 28th of that month the jet had completed its initial carrier operations. Two days later test pilot Bill Miller was killed in this aircraft when it crashed into Chesapeake Bay while he was practising for an airshow. *(Grumman History Center)*

LEFT Newly built F-14A BuNo 158980 was involved in the NATC's carrier compatibility trials in December 1973, embarking in CVA-59 from its NAS Patuxent River home. Here, the jet rides bow catapult one at the very start of a test flight, the fighter carrying an inert YAIM-54A test round on its forward port under-fuselage pallet. *(Grumman via Tailhook)*

21

THE TOMCAT STORY

*the end. Had there been someone in the
back seat to warn him, the accident would
never have happened.*

*Most accidents are stupid, and this was
no exception. Incidentally, it was 18 months,
exactly, after the loss of the prototype on
30 December 1970.*

For the duration of the trials period, Grumman
employed a small fleet of KA-6 Intruder tankers
to extend the Tomcat missions. It also made
use of an automated telemetry system to relay
in-flight data to the ground in real time for rapid
evaluation. These aspects of the test programme,
together with integrated service trials and
operational instruction for air- and groundcrews,
combined to cut 18 months off the projected
development time for the F-14. This meant that
the first production aircraft reached the Pacific
Fleet's fleet replacement squadron VF-124 at
NAS Miramar, California, in October 1972.

Although the aircraft had successfully
completed initial service trials and was
now being integrated into fleet service, its
manufacturer was at that point losing money on
every Tomcat delivered to the US Navy due to
the fixed-priced contract it had signed when the
jet was ordered in January 1969. This had been
negotiated as part of a 'total package' by Robert
S. McNamara during Grumman's boom years
in the 1960s, when the company's order books
were full to near capacity producing aircraft
for the US Navy, USAF and US Marine Corps
at the height of the Vietnam War. The harsher
economic climate of the early 1970s, when
raging inflation destroyed the manufacturer's
profits on the programme, left Grumman losing
$1 million on each Tomcat it was delivering up
to those ordered as part of Lot V. When the
US Navy and the manufacturer failed to agree
a revised price, resulting in the fiscal year 1974
contracts being left unsigned, Grumman, faced
with bankruptcy, threatened to cease production
and not deliver Lot V jets at all.

LEFT BuNo 158613, the second production standard Tomcat built and delivered to the US Navy in June 1972, also participated in the December 1973 AIM-54 deck trials at 'Pax River'. Seen here with a full load of dummy missiles and a blown starboard main gear tyre, the aircraft is being towed out of the arrestor wires after making an eventful landing on board CVA-59. (Grumman History Center)

The disadvantages of the fixed-price contract system are explained here by F-14 Programme Project Coordinator Capt L.S. 'Scotty' Lamoreaux, who was subsequently employed by aerospace giant Hughes to support the Tomcat procurement process after he left the US Navy:

This was a difficult way to produce a complex aircraft that is undergoing constant changes in specification and configuration during the formative R&D [research and development] phase of the contract. The fixed-price R&D contract was widely used and widely condemned, but little has been done to change the practice. Additionally, the contract stipulated an inflation rate that was far below the actual rate experienced at the time. The crisis was not that the cost had escalated that much, but that it had escalated to a point that exceeded Grumman's contract ceiling price, which had allowed only a ten per cent profit [to be made on each aircraft delivered]. When the inflation rate gap was subtracted from the profit, it did not take much of a price increase to put Grumman into a loss position well below the ceiling price.

Although the company had made a small profit on the first 38 aircraft delivered as part of Lots I–III, it had been warning since late 1969 that the contract needed to be renegotiated due to general inflation having steadily increased until it was almost 5% higher than the most

pessimistic predictions when the deal had been struck. Other costs had also risen steeply, with titanium, for example, increasing in price by 40–50% in just 12 months – only the SR-71 used a higher proportion of titanium in its construction than the F-14.

The fixed-price contract problems rumbled on until the Lot V jets had been completed, by which point Grumman was in deep financial trouble. The company's bankers had refused to extend its unsecured line of credit until the F-14 pricing problem was resolved in a way that did not impair the financial viability of Grumman. A compromise was finally reached in March 1973 that saw the company accept the fixed-price contract for the first 134 aircraft delivered (and therefore absorb a $220 million loss) and the US Navy agree to renegotiate the price of follow-on orders and provide a $200 million loan to tide Grumman over. The latter was soon terminated, however, when it was discovered that the company had invested it in short-term securities in order to generate a $2.8 million profit in an attempt to offset the losses it had incurred to date.

By then Grumman was close to securing an order from Iran for the F-14, and the Iranian Melli Bank stepped in to supply the company with a $75 million loan. This show of confidence in the manufacturer persuaded a syndicate of nine American banks to lend Grumman the remainder of the money that had been withdrawn by the US Navy. Eventually, from 1975, the company started to turn a profit from the Tomcat once again.

Chapter Two

Anatomy of the Tomcat

Grumman fighters had a reputation for being incredibly strong, and the Tomcat was probably the most rugged of them all.

All 712 Tomcats constructed by Grumman between 1970 and 1992 were assembled at the company's Calverton facility. The actual process of manufacture took place at several locations, with 60% of F-14 production being handled by more than 150 subcontracting companies. The main suppliers are detailed as follows.

OPPOSITE The Tomcat's afterburner plume was impressive to behold in low-light conditions, as seen here with VF-154's 'Nite 107' (BuNo 161296) launching from CV-63 on a dusk sortie during Annual Exercise 14G off the coast of Japan in November 2002. The TF30 was the first Western turbofan engine to be equipped with an afterburner, and when it was employed by the pilot the Tomcat's fuel usage suffered a four-fold increase. (US Navy)

ABOVE With its canopy removed, FSD No 5 BuNo 157984 is swarmed over by Grumman technicians at Calverton during the early stages of its flight test programme. The jet's spine fairings have been removed, exposing control rods and cables. The wing pivot bearings and swing-wing actuator spindles are also visible, as are the hydraulic actuators for the 'tailerons'. *(Grumman via Tailhook)*

BELOW F-14As come together in Grumman's crowded Plant 6 at Calverton in the mid-1970s. The Intruders seen behind the Tomcats are A-6As being rebuilt as E-models. Grumman employed a modular concept when it came to F-14 assembly, with seven separate stations being responsible for different aspects of this process. *(Cradle of Aviation Museum)*

The entire aft fuselage was built by Fairchild Republic at its Farmingdale factory, located on Long Island not far from Grumman's Bethpage works. The same company's Hagerstown plant built the tailfin and rudder assemblies, while Rohr Industries constructed the engine inlet ducts and aft nacelles. Aeronca built the jet's distinctive speed brakes on the upper and lower fuselage 'boat tail' between the engine exhausts, as well as the tail-section access doors. Kaman Aerospace was responsible for the wing surfaces, leading edge devices, slats, flaps and spoilers. Sargent Industries built the titanium wing pivot bearings and Hamilton Standard produced the wing-sweep actuator. The main landing gear strut, main landing gear trace and nose landing gear strut were all built by Bendix, while B.F. Goodrich supplied the wheels, tyres and brakes. Goodyear Aerospace provided the carbon brakes, Martin-Baker supplied two GRU-7A ejection seats (for the F-14A), the canopy and windscreen were manufactured by Swedlow and the nose radome by Brunswick.

In respect to systems fitted within the airframe, Garrett AiResearch was responsible for supplying the environmental control refrigeration system, temperature control system, Central Air Data Computer (CADC), air inlet control system, cabin pressure system and ARS100 air turbine starter. Gull Airborne Instruments provided the fuel quantity measuring system, engine instruments, flap indicator and AOA indicator, while the emergency generator and integrated drive generator were supplied by Sundstrand Aviation. Actuators were built by Bendix (horizontal stabiliser, servo cylinder and rudder servo actuator), Marquardt (inlet control servo cylinder), Pleaseu Dynamics (ram air door actuators) and the National Water Lift Division of Pneumo (spoiler and pitch servos, as well as flight control components).

Eventually, all of these parts, and many more besides, would come together with those manufactured in-house by Grumman at Calverton's Plant 6, which served as an assembly hall for the A-6 Intruder and EA-6B Prowler, as well as the F-14.

Grumman employed a modular concept when it came to Tomcat assembly, with seven separate stations being responsible for different aspects of this process. Station A was where construction started, with the mating of the nacelle assembly to the forward/centre-fuselage module, mating of the aft fuselage and nacelle assemblies, fitting of the inlet/glove assemblies and attachment of the cockpit canopy. Moving on to Station One, the aircraft had its vertical tail surfaces and main undercarriage members added here. The fitment of the latter allowed the aircraft to move freely on its own wheels throughout the remaining stages of the manufacturing process. Wings and engines were installed at Station Two, with rigging and the testing of flight control systems being carried out at Station Three. Engineers working here also oversaw the installation of the Hughes AN/AWG-9 radar, CADC and other mission-optimised avionics at this point. Testing of avionics equipment took place at Station Four, after which the completed aircraft was wheeled outside for engine runs and fuel flow calibration with technicians from Station Five. The jet was painted – originally in grey polyurethane gloss over white – at Station Six and the weapons racks were added and the weapon system tested (including firing 500 rounds from the cannon) at Station Seven.

Having taken 65–70 days to pass along the production line, the aircraft was cleared for flight and taken aloft by Grumman test pilots. The company adopted a 'fly–fix–fly' cycle for its newly built F-14s until all the defects found in the aeroplane had been rectified. Grumman's target was, of course, to produce an aircraft that was faultless, but during the early stages of the programme such 'zero-defect' jets were rare. However, as experience built up on the production line, a growing number of Tomcats were accepted by the US Navy's Calverton-based acceptance team following only a single test flight. After the handover, a Naval Aviator and a Radar Intercept Officer (RIO) would usually complete two local sorties prior to delivering the F-14 to a fleet unit either at NAS Miramar or NAS Oceana, Virginia.

Despite the Tomcat being hailed as the most advanced fighter of its time when production commenced in 1970, the aeroplane's construction was largely conventional. The most important part of the aircraft was its single-cell titanium wing box, which was truly cutting edge.

ABOVE This head-on view of Station A shows three forward/centre-fuselage modules, while the airframe closest to the camera also has the aft fuselage, nacelles and inlet/glove assemblies attached to a forward/centre-fuselage module. Finally, the partially completed jet also boasts a suitably protected cockpit canopy. *(Grumman via David F. Brown)*

BELOW The wings were fitted and engines installed at Station Two in Plant 6 – the F-14A in the foreground of this photograph is in the process of having its port TF30 installed. Rigging and the testing of flight control systems was the next phase of production at Station Three. All of the Tomcats visible here were destined for service with the Imperial Iranian Air Force. *(Cradle of Aviation Museum)*

Grumman F-14A Tomcat. *(Mike Badrocke)*

1 Pitot tube
2 Radar target horn
3 Glass-fibre radome
4 IFF aerial array
5 Hughes AWG-9 flat plate radar scanner
6 Scanner tracking mechanism
7 Ventral ALQ-100 antenna
8 Gun muzzle blast trough
9 Radar electronics equipment bay
10 AN/ASN-92 inertial navigation unit
11 Radome hinge
12 In-flight refuelling probe (extended)
13 ADF aerial
14 Windscreen rain removal air duct
15 Temperature probe
16 Cockpit front pressure bulkhead
17 Angle of attack transmitter
18 Formation lighting strip
19 Cannon barrels
20 Nosewheel doors
21 Gun gas vents
22 Rudder pedals
23 Cockpit pressurisation valve
24 Navigation radar display
25 Control column
26 Instrument panel shroud
27 Kaiser AN/ANG-12 head-up display
28 Windscreen panels
29 Cockpit canopy cover
30 Face blind seat firing handle
31 Ejection seat headrest
32 Pilot's Martin-Baker GRU-7A ejection seat
33 Starboard side console panel
34 Engine throttle levers
35 Port side console panel
36 Pitot static head
37 Canopy emergency release handle
38 Fold out step
39 M-61-A1 Vulcan 20mm six-barrel rotary cannon
40 Nose undercarriage leg strut
41 Catapult strop link
42 Catapult strop, launch position
43 Twin nosewheels
44 Folding boarding ladder
45 Hughes AIM-54A Phoenix air-to-air missile (6)
46 Fuselage missile pallet
47 Cannon ammunition drum (675 rounds)
48 Rear boarding step
49 Ammunition feed chute
50 Armament control panels
51 Kick-in step
52 Tactical information display hand controller
53 Naval Flight Officer's instrument console
54 NFO's ejection seat
55 Starboard intake lip
56 Ejection seat launch rails

57 Cockpit aft decking
58 Electrical system controller
59 Rear radio and electronics equipment bay
60 Boundary layer bleed air duct
61 Port engine intake lip
62 Electrical system relay controls
63 Glove vane pivot
64 Port air intake
65 Glove vane housing
66 Navigation light
67 Variable area intake ramp doors
68 Cooling system boundary layer duct ram air intake
69 Intake ramp door hydraulic jacks
70 Air system piping
71 Air data computer
72 Heat exchanger
73 Heat exchanger exhaust duct
74 Forward fuselage fuel tanks
75 Canopy hinge point
76 Electrical and control system ducting
77 Control rod runs
78 UHF/TACAN aerial
79 Glove vane hydraulic jack
80 Starboard glove vane, extended
81 Honeycomb panel construction
82 Navigation light
83 Main undercarriage wheel bay
84 Starboard intake duct spill door
85 Wing slat/flap flexible drive shaft
86 Dorsal spine fairing
87 Fuselage top longeron
88 Central flap/slat drive motor
89 Emergency hydraulic generator
90 Bypass door hydraulic jack
91 Intake bypass door
92 Port intake ducting
93 Wing glove sealing horn
94 Flap/slat telescopic drive shaft
95 Port wing pivot bearing

96 Wing pivot carry through (electron beam welded titanium box construction)
97 Wing pivot box integral fuel tank
98 Fuselage longeron/pivot box attachment joint
99 UHF datalink/IFF aerial
100 Honeycomb skin panelling
101 Wing glove stiffeners/dorsal fences
102 Starboard wing pivot bearing
103 Slat/flap drive shaft gearbox
104 Starboard wing integral fuel tank (total internal fuel capacity 2,364 USgal/8,951 litres)
105 Leading edge slat drive shaft
106 Slat guide rails
107 Starboard leading edge slat segments (open)
108 Starboard navigation light
109 Low-voltage formation lighting
110 Wing tip fairing
111 Outboard manoeuvre flap segments (down position)
112 Port roll control spoilers
113 Spoiler hydraulic jacks
114 Inboard, high lift flap (down position)
115 Inboard flap hydraulic jack
116 Manoeuvre flap drive shaft
117 Variable wing sweep screw jack
118 Starboard main undercarriage pivot fixing
119 Starboard engine compressor face
120 Wing glove sealing plates
121 Pratt & Whitney TF30-P-412 afterburning turbofan
122 Rear fuselage fuel tanks
123 Fuselage longeron joint
124 Control system artificial feel units
125 Tailplane control rods
126 Starboard engine bay

127 Wing glove pneumatic seal
128 Fin root fairing
129 Fin spar attachment joints
130 Starboard fin leading edge
131 Starboard all-moving tailplane
132 Starboard wing (fully swept position)
133 AN/ALR-45 tail warning radar antenna
134 Fin aluminium honeycomb skin panel construction
135 Fin-tip aerial fairing
136 Tail navigation light
137 Electronic countermeasures antenna (ECM)
138 Rudder honeycomb construction
139 Rudder hydraulic jack
140 Afterburner ducting
141 Variable area nozzle control jack
142 Airbrake (upper and lower surfaces)
143 Airbrake hydraulic jack
144 Starboard engine exhaust nozzle
145 Anti-collision light
146 Tail formation light
147 ECM aerial
148 Port rudder
149 Beaver tail fairing
150 Fuel jettison pipe
151 ECM antenna
152 Deck arrester hook (stowed position)
153 AN/ALE-29A chaff and flare dispensers
154 Nozzle shroud sealing flaps
155 Port convergent/divergent afterburner exhaust nozzle
156 Tailplane honeycomb construction

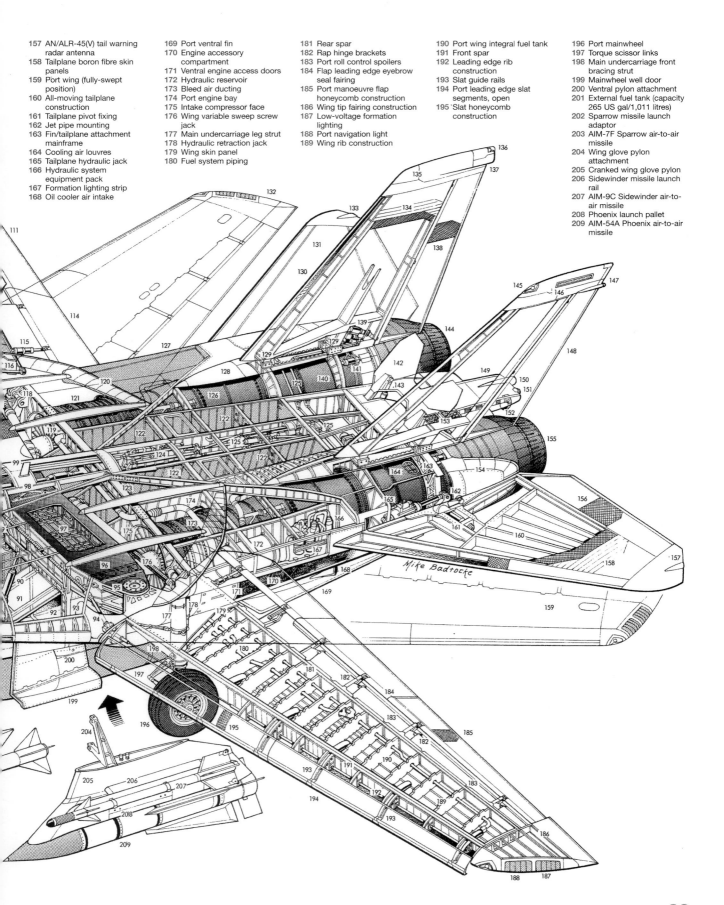

157 AN/ALR-45(V) tail warning radar antenna
158 Tailplane boron fibre skin panels
159 Port wing (fully-swept position)
160 All-moving tailplane construction
161 Tailplane pivot fixing
162 Jet pipe mounting
163 Fin/tailplane attachment mainframe
164 Cooling air louvres
165 Tailplane hydraulic jack
166 Hydraulic system equipment pack
167 Formation lighting strip
168 Oil cooler air intake

169 Port ventral fin
170 Engine accessory compartment
171 Ventral engine access doors
172 Hydraulic reservoir
173 Bleed air ducting
174 Port engine bay
175 Intake compressor face
176 Wing variable sweep screw jack
177 Main undercarriage leg strut
178 Hydraulic retraction jack
179 Wing skin panel
180 Fuel system piping

181 Rear spar
182 Rap hinge brackets
183 Port roll control spoilers
184 Flap leading edge eyebrow seal fairing
185 Port manoeuvre flap honeycomb construction
186 Wing tip fairing construction
187 Low-voltage formation lighting
188 Port navigation light
189 Wing rib construction

190 Port wing integral fuel tank
191 Front spar
192 Leading edge rib construction
193 Slat guide rails
194 Port leading edge slat segments, open
195 Slat honeycomb construction

196 Port mainwheel
197 Torque scissor links
198 Main undercarriage front bracing strut
199 Mainwheel well door
200 Ventral pylon attachment
201 External fuel tank (capacity 265 US gal/1,011 litres)
202 Sparrow missile launch adaptor
203 AIM-7F Sparrow air-to-air missile
204 Wing glove pylon attachment
205 Cranked wing glove pylon
206 Sidewinder missile launch rail
207 AIM-9C Sidewinder air-to-air missile
208 Phoenix launch pallet
209 AIM-54A Phoenix air-to-air missile

Stronger than steel, but appreciably lighter, titanium is a difficult material to work with. Earlier naval fighters like the F-4 Phantom II used only limited amounts of titanium, reserving its use for areas of high thermal or physical stress. On the F-4, titanium accounted for only 9% of the structure, but with the Tomcat it made up around 25% of the empty weight. Titanium was used in the construction of the wing box, wing pivots, wing upper and lower skins, the intakes, rear fuselage skins and in the hydraulic lines.

Titanium was chosen by Grumman engineers for the Tomcat's wing box in an effort to save both cost and weight. General Dynamics had elected to use a bolt-assembled component manufactured from D6AC steel when it designed the F-111's wing box in the early 1960s. Grumman could have simply copied this design, but it realised that weight savings could be made if a titanium wing box could be fabricated using electron-beam welding instead of bolts. This was cutting-edge technology at the time, and Grumman's engineers led the way with titanium construction in fighter aircraft following several years of experimentation with electron-beam welding that fused this ultra-strong metal with other materials. Employing a small vacuum chamber, they had discovered that thick sections of 6AL-4V titanium could

be welded with a minimum of distortion. Conventional welding operations on thick sections of material demanded multiple passes and subsequent inspections, all of which added time and expense to the manufacturing process, but a single pass sufficed for electron-beam-welded titanium.

The F-14's wing box structure had been designed, built and tested to destruction by 1968 – the prototype box finally failed at 112% load factor, and not at a weld but at a tooling mark in the lower cover.

Aviation historian Doug Richardson explained:

Design of a wing box for any variable-geometry aircraft poses severe engineering problems. For a start, the moving outer wing sections transmit large and variable bending and torsional moments as wing angle is varied. The wing/fuselage pivots must be positioned to minimise adverse pitching moments, particularly at high altitudes and high-rate turns. The wing box used to carry these pivots is located at the point on the aircraft where cross-section is greatest, forcing the designer to shape the wing box to follow the contours dictated by features such as air intake ducting. In the case of the F-14, these factors resulted in a 20ft long component which also served as an integral fuel tank.

When fully assembled (at Grumman's Bethpage plant) from 33 machined parts fused together via 3 Sciaky electron-beam welding machines, the wing box was 22ft long, 33–36in wide and 14in deep. It transmitted its wing loadings to the fuselage via two sets of wing pivots. The box was attached to the fuselage via four pin joints. Titanium alloy was also used in the construction of the two annular, spherical bearings that made up the wing pivots, these being Teflon-coated. The pivots were then bolted to the wing box. Each wing was mated with the pivots via two sets of lugs. One lug of any two could fail without endangering the aircraft.

The resulting weight reduction through using titanium was significant, for not only was there a direct saving of 900lb on the box structure itself, but the savings in fuel and structure shaved

more than 22,000lb off the Tomcat's gross take-off weight.

The fuselage was assembled around conventionally machined steel frames. The latter were used for the aft fuselage and undercarriage support frames, as well as for the spectacle beam on to which the rear engine and stabiliser mounts were attached. Bonded honeycomb panels were also widely used for fuselage skinning throughout the aircraft as a weight-saving device, although the aft 'hot section' panels near the engine were made of titanium. The latter material could better withstand the high temperatures found in these areas, and it was also corrosion resistant. Titanium was also used for the upper and lower wing skins, engine intakes, hydraulic lines, main and aft fuselage longerons and the engine support beam.

Elsewhere, bonded honeycomb material formed the glove vanes in the wing leading edges, the inlet duct sidewalls, the leading and trailing edges of the wings, the moveable control surfaces and the jet's distinctive twin tails. The horizontal tail surface skins, dubbed 'tailerons' by Tomcat crews, were made up of boron-epoxin y composite materials, however. This was the first time that any Western military aircraft that had attained series production used composites for loading-bearing structures.

'Swing-wings' and 'pancakes'

The F-14's distinctive moving wing sections incorporated plain trailing edge flaps, full-span leading edge slats, lift dumpers and spoilers. The latter, working in conjunction with the horizontal stabilisers, allowed the pilot to maintain roll control when the wings were swept fully forward. Unlike early variable-geometry aircraft, which used manually controlled wings, the F-14 was the first to rely on an automatic system. The wings were moved to the optimum position for the best lift/ drag ratio (the ratio of wingspan, squared, to wing area) by the CADC as the Mach number varied.

Doug Richardson explained:

Wing sweep could be varied from 20 [used for take-off and landing] to 68 degrees [attained at about Mach 0.9 and locked there from Mach 1.2 all the way up to maximum Mach], with a special 75-degree position which overlapped the tailplane being provided for use on the ground in order to minimise parking space. Sweep angle was automatically controlled by the CADC in order to optimise the lift/drag ratio. This was particularly effective between Mach 0.6 and 0.9 – the range of speeds most likely to be met in aerial combat. To improve combat manoeuvrability, the slats and outboard flap sections could be deployed while the wings were in the fully-forward position.

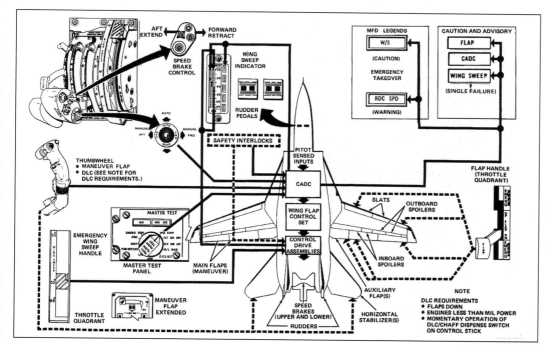

LEFT The wing sweep and control surfaces schematic diagram published in NAVAIR 01-F14AAD-1 publication *NATOPS Flight Manual Navy Model F-14D Aircraft*, dated 1 February 1997. *(US Navy)*

RIGHT Its wing box panels having been removed by squadron maintainers, this VF-101 F-14A has its port wing pivot bearing (centre right) and actuator spindle exposed. The wing box beam that surrounded the pivot area was fabricated from electron-beam-welded titanium (as was the pivot itself). *(Danny Coremans)*

Controlling the wing sweep manually would have been difficult, especially in the high-pressure environment of aerial combat, with minor changes being required depending on airspeed, altitude and wing loading. The F-14, therefore, was almost always flown with the wing sweep control on automatic. The Mach Sweep Programmer, which oversaw the operation of the 'swing-wings', relied on

outputs from the CADC to determine the best sweep angle. The F-14 was also fitted with a manual override that allowed the pilot to go to full sweep even at low speeds so as to improve acceleration, but decreasing sweep for a greater lift/drag ratio required an emergency setting. This was done to prevent overenthusiastic pilots 'popping' the wings in an attempt to pull sudden 'bat turns' during air combat manoeuvring (ACM), overstressing the jet in the process. The scissoring of the wings backwards and forwards was physically impossible in any case, as the sweep angle change rate dropped from 7.5 degrees per second to 4.0 degrees per second when the fighter was under its maximum designed load of 7.5g.

In order to maintain a smooth, flush fit between the trailing edge of the wing and the top of the rear fuselage, the latter incorporated inflatable canvas bags, pressurised with air from the 12th stage of the TF30 engines via a regulator, in its upper surface. Teflon paint on the underside of the wing prevented abrasion of the bags.

In another break from convention, no ailerons were fitted to the F-14's 'swing-wings'. Instead, as noted earlier, roll control was maintained by the pilot via wing-mounted spoilers and the differentially moving 'tailerons'. The wing spoilers would be locked down at sweep angles in excess of 57 degrees, leaving roll control entirely to the composite horizontal stabilisers. 'Having gained experience with boron epoxy structure by flight testing limited components on the F-111 and A-6', noted Doug Richardson. 'Grumman started development of the F-14A stabilisers in 1968. By 1970 the resulting structures had completed demonstration fatigue and static-load tests'.

As previously detailed, the leading edge slats and trailing edge flaps, unlike the composite 'tailerons', were constructed from bonded honeycomb material. The flaps were of the conventional single-slotted trailing edge type, with three sections being fitted on each outer wing panel. These consisted of two outer main segments and one inner auxiliary segment, with the latter becoming inoperative at sweep angles exceeding 22 degrees so as to prevent the possibility of wing glove damage. Operation of the main flap sections was also inhibited when 50 degrees of wing sweep was reached.

RIGHT To achieve a flush fit between the trailing edge of the wing and the top of the rear fuselage, the latter incorporated inflatable canvas bags in its upper surface, pressurised with engine bleed air. When first installed, the fabric of the over-wing fairing airbags was light grey in colour, but this quickly changed to a darker shade with the harsh conditions of operational flying. *(Danny Coremans)*

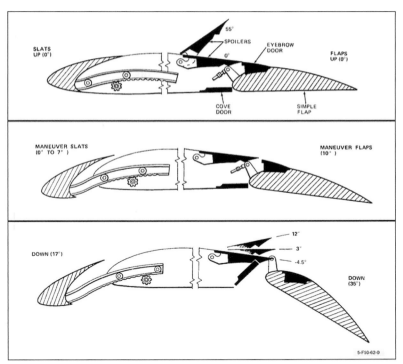

Grumman believed that the three flap sections, operating in unison with the conventional leading edge slats, offered optimum lift-generating characteristics for the jet when being flown at low speeds. In subsonic and transonic flight, however, the outer sections could also double as manoeuvring flaps. Their employment rested with the CADC, and when extended in combat they delayed buffet and wing airflow separation at high AOA. Additionally, from the 185th Tomcat onward, hydraulically actuated manoeuvring slats were fitted to the wing upper surfaces to further alleviate buffet, particularly during ACM training.

In an effort to improve supersonic manoeuvrability when the wings were fully swept, Grumman created two retractable vanes that extended from the leading edges of the wing gloves. Doug Richardson explained:

The small triangular-shaped vanes extended at supersonic speeds under the control of the CADC. Maximum extension was 15 degrees. When extended, these destabilised the forward area of the F-14 at speeds above Mach 1.4 and allowed an exceptional 7.5g turn to be performed at Mach 2 by generating additional lift ahead of the aircraft's centre of gravity.

ABOVE LEFT The F-14's distinctive moving wing sections incorporated plain trailing edge flaps, full-span leading edge slats, lift dumpers and spoilers. The latter, working in conjunction with the horizontal stabilisers, allowed the pilot to maintain roll control when the wings were swept fully forward. Here, the port wing can be seen in its fully extended position, with the spoilers extended and leading and trailing edge flaps deployed. *(Danny Coremans)*

ABOVE The wing control surfaces diagram, showing the various slat, spoiler and flap positions, published in NAVAIR 01-F14AAA-1 publication *NATOPS Flight Manual Navy Model F-14A Aircraft*, dated 15 May 2003. *(US Navy)*

BELOW The F-14's trailing edge flaps (and leading edge slats) were constructed from bonded honeycomb material. The flaps were of the conventional single-slotted trailing edge type, with three sections being fitted on each outer wing panel. Note the heavy staining and weathering of the wing by the glove-sealing canvas bags, despite Teflon-based paint being used to try and reduce such abrasions. *(Danny Coremans)*

ABOVE To improve supersonic manoeuvrability when the wings were fully swept, Grumman created two retractable vanes extending from the leading edges of the wing gloves. As seen here, these vanes could be extended at any wing-sweep angle – the pilot of fully armed, and brand new, VF-2 jet BuNo 162606 has selected mid-sweep prior to positioning his aircraft for the photographer, fellow 'Bullet' Lt Dave Baranek.

BELOW F-14As from VF-114 'Aardvarks' and VF-213 'Black Lions' crowd the flight deck of *Enterprise* between missions in the Pacific Ocean in July 1984. The wings of these aircraft are locked in the 75-degree over-sweep position that was the norm for Tomcats when chained down to a carrier flight deck. 'Blacklion 202' (BuNo 159859), was lost in a fatal crash shortly after this photograph was taken. *(US Navy via Peter Mersky)*

The vanes also helped compensate for the nose-down pitching moment associated with supersonic speeds and offloaded the rear fuselage and horizontal stabilisers, reducing the bend stresses on the rear of the aircraft and making that section of the Tomcat lighter than it otherwise would have had to be. Finally, torsional loads on the wing pivots were also reduced thanks to the vanes.

Although the performance numbers mentioned above checked out during the aeroplane's flight testing with both Grumman and the US Navy, once the F-14 was in front-line service it was found that the vanes had limited overall effectiveness. Mike Pelehach confirmed this:

The whole concept of having vanes was a good one, but what did it really cost you to fit the associated mechanism and interlocks? Those got a lot more complicated and heavier and more costly than we had envisaged initially. The airplane was designed for Mach 2.4, but we found that in many cases it was an academic number. People didn't fly the airplane at Mach 2.4. The faster you move, the more the lift moves back on the wing, and it really moves back at the last two-tenths of a Mach number. At Mach 2.25 the need for the vanes became marginal. For what the airplane was designed to do, vanes made it better, but I don't think they were worth the penalty.

Indeed, from the early 1980s they were locked shut by front-line units, with the vane actuators removed to save weight. B- and D-model F-14s did not mount them at all.

The centrebody area between the engine nacelles, housing the wing box and leading edge vanes, provided the aircraft with about half of its

LEFT VF-1 F-14A BuNo 160887 accelerates along waist catapult two at the start of an Operation Desert Storm mission from USS *Ranger* (CV-61) in early February 1991. The aircraft's leading edge slats and trailing edge flaps have been extended and the all-moving tailerons set at full deflection to raise rapidly the compressed nose and give the Tomcat maximum lift when it reaches the end of the catapult. *(Pete Clayton)*

lifting area. Boasting an aerofoil-like cross section, this shallow, flat area was dubbed the 'pancake' by Grumman designers. Not subjected to the bending and twisting motion associated with a traditional, larger wing, this low aspect ratio area complemented the 'swing-wings' when unswept, albeit at a cost of additional drag. Thanks to its rigid, fixed structure, the 'pancake' proved critically important in reducing wing loading. This in turn allowed the Tomcat to be flown at a very high AOA when needed – specifically in ACM. High aspect ratio wings usually break away from controlled flight without any real warning at 16 degrees AOA, leading to a stall. The low aspect ratio of the 'pancake' gave the Tomcat a slower and steadier decrease in lift, which meant that the jet did not really stall. Indeed, despite its size, the F-14 possessed remarkable agility, with pilots routinely pulling 30 or even 50 degrees of AOA in ACM.

Intakes

Having experienced at first hand the problems associated with the F-111B and its complex engine intake ducting, Grumman was determined not to saddle the Tomcat with a similar layout. Doug Richardson noted:

In designing the F-14 engine installation, Grumman was able to draw on experience gained as far back as 1966, when the company undertook a series of wind tunnel studies of advanced inlet and ejector designs as part of an F-111B improvement programme. The two engines were installed within nacelles located as far apart as possible on the rear fuselage.

On fighters with conventional fuselage-mounted intakes, a system has to be devised to divert turbulent boundary air, preventing it from reaching the engines. In the case of the F-111, this was particularly complex, since the intake ducting was short and the TF30 engines were prone to stall. Since the F-14 engine nacelles were positioned well out from the fuselage, the inlets ran little risk of ingesting boundary layer turbulence. The variable-geometry intakes were of multi-ramp wedge configuration and offered a straight path for the incoming air. This simple scheme avoided the complex inlet/intake interface problems that dogged the TF30-powered F-111.

ABOVE **VF-41's 'Fast Eagle 105' (BuNo 161615) has its wings spread at the 20-degree position in preparation for aerial refuelling from a USAF KC-135 during a cross-country flight from NAS Oceana to NAS Fallon in late 1998. The aircraft's excellent slow-speed handling characteristics meant that pilots could accurately position the F-14 behind the tanker and fly the jet's extended probe into the trailing basket without too many issues.** *(Ted Carlson)*

BELOW LEFT **The F-14's rectangular intakes featured forward-facing variable-position deflection ramps that had the ability to 'over-collapse' so as to provide additional area when the aircraft was taking off or landing. The ramps were operated automatically by the Inlet Control Computers, calculating their optimum position 40 times per second according to parameters such as engine speed, air temperature and pressure and the aircraft's AOA.** *(Danny Coremans)*

BELOW RIGHT **Here the port variable-position deflection ramps have been fully lowered. At speeds up to Mach 0.5 the ramps would remain retracted, but when the aircraft went faster they were lowered – as seen here – by actuators in order to slow the incoming air to a more digestible subsonic speed prior to passing to the face of the engine.** *(Danny Coremans)*

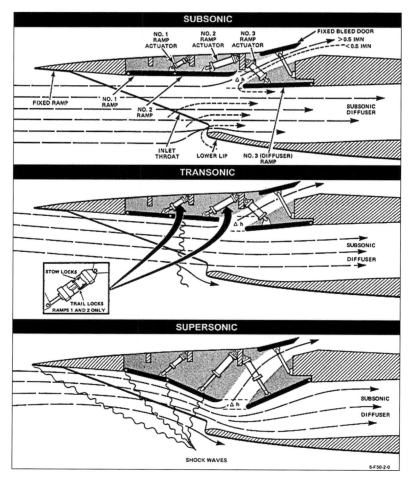

LEFT The variable-geometry inlet configuration diagram, showing the various slat, spoiler and flap positions, published in NAVAIR 01-F14AAA-1 publication *NATOPS Flight Manual Navy Model F-14A Aircraft*, dated 15 May 2003. *(US Navy)*

The air that flowed through the intakes was compressed by forward-facing variable-position ramps that had the ability to 'over-collapse' so as to provide additional area when the aircraft was taking off or landing. This feature meant that there was no need for suck-in doors or hinged cowls to facilitate additional airflow at slower speeds. A single rear-facing throat-bleed slot was fitted on the upper wing surface above each of the intakes, these being used to disperse boundary layer air via hydraulic actuators. The remaining air was compressed in a subsonic diffuser duct before passing to the face of the engine. The intake deflection ramps were operated automatically by the Inlet Control Computers (part of the CADC), calculating the optimum position for the ramps 40 times per second according to parameters such as engine speed, air temperature and pressure and the aircraft's AOA.

The dual-position throat-bleed doors mounted on the upper surface of the inlets were supposed to inhibit the possibility of engine compressor stalls due to disturbed airflow (prevalent during high AOA flight and when there were sudden, sharp throttle movements – both characteristics of ACM), but numerous Tomcats were lost as a result of single-engine flameouts. With the engines 9ft apart, if one flamed out, the other – especially if it was in afterburner – produced a significant yawing moment known as 'nose slice' to F-14 crews. The aircraft could quickly be thrown into an unrecoverable fast flat spin as a result of an engine flameout, which the TF30 was, unfortunately, very prone to. Such stalls were first encountered during the early stages of flight when pre-production aircraft were flown at high AOA at high altitude and low speeds, engines stalling when coming out of afterburner and at low power settings.

At some airspeed/power setting combinations, an engine flameout could result in a very violent departure from controlled flight. This in turn could rapidly develop into a self-

BELOW A brown-shirted plane captain from VF-211 closely inspects the starboard intake, ramps and actuators in 'his' F-14A prior to the veteran jet flying an operational mission over Iraq from *Enterprise* in January 2004. The sailor's presence lends a sense of scale to the Tomcat's intakes. *(US Navy)*

sustaining irrecoverable flat spin if the pilot did not take the appropriate recovery actions within a matter of seconds. At the very high levels of negative g associated with such a spin, it quickly became impossible for crew members to reach their ejection seat handles. If the yaw rate was allowed to build up, the spin flattened – it could increase to 180 degrees per second, nose slightly down, with zero AOA and zero airspeed. The crew would soon lose consciousness. Even if the pilot and RIO managed to eject prior to blacking out, the low airspeeds associated with a flat spin meant that the large, heavy canopy separated slowly from the jet and the crew ran the risk of hitting it as they left the Tomcat; a fate that befell 'Goose' in *Top Gun*.

Grumman, Pratt & Whitney and the US Navy struggled to find a solution to this problem, which specifically afflicted the F-14A, for many years until the adoption of the Digital Flight Control System in the late 1990s.

Flight controls

The Tomcat's flight controls reflected the state of aerospace technology when the jet was designed in the 1960s, relying on metal and hydraulic rods and cables, springs and weights and servos and boosters to impart the pilot's control inputs from the cockpit to the moveable surfaces. Indeed, the F-14 was the last American non-Fly By Wire (FBW) fighter to enter front line service, the pilot moving the controls with a solid mechanical action – only the wing spoilers were electrically driven.

Although pilots generally considered the F-14 to be a very stable and forgiving aircraft in most flight regimes, they had to fly it in the traditional way – by hand. For example, there was no computer to automatically trim the jet for the pilot. If the Tomcat left the flight envelope and went out of control, there was a long series of emergency procedures that were read out loud – usually by the RIO – as an aid to the pilot as he attempted to regain control of the 'Big Fighter'. Conversely, in an F/A-18, for example, when the aircraft departed controlled flight the pilot simply released the joystick, locked his harness and allowed the flight computer to right the jet. One distinct advantage enjoyed by the Tomcat pilot thanks to the aircraft's manual-only controls was that he had the ability to exceed

the jet's 'safe' flight envelope in an emergency – usually during ACM. His counterpart in a Hornet could attempt to do this, but the flight computer usually restricted such manoeuvres to 7g. Tomcats were regularly pushed well beyond

LEFT A single rear-facing throat-bleed slot was fitted on the upper wing surface above each of the intakes to disperse boundary layer air via the intake ramps. Forward and inboard of each of the slots were heat exchanger exhausts for the Environmental Control System. This F-14D from VF-213 was photographed being marshalled on to one of CVN-71's bow catapults during Operation Iraqi Freedom in March 2003. *(US Navy)*

BELOW Green-shirted maintenance personnel from VF-143 have removed some of the spine panels from this F-14B, chained down over the fantail of USS *George Washington* (CVN-73), in order to investigate a minor flight control issue with the jet. The spine of the Tomcat housed control rods and cables, electrical wiring and the emergency hydraulic generator, as well as numerous cooling ducts. *(US Navy)*

LEFT Despite its size, the Tomcat was highly regarded by pilots for its capabilities as a dogfighter – particularly if they were at the controls of an F110-powered variant. Having selected wings fully forward, the pilot of this F-14 is working hard as he pursues a highly agile A-4F 'Super Fox' out over the NAS Fallon range during a Topgun ACM training mission in the early 1990s. *(Ted Carlson)*

LEFT Tomcats from NAWC's Aircraft Division at 'Pax River' prepare to run in over USS *John C. Stennis* (CVN-74) and pitch out into the recovery pattern during the highly successful Digital Flight Control System trials staged off the Virginia coast in 1996. Leading the section is an F-14A, with a D-model jet in trail. *(US Navy)*

the recommended 6.5g in training, without the airframe suffering any ill effects.

Although the F-14 was superior to the legendary F-4 Phantom II (the fighter it replaced in the fleet) in respect to weapon systems, manoeuvrability and range, the Tomcat was not as smooth or as stable as its predecessor on the glideslope when coming in to land on a carrier. It was not as good at holding an accurate approach speed or glideslope angle either, and it tended to veer away from a heading. The aircraft also suffered from high pitch inertia, causing it to float when in the final stages of landing. High residual thrust meant that pilots had to use low throttle settings, giving poor engine response when more power was required. Finally, indifferent lateral control made precise heading control difficult. Nevertheless, the aircraft demonstrated the ability to land successfully and go around (bolter) in a number of simulated emergency configurations during the US Navy's exhaustive test and evaluation programme.

Although passed fit for fleet service, the Tomcat would suffer an unenviably high loss rate due to poor TF30 engine performance and challenging handling characteristics in certain flight regimes – specifically flameouts when at high AOA, and Dutch roll and uncontrollable sideslipping during landing. In 1996 a new Digital Flight Control System (DFCS) that had

BELOW Although the Tomcat had good low-speed handling characteristics the aircraft could be a handful in the final stages of a carrier landing. It was poor at holding an accurate approach speed or glideslope angle and it tended to veer away from a heading. The jet also suffered from high pitch inertia, causing it to float in the final stages of landing. High residual thrust and indifferent lateral control added to these woes. *(US Navy)*

been developed by British firm GEC-Marconi Avionics was acquired for the surviving F-14 fleet as a replacement for the jet's original analogue flight controls. Based on the system built for the Eurofighter Typhoon, the DFCS used FBW software to send commands to the rudders and 'tailerons' to dampen Dutch roll (both rolling and yawing – an out-of-phase combination of 'tail-wagging' and rocking from side to side) oscillations and adverse sideslip when on the glideslope for landing. It also controlled wing rock on take-off. During ACM, the DFCS improved departure resistance when manoeuvring at high AOA and gave the pilot a far greater chance of recovering the jet should it in fact depart from controlled flight.

The Cat's claws – air-to-air weapons

The Tomcat's primary mission for much of its career with the US Navy was to protect the carrier and its battle group from prowling Soviet long-range bombers equipped with anti-ship missiles. The F-14's principal air-to-air weapon when performing this role was the AIM-54 Phoenix missile, which had been in development for more than ten years by the time the Tomcat made its first flight. Indeed, the AIM-54 could trace its lineage back to the Bendix XAAM-M-10 Eagle, which was supposed to arm the Missileer bomber interceptor. The XAAM-M-10 suffered persistent development problems, however, resulting in the Missileer being abandoned in December 1960. Two years later, the Eagle was reborn as the AAM-N-11 Phoenix, with its prime contractor now being the Hughes Aircraft Company. Subsequently redesignated the AIM-54, the missile (and its all-important

ABOVE With the arrival of the agile F/A-18 Hornet from the mid-1980s, the previously unrivalled F-14 had a serious contender to its crown. More 'showboating' than dogfighting, an F-14B from VF-103 and an F/A-18C from VFA-34 perform a mirror formation pass off the portside of CVN-73. *(US Navy)*

ABOVE This heavily modified NA-3A Skywarrior was used by the Hughes Aircraft Company during the 1960s as a flying testbed for the Phoenix Airborne Missile Control System (AMCS). It is seen here test-firing a development AIM-54 over the Pacific Missile Range in 1967, shadowed by an F-9 Cougar chase aeroplane. The Skywarrior was fitted with an F-111B radome to house the AMCS antenna, radar and infrared subsystems. *(Mike Glenn)*

RIGHT FSD No 6 BuNo 157985 was delivered to the PMTC at NAS Point Mugu on 18 December 1971. Heavily involved in missile separation and weapons tests (it is seen here firing AIM-54 practice rounds), the aircraft managed to shoot itself down during AIM-7E-2 trials on 20 June 1972. The weapon pitched up on firing and ruptured several fuel cells, which duly ignited. The crew successfully ejected. *(US Navy)*

AN/AWG-9 advanced fire control system, which is detailed in Chapter 5) survived the cancellation of the F-111B.

Flight trials of the weighty weapon, which tipped the scales at 1,008lb, commenced in 1965 with unguided rounds. The first fully guided XAIM-54 flights were undertaken the following year, with two NA-3A Skywarriors and an F-111B employing weapons over the Pacific Missile Test Range at Point Mugu. The first guided shot scored a hit at a range twice that of the best air-to-air missiles of the time. More test rounds were fired in 1968–69, and in December 1970 Hughes received a contract to put the AIM-54A into production. Testing of this initial version of the weapon continued into the early 1970s, and by the time the last example was delivered to the US Navy nine years later, Hughes had built more than 2,500 AIM-54As at its Tucson, Arizona, plant.

The myriad tests undertaken by Hughes, Grumman and the US Navy demonstrated the missile's unrivalled capabilities against a variety of small, medium and large targets (principally BQM-34E Firebee, QT-33 and QT-86 drones and CQM-10B Bomarc surface-to-air missiles) flying at high, medium and low altitudes replicating Soviet aircraft/missile and mission profiles. A typical test, performed in April 1973, saw an AIM-54 pass within a lethal distance of a BQM-34E flying at Mach 1.5 at 50,000ft simulating a Tu-22 'Backfire' bomber-type target. The weapon was launched at a distance of 126 miles, and it took just over 2 minutes 30 seconds to reach its target. The latter was still more than 70 miles from the Tomcat when it was destroyed. Seven months later, a single F-14 fired a maximum load of six AIM-54s at three QT-33s, two BQM-34As and a BQM-34E flying at medium altitude at speeds varying from Mach 0.6 (QT-33s) to Mach 1.1 (BQM-34s). Two of the QT-33s and two BQM-34s were destroyed (three by direct hits and one by a near miss), one missile failed and one shot was declared a 'no test' due to a drone malfunction.

The fuselage of the Phoenix was made of metal, while the aerodynamic surfaces (wings and fins) of the A-model were of a honeycomb structure – though this was replaced by sheet-metal from the AIM-54B onwards as a cost-cutting measure. Directly behind the

ABOVE Brand new F-14B BuNo 163227 of VF-211 was sent aloft from NAS Miramar in late 1989 with a 'Doomsday' load of six AIM-54C Phoenix drill rounds. Such a configuration was never seen during blue water operations from a carrier as the Tomcat would have been too heavy to land back if none of the missiles had been expended. *(US Navy)*

RIGHT The AIM-54A preflight check page from the NAVAIR 01-F14AAA-1T(B) publication *Tactical Manual Pocket Guide F-14 Aircraft*, dated July 1985. *(US Navy)*

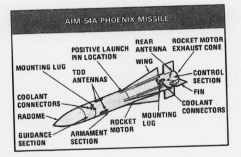

NWP 55-5-F14 (Rev. B) PG

AIM-54A PHOENIX MISSILE

MOUNTING LUG
POSITIVE LAUNCH PIN LOCATION
REAR ANTENNA
ROCKET MOTOR EXHAUST CONE
WING
TDD ANTENNAS
CONTROL SECTION
COOLANT CONNECTORS
FIN
RADOME
COOLANT CONNECTORS
MOUNTING LUG
GUIDANCE SECTION
ARMAMENT SECTION
ROCKET MOTOR

PREFLIGHT

1. Radome free of cracks, scratches, grease deposits
2. No damage to TDD antennas
3. No excessive hydraulic fluid (pink) or coolanol (clear) accumulations or leaks
4. No dents, deformities in rocket motor or armament sections
5. Wings and fins for security
6. No dents, deformities, broken welds in fins and wings
7. Battery electrolyte vent port free of fresh or aged electrolyte (Port is covered by a white plastic cap located inside the tailcone at the 9 o'clock position)

WARNING

Electrolyte is caustic; fumes are toxic.

8. No cracks or deformities in rocket motor exhaust cone
9. No damage to rear antenna

nose radome was the planar array seeker antenna, followed by the transmitter receiver and the electronics unit. The fusing (Downey Mk 334 proximity, Bendix infrared or contact) and arming system came next, followed by the 132lb high-explosive warhead. The aft section of the missile (roughly half of its length) contained the single-stage Rocketdyne Mk 47 solid-propellant motor. This steel-cased unit had a long burn time – on a maximum range shoot the missile could have a flight time of up to 3 minutes – and the power required to accelerate the AIM-54 to speeds of up to Mach 5 at high altitude. The weapon was appreciably slower at lower altitudes, however.

The Phoenix was steered by tail-mounted control surfaces, following on from previous air-to-air weapons built by Hughes, such as the AIM-4 Falcon. The company believed that this layout offered lower drag and higher manoeuvrability than the moving wings used by the AIM-7 Sparrow, for example. This was proven during development testing, when Phoenix rounds had manoeuvred at up to 17g. The hydraulic actuators, and their associated power system, used to achieve such eye-watering turns were packed into the rear of the missile, being wrapped around the motor tailpipe.

The follow-on AIM-54B, manufactured from the end of 1977, featured improved resistance to enemy signals jamming and re-engineered software modules. Other changes were aimed at enhancing reliability, and these included all-digital guidance equipment and non-liquid environmental conditioning and hydraulic systems – the A-model weapon required a continuous feed of cooling oil from the F-14 itself when attached to the jet due to the incredible internal heat generated by its electronics when powered up.

The definitive Phoenix variant was the AIM-54C, development of which was commenced at the company's expense in the autumn of 1976. Flight trials got under way four years later. Once again, improved reliability was the primary focus of the upgrade, with the missile having much greater resistance to electronic countermeasures (ECM). According to F.B. Newman of the Hughes Aircraft Company, 'the AIM-54C was the model that had everything they'd [the US Navy] ever wanted in it – a

higher thrust motor, an improved warhead and an improved fuse'. The latter, controlled by a Motorola target detection device that detonated the warhead at the optimum moment to inflict maximum damage, allowed the C-model Phoenix to 'take down targets such as high-diving air-to-surface missiles like the AS-4 and AS-6 launched by "Badgers", "Bears" and "Backfires"'. Newman went on to say:

Until the C-model fuse came along, we had the problem that they [anti-ship missiles] cruised at very high altitude at Mach 2.0 to 3.0, and when they 'tipped over' into a steep, high-angle, high-velocity dive it was impossible to intercept with Phoenix. The AIM-54C changed that.

The modestly improved AIM-54C+ was introduced during the late 1990s, this version having enhanced electronic counter-countermeasures (ECCM), a revised proximity fuse that could handle all-altitude operations, improved target discrimination and increased engagement range.

The Tomcat's medium-range air-to-air missile was the venerable Raytheon AIM-7 Sparrow, which, although being less effective in every way when compared with the Phoenix, was considerably cheaper, half the weight of the long-range weapon, inflicted much less drag on the F-14 and did not require heavy pallets when tunnel-mounted beneath the jet's centre section. Serving as the long-range weapon for

BELOW Four US Navy Reserve units were issued with F-14As in 1985-87 – VF-201 'Hunters' and VF-202 'Superheats', both based at NAS Dallas, Texas, and VF-301 'Devil's Disciples' and VF-302 'Stallions' at NAS Miramar. This 'Hunters' jet – BuNo 162709, which was the third-to-last A-model Tomcat built – is firing an AIM-54C during an active duty training exercise. *(US Navy)*

most other US fighters from the 1960s through to the 1990s, the semi-active radar missile was developed in the 1950s by Sperry as the XAAM-N-2. Entering service in 1958, the weapon was redesignated the AIM-7 in 1962. More than 34,000 examples of the C, D and E

models of the missile were produced, and these were widely used during the Vietnam War.

Designed at a time when the most likely target for the weapon was a subsonic non-manoeuvring bomber flying at high altitude, the Sparrow proved disappointing when employed against highly agile North Vietnamese MiG-17s and MiG-21s that were typically encountered at altitudes below 8,000ft. A rapid redesign effort by Raytheon produced the more manoeuvrable and reliable AIM-7E-2, followed by the E-3, with clipped wings, and the E-4, which was specifically built to work in conjunction with high-powered fighter radars such as the AN/AWG-9 installed in the F-14. In 1975 production switched to the AIM-7F, which had been redesigned from nose to tail. The adoption of solid-state electronics had allowed Raytheon to move the weapon's warhead (which had been enlarged) forward of the guidance wings, while a new dual thrust sustainer motor boosted the missile's range to 30 miles – twice that of the -7E.

The final model acquired by the US Navy was the AIM-7M, which entered service in the early 1980s. Costing $203,000 per missile (less than half the price of an AIM-54), the -7M featured an ECM-resistant monopulse seeker with improved look-down capability and a digital signal processor. In all other respects, this variant was similar to the -7F, and most surviving examples of the latter weapon were upgraded to -7M specification.

The Sparrow was scheduled to be replaced by the AIM-120 Advanced Medium-Range Air-to-Air Missile (AMRAAM) from the mid-1990s, but funding for the software upgrade that would have allowed the weapon to be employed by the F-14D was cancelled when the Tomcat's primary mission began to shift from fighter to precision bomber.

For short-range combat, the F-14 was armed with up to four AIM-9 Sidewinder missiles, this weapon having been developed by the US Navy as the XAAM-N-7 in the 1950s. A simple, but effective, heat-seeking missile built in huge numbers, the AIM-9J variant was the model initially used by early-production F-14s. Embodying lessons learned during the early years of aerial combat in the Vietnam War, when the AIM-9B/D/E/G enjoyed a degree of success, the J-model had an expanded target-

ABOVE Chained to the flight deck of CVN-73 between OSW patrols over Iraq in December 1997, this F-14B of VF-102 is armed with AIM-54C and AIM-9L missiles, and two 500lb Mk 82 bombs on BRU-32 racks. Mixed loads became commonplace as Tomcat units took on the precision strike role from the mid-1990s. RIO Lt Steve Nevarez sits on the forward spine of the jet awaiting the arrival of his pilot. *(US Navy)*

RIGHT The AIM-7E/F/M preflight check page from the NAVAIR 01-F14AAA-1T(B) publication *Tactical Manual Pocket Guide F-14 Aircraft*, dated July 1985. *(US Navy)*

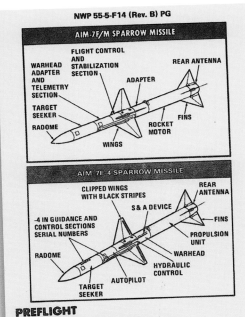

ABOVE Having dispensed with its under-fuselage weapons pallets, this VF-1 jet is armed with four live (denoted by their yellow bands) AIM-7Ms and four AIM-9Ls in a fleet air defence maximum loiter loadout – the fighter was photographed during an Operation Desert Storm combat air patrol. This particular jet, BuNo 162607, has been on display in the Yanks Air Museum at Chino, California, for almost 20 years. *(US Navy)*

ABOVE VF-2 F-14D BuNo 164349 has a weapons loadout that was again rarely seen in the front line – four AIM-7Ms, two AIM-54Cs and two AIM-9Ls. Having previously served with VF-11 and VF-124 prior to being issued to VF-2, this aircraft participated in the F-14's final operational deployment in 2005-06 as VF-213's 'Blacklion 212' – the jet dropped two GBU-38 JDAM on insurgent targets in Iraq during its time in-theatre. *(US Navy)*

engagement zone that allowed it to be launched at any spot in the rear half of a target aircraft, rather than just at its exhaust. The Tomcat also used the follow-on H-model, which embodied still more improvements to the missile's target acquisition capabilities.

The AIM-9L, which went into production in 1977, was the first 'all-aspect' Sidewinder variant that was capable of attacking a target aircraft from all directions, including head-on. A completely re-engineered weapon, it boasted a highly sensitive seeker head that could pick up heat created by friction off the leading edge of an aircraft wing and differentiate between an aircraft and decoy flares. The L-model also

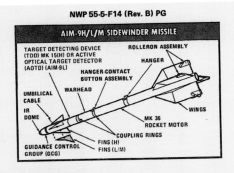

NWP 55-5-F14 (Rev. B) PG

AIM-9H/L/M SIDEWINDER MISSILE

PREFLIGHT

1. Dome cover installed
2. Fins secure, but rotate freely
3. Retainer springs attached on inside fins
4. Rubber seals at base of fins intact
5. Umbilical connected, umbilical block hooks in place
6. AOTD windows clean and undamaged, replace AOTD protective cover (AIM-9L/M only) (Do not touch windows)
7. No evidence of smoke or carbon around gas grain generator exhaust port
8. No dents in rocket motor casing
9. Wings secure
10. Rollerons caged and wheels free to turn
11. Motor weather seal intact

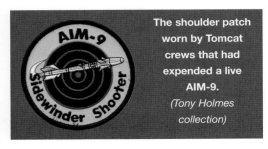

The shoulder patch worn by Tomcat crews that had expended a live AIM-9. *(Tony Holmes collection)*

LEFT The AIM-9H/L/M preflight check page from the NAVAIR 01-F14AAA-1T(B) publication *Tactical Manual Pocket Guide F-14 Aircraft*, dated July 1985. *(US Navy)*

introduced a higher-impulse rocket motor, larger warhead and a proximity directional blast fragged fuse that was rigged to detonate outward towards the target – these fuses were also fitted to the AIM-54C and AIM-7M. The final Sidewinder model employed by the Tomcat was the AIM-9M, which entered production in 1982. Very similar to the L-model, the 'Mike' had improved capability against infrared countermeasures (specifically decoy flares), increased reliability and a reduced-smoke motor.

The final weapon fielded by the Tomcat that could be used in aerial combat was the 20mm General Electric M61A1 Vulcan rotary cannon, fitted in the port side of the forward fuselage. The weapon was 74in long and weighed 265lb. A muzzle gas diffuser was fitted to the jet to avoid structural damage being inflicted on the airframe when the weapon was in operation, while a muzzle clamp reduced the dispersal of

rounds fired from the cannon's six barrels. The M61A1's ammunition drum carried a total of 678 rounds. In order to prevent the possibility of spent cases being sucked into the left intake after firing, they were returned to the drum after their removal from the gun breech. Capable of being fired at a rate of 6,000 rounds per minute, the Vulcan cannon could empty the ammunition drum in just 7 seconds.

The Tomcat's air-to-ground arsenal is described in Chapter 3, under the heading 'Bombcat' evolution.

ABOVE LEFT 'Ordies' from VF-103 load 20mm PGU-28 semi-armour-piercing high-explosive incendiary rounds into the magazine of an F-14B on the flight deck of CVN-73 during the carrier's deployment in 2002. A gun jam on 20 July that year ruined VF-103's one and only chance of seeing combat in OEF. *(US Navy)*

ABOVE The pilot of VF-31 F-14D BuNo 164342 'Tomcatter 100' rolls in hot and squeezes off 100 rounds of 20mm ammunition at the grey waters of the NAG in early January 2006. The M61A1 is fed by a linkless ammunition storage and handling system containing linkless M-50 of PGU-series electrically primed ammunition. *(Erik Hildebrandt)*

Powerplants

The original engine fitted into the F-14A was the 12,350lb (5,600kg) thrust Pratt & Whitney TF30-P-412 axial-flow turbofan, which was an improved version of the TF30-P-12 that had been rigorously tested in the F-111B. Even before the first prototype had flown, Grumman knew that this powerplant had some serious flaws. It was underpowered – despite thrust increasing to 20,900lb when in afterburner – and was particularly susceptible to compressor stalls if intake airflow was disturbed. The stalling problem was further amplified by the fact that the TF30s were widely spaced on the Tomcat.

If an engine stalled while the aircraft was in afterburner, the sudden onset of asymmetric thrust could cause the nose to 'slice' (rotation in yaw) so violently that the jet suffered a flat spin departure that was often impossible for the pilot to recover from.

Developed by Pratt & Whitney as a private venture for civilian airliners in the late 1950s

RIGHT A TF30-P-414 turbofan sits on an engine trolley following its removal from the VF-14 F-14A seen parked behind it at NAS Oceana. More than 3,000 examples of the TF30 were built by Pratt & Whitney during its 22-year production run. *(Danny Coremans collection)*

ABOVE When it came to sheer spectacle, the sight and sound of an F-14A launching in Zone Five afterburner had few rivals on a carrier deck. Having just been released by the catapult shuttle (the small white protuberance in the flight deck immediately beneath the jet), VF-154's 'Nite 107' (BuNo 161296) is just milliseconds away from taking flight off *Kitty Hawk*'s waist catapult two during OIF. *(US Navy)*

and originally designated the JTF10A, this high-compression, axial-flow, twin-spool turbofan failed to attract any orders despite it being available in no fewer than six versions. Although a commercial failure, the JTF10A boasted significant improvements over previous powerplants. Indeed, it was the first Western turbofan engine

BELOW The TF30 suffered from poor reliability in fleet service, with compressor stalls and in-flight fires causing the loss of more than 50 F-14s during the jet's three decades of front-line use. The crew of this Phoenix missile-equipped F-14A from VX-4 were lucky to get their fighter back to NAS Point Mugu after its port engine spectacularly failed during a routine test flight over the Pacific Missile Test Range. *(US Navy)*

to be equipped with an afterburner. In the mid-1960s the engine was chosen – in TF30 form – to power the USAF's F-111 fighter-bomber and the US Navy's F-111B fighter. When the latter was cancelled and the F-14 selected in its place, the US Navy was forced to persevere with the TF30-P-412 as there was no alternative powerplant then readily available.

Little changed during its 22 years in production (when more than 3,000 engines were built), the TF30 featured an annular intake made from a single-piece casting that led directly to a three-stage titanium fan mounted within a steel containment case. The latter was located at the forward end of the low-pressure (LP) compressor shaft, which had a pressure ratio of greater than 2-to-1 and a bypass ratio of 0.91-to-1. The remaining six stages on the LP spool were those of the LP compressor, whose titanium rotor blades operated in conjunction with steel stator blades. A seven-stage high-pressure (HP) compressor made from nickel-based alloy offered a further pressure ratio of around 18-to-1, delivering its airflow into eight Hastelloy X annular chambers. The TF30 could burn either JP-4 or JP-5 fuel, which was fed to the four nozzles in each chamber by a Chandler Evans two-stage fuel pump.

Hot gas from the chambers then passed through a single-stage HP turbine with air-cooled cobalt-alloy blades, followed by a three-stage uncooled LP turbine fitted with nickel-alloy blades. The two-piece turbine casing was of steel construction. The final engine section housed the five-zone afterburner, which ended in a convergent/divergent nozzle. The engine was started by an AiResearch ARS100 air turbine starter located on the left forward drive pod of the accessory gearbox.

The TF30 was originally only meant to power the RDT&E airframes and the first 61 production F-14As. From 1973 onward all new Tomcats (as well as those A-models already delivered) would be fitted with the Pratt & Whitney F401-PW-400, which had 30% more thrust than the TF30. The new engine was being primarily built for fitment to the USAF's F-15 Eagle, with the US Navy sharing development costs with the air force on a 60%/40% basis. It was to be fitted into a new variant of Tomcat designated the F-14B (not to be confused with the F-14B that entered fleet service in the late 1980s). However, by the time the F401 commenced flight-testing in a modified A-model, the Tomcat was running considerably over budget to the tune of more than $400 million.

As early as April 1971, Grumman had been warned by the Department of Defense that costs would have to be cut or the F-14 may be cancelled. Rampant inflation made the problem worse, as Grumman struggled to meet the fixed-price stipulation in the contract that it had signed with the US Navy in 1969. With funding tight and some members of Congress calling for the Tomcat programme to be terminated, Deputy Secretary of Defense David Packard had little choice but to perform merciless major surgery on the project in May 1971 so as to ensure the F-14's long-term future. Among the many cuts imposed on the programme was the cancelling of the F401 engine (which was proving too complicated for fleet use in the short term in any case). Both the F-14B and improved F-14C also fell victim to Packard's 'knife'.

With the TF30 being its only option for the Tomcat, the US Navy implored Pratt & Whitney to improve the engine's reliability. The end result was the TF30-P-414, which was fitted to all A-model jets from the 235th airframe onward. It had taken a decade for this to happen, the upgraded engine featuring steel containment cases around the first three fan stages as a 'damage control' measure following numerous fan blade failures with the TF30-P-412. Disintegrating blades often scythed through anything that got in their way after breaking off the rapidly spinning turbine, causing catastrophic damage to the rest of the engine that frequently resulted in the loss of an aircraft due to fire. Slightly different materials were also employed in the blades' manufacturing process, and additional steps taken (including the fitment of more titanium sheeting and ablative substances) to improve fire prevention should a failure occur.

TF30-P-414s were retrospectively fitted to early-build F-14As as well, with the final TF30-P-412 being retired in the summer of 1979. Although the -414 was indeed an improvement over the original engine, it was still somewhat lacking when it came to durability. Pratt & Whitney duly produced the -414A from late 1982 in an attempt to address these lingering problems,

ABOVE The pilot of 'Bullet 212' (BuNo 161275) selects afterburner for the benefit of Dave Baranek's camera during a dusk training mission from USS *Ranger* (CV-61) in 1989. The shock diamonds synonymous with an engine operating in afterburner are clearly visible in the reduced light, these standing wave patterns that appear in supersonic exhaust plumes being formed from a complex flow field. *(Dave Baranek)*

the new engine offering increased mean times between overhaul, better reliability and greater resistance to compressor stalling. This version of the TF30 would remain the powerplant for all A-model aircraft until the jets' retirement in 2004.

By then more than 50 Tomcats, worth $1.5 billion, had been lost through engine-related

BELOW The wide spacing between the F-14A's TF30s is dramatically revealed in this photograph of VF-51 jet BuNo 162602, which broke in two after suffering a ramp strike attempting to land at night on board *Kitty Hawk* in the Sea of Japan on 11 July 1994. The cockpit section slid down the deck and over the side, with the pilot, Lt Cdr D. Jennings, and the RIO, Lt R. Arnold, successfully ejecting. *(US Navy)*

MEETING THE MISSION
The F110 Augmented Turbofan

GENERAL ✦ ELECTRIC

ABOVE This press handout was created by General Electric for the F110 shortly after the engine had been ordered into production for both the F-14 and F-16 in the 1980s. It featured the re-engined F-14B BuNo 157986, which initially flew with F101-DFEs before receiving F110s, and a similarly powered USAF F-16C from one of the test units at Edwards AFB. *(Peter Mersky collection)*

problems – primarily compressor stalls caused as a result of the jet being at high AOA while vigorously manoeuvring during air combat training. Such failures caused high-profile Navy Secretary and Naval Flight Officer (NFO), John F. Lehman to tell Congress in 1984 that the 'F-14/TF30 combination was probably the worst airframe/engine mismatch we have had in many years. The TF30 is simply a terrible engine'. His opinion was echoed by veteran fighter pilot Rear Admiral Paul T. Gillcrist, who flew the Tomcat in the early 1980s while a wing commander for all Pacific Fleet fighter squadrons at NAS Miramar:

I do not believe that anyone who has ever flown the F-14A Tomcat would argue with

the statement that the airplane's greatest single weakness is the engine. The decision to cut the F401-PW-400 destined US Navy fighter aircrews to fly on the pointed end of the spear in F-14s powered by what they referred to as 'two pieces of junk' for an unprecedented 18 years. It was not until April 1988 that the first F-14A+ [subsequently redesignated the F-14B] configured with the new General Electric F110-GE-400 engine reached VF-101 at NAS Oceana.

Grumman had been given approval by the US Navy to look into fitting a number of F-14As with a new powerplant in the early 1980s, the company having actually resumed flight operations with the original F-14B prototype now fitted with General Electric F101-DFE engines in July 1981. Chosen by the USAF for its B-1B bomber and F-15 and F-16 fighters, the engine (redesignated the F110 in October 1982) was capable of producing 26,950lb of thrust when installed in the F-14. The F110-GE-400 greatly enhanced the Tomcat's mission performance thanks to its thrust levels being 32% higher than those of the TF30. Its lean fuel burn rate also boosted the jet's combat air patrol (CAP) loiter time by no less than 34%. Being 20 years younger than the Pratt & Whitney engine, the F110 was also designed from the outset to be far less susceptible to stalling at high AOA.

RIGHT The F110 was a large engine for a big fighter, this particular example sitting on a wheeled trolley in the VF-213 hangar at NAS Oceana in front of F-14D BuNo 164347. Sandwiched between the exhaust nozzle extension ducting to the left and the shroud to the right is the mounting ring that secures the engine to the airframe.

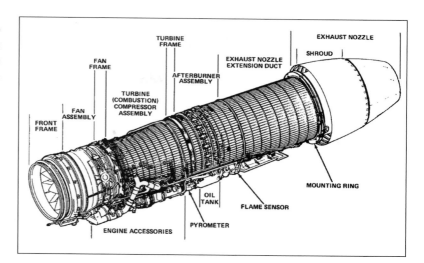

RIGHT A diagram of the F110-GE-400 engine published in NAVAIR 01-F14AAD-1 publication *NATOPS Flight Manual Navy Model F-14D Aircraft*, dated 1 September 2004. *(US Navy)*

The F110 proved to be almost completely installationally interchangeable with the TF30, the new engine needing just an extra 50in section 'downstream' of the turbine because it was appreciably shorter – 182in in length compared with 236in. The only other change of note was rearrangement of the engine accessories and their drive gearbox. Although the diameter of the F110 was less, at 46.5in, than the TF30, airflow at take-off was increased from 242 to 270lb per second – hence the increase in power to 26,950lb (the F110 was actually rated at 29,000lb, although it was restricted to 26,950lb to match the US Navy requirement). This in turn meant that no afterburner was needed for catapult launches, greatly reducing fuel consumption – employing the 'burners multiplied fuel use fourfold. Furthermore, the F110's relative frugality in MIL power (non-afterburner) boosted the re-engined Tomcat's mission radius by more than 62%, while its increased thrust reduced the jet's time to high altitude by a whopping 61%.

Although the TF30 had been an advanced engine in the 1960s, the F110 clearly showed the progress made in turbofan technology in the intervening two decades. The TF30 had 16 stages of compression, with the 3-stage fan rotating on the same shaft as the 6-stage LP compressor. By contrast, the F110 had just 12 stages in total, comprising a 3-stage bypass fan and a 9-stage HP compressor and, crucially, hundreds of fan blades fewer. Despite this, the F110's overall HP ratio of 31-to-1 was appreciably higher than the TF30's 18-to-1, which in turn led to better fuel economy for the General Electric engine. Furthermore, the F110 could effectively burn fuel in a much

ABOVE Recently delivered F110 engines sit in Calverton's Plant 6 awaiting their installation in new-build and remanufactured B- and D-model F-14s in the late 1980s. These would be fitted at Station Two, along with the outer wing sections. *(Grumman via Tailhook)*

RIGHT A diagram of the fuel tanks, and their associated systems, for the Tomcat published in NAVAIR 01-F14AAD-1 publication *NATOPS Flight Manual Navy Model F-14D Aircraft*, dated 1 September 2004. *(US Navy)*

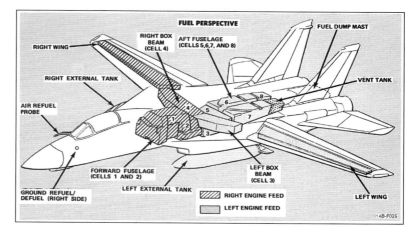

RIGHT AND FAR RIGHT Afterburner nozzles fitted to an F110 installed in an F-14D from VF-213. The nozzles would be in the fully open position when the pilot selected afterburner. According to Lt Brandon Hammond of VF-154, 'The Tomcat has "weight on wheels" and "weight off wheels" switches. When weight is "on wheels" [on deck] the nozzles are commanded open to reduce thrust produced by the engines to keep from blowing over ground personnel. When the weight is "off wheels" [airborne] the nozzles will close any time when in "basic engine" from idle to military power [highest thrust without selecting afterburner], and will open up as afterburner is staged. This feature gives added thrust at idle when airborne.'
(Danny Coremans)

shorter distance than the TF30, particularly in its afterburner section. The distance from the augmentation fuel nozzle rings to the end of the exhaust nozzle of the F110 was just over half that of the TF30, but it was cheaper for the US Navy to have General Electric add an unnecessary extra section to its engine than to shorten the F-14.

Of the 712 Tomcats built by Grumman, just 86 F-14Bs and 55 F-14Ds would be fitted with F110-GE-400 engines. The remaining jets had to rely on the TF30-P-412/414, dubbed 'The

little engine that couldn't' by Rear Admiral Paul T. Gillcrist.

BELOW The F110-engined F-14 did not require afterburner during a catapult shot thanks to the increased power of its GE turbofans. On the cat, the B/D-model was not allowed to be in afterburner because insufficient cooling for the jet blast deflector would warp the metal. Here, VF-31's 'Tomcatter 101' (BuNo 164603) accelerates away from CVN-71 at the start of a training mission in July 2005. *(US Navy)*

The maintainer's perspective

Daniel 'Dsquare' Dixon is typical of the myriad – largely unsung – maintainers who toiled away for countless hours keeping the highly complex Tomcat serviceable in the world's harshest operational environment for a combat aircraft – a carrier flight deck. He was a jet mechanic with the US Navy for more than 20 years, serving with no fewer than six F-14 units during this time. Dan's personal experience of working on the TF30 and the follow-on F110 provide a unique 'owner's manual' insight into the Tomcat community from a maintainer's perspective:

The beginning of my Navy career wasn't exactly at the beginning of the Tomcat's service lifespan, but it was close, and the F-14A was still a relatively new addition to the Navy's flightline. By the time that I heard my first Tomcat roar in 1977, the airplane had been in the fleet for about four years, and still had a large number of its infancy quirks and troubles. The original TF30-P-412 engines were being replaced with the modified TF30-P-414, and afterburner malfunctions were reaching epidemic proportions in the late 1970s. I learned first-hand what it is like to change six afterburner fuel control systems in a week – an undertaking that was one of the most laborious, time-consuming, messy and challenging tasks that I ever experienced during my many years of maintaining the jet. These problems stemmed from the fact that the Pratt & Whitney TF30 was not originally designed with an afterburner.

When General Electric could not deliver the engine it had promised for the F-14, Pratt & Whitney had the brilliant idea of slapping an afterburner on to an existing turbofan engine and the US Navy bought it. The design had an abundance of flaws, and it took the best part of ten years for the US Navy and Pratt & Whitney to work out most of the bugs. All of that effort never really overcame the fact that the rest of the engine was not designed for the flight characteristics of a supersonic fighter jet, so the F-14A always had flight restrictions based on the compressor stall limitations of those engines.

Certain flight manoeuvres at high speed could starve an engine of adequate airflow, resulting in a compressor stall. When a jet engine compressor stalls, it will reverse its rotation, resulting in reverse airflow through and from that engine. The Tomcat's flight manual outlined the prescribed envelope for safe manoeuvres at high speeds, and clearly listed the restrictions. Most, if not all, of the manoeuvres that were attempted outside of the prescribed flight envelope would generate the disturbed turbulence that quickly resulted in a compressor stall, followed by the urgent need to stabilise flight in order to restart the stalled engine. The lower the altitude, the greater that urgency became, and in ACM, an engine stall would often be fatal.

My first experience at sea was on a carrier qualification (CQ) detachment on board *Ranger* off the coast of California in 1978. CQ detachments were periods in which the aircrew would practice and qualify, or requalify, in carrier landings during day and night operations. In these early years the use of afterburner during shipboard catapult launches was restricted as a flight deck crew safety precaution, with 'burner shots having to be approved on a case-by-case basis by the ship's Executive Officer or Commanding Officer. On this detachment, the aircrew were given the go-ahead to use their afterburners on the last night launch of the detachment.

It was a brisk, cold winter night, but I was not about to miss the show. I found a great

BELOW Aviation Machinist's Mate Petty Officer 3rd Class Dan Dixon checks for oil leaks in the starboard TF30 of F-14A BuNo 159460, assigned to VF-211 during CV-64's WestPac of 1980. Nicknamed 'Dsquare', Dan was a jet mechanic with the US Navy for more than 20 years, serving with no fewer than six F-14 units during this time. *(Dan Dixon)*

ABOVE Dan Dixon's love affair with the F-14 began in 1978 on board *Ranger*. In those days, afterburner launches were restricted as a flight deck crew safety precaution. Dan duly witnessed a series of spectacular departures similar to this one, which features VF-211 jet 'Nickel 104' (BuNo 158618) about to launch from USS *John C. Stennis* (CVN-74) on 1 January 2002. *(US Navy)*

ABOVE RIGHT Aviation electricians use a fluke meter to check wiring on the starboard F110 fitted to a VF-31 F-14D chained down in the hangar deck of USS *Abraham Lincoln* (CVN-72) in February 2003. *(US Navy)*

observation spot to the right and aft of the jet blast deflector, next to a parked and secured helicopter about 150ft away. The pilot hit Zone Five (maximum) afterburner and I was pinned to the side of the helicopter from the thrust of the jet blast. I felt like I was being slow roasted in its radiated heat. The afterburner flame illuminated half of the flight deck. The vibration from all of that harnessed power seemed to be enough to rattle one's dental fillings. Less than a minute later the catapult shuttle released and the Tomcat streaked down to the end of the cat track. Once airborne, the pilot pulled back on the control column and the jet rocketed vertically until the afterburner flames disappeared from our view. That launch was the most awe-inspiring event of my young life to that point, but there were many more to follow in my career.

The operational tempo and adventure of that shipboard detachment inspired me to terminate my shore-based tour of duty and take my intensely compact and rich experience to sea with VF-211, where I continued to build a reputation for mechanical aptitude and technical knowledge growth. During my first WestPac [Western Pacific] cruise on board USS *Constellation* (CV-64) in 1980, I witnessed a shift in operational policy for the Tomcat. The long-standing catapult launch restriction was lifted after we almost lost a jet from a 'cold' cat shot (sudden loss of adequate steam pressure in the catapult piston, impacting its speed and power), which I had the nerve-racking experience of witnessing from the ultimate

front row 'seat'. As one of the final checkers standing near the catapult launch area, I saw the jet drop almost completely from view below the bow of the ship, felt the salt water spray that the Tomcat's afterburners blew around, and saw the mighty jet reappear as it grasped for airspace, rocketing clear from the wave tops. That event led to maximum afterburners on catapult launches becoming Standard Operating Procedure, much to the relief of the aircrew and the excitement of the deck crew.

The more experience that I gained in working on the Tomcat, the more obvious it became that the jet was not designed with maintenance in mind. Access to some parts, and their removal and replacement, often required great ingenuity and/or airframe modifications. Indeed, it was apparent that the airframe was built around its internal systems in many areas. Frequently, special tooling had to be fabricated for the removal of certain parts, and the flexibility of a contortionist was required to reach and repair something that had broken 'deep in the guts' of the jet.

Like any airplane that ever flew, the early versions of the Tomcat were never as good as the next modification or model. The F-14 had its growing pains, and bugs to be worked out. Improvements were made to all of the systems throughout its service life. The first crash, for example, was a result of a ruptured hydraulic line that simply needed another clamp to properly secure it under its high load pressure pulsations. Improvements are always a part of the evolution of any aircraft. The engine modifications introduced with the TF30-P-414, for example,

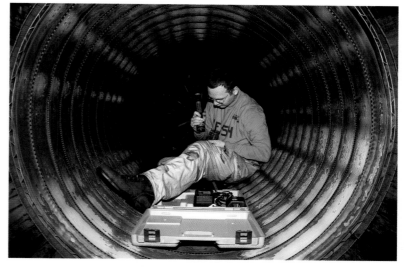

lessened the damage to the airframe and aircraft fuel system in the event of a compressor failure. The multitude of revisions to the afterburner fuel controls over the years helped to stabilise that system and improve its reliability.

High-rate component failures brought improvements to the materials and manufacturing of those parts. Some systems like the glove vanes were determined to be ineffective and were disabled or eliminated in later models of the aircraft. As the airframe aged under the regular stresses imposed on a supersonic fighter jet, modifications became necessary to strengthen its structure through bulkhead reinforcement and the installation of large structural staple assemblies.

The greatest improvement to the F-14 in my experience was when the Navy bought the F110-GE-400 engine. Where the old Pratt & Whitney TF30 had a clearly defined stall margin, the F110 could withstand any flight manoeuvre without a hiccup. It is rumoured that General Electric posted a bounty (reward) for the first pilot that could outfly its engine, causing a pilot-induced stall. I cannot attest to the validity of that rumour, but I do know that the core engine design provided greater internal airflow stability, which directly contributed to its reliability during all phases of flight. The F110 produced a maximum thrust of 26,950lb, with a thrust-to-weight ratio of 6.1-to-1, compared

ABOVE Another 'Green Shirt' from VF-31 casts his expert eye over an F110 that has recently undergone routine servicing in the hangar deck of CVN-72 during CVW-14's marathon ten-month combat cruise in 2002–03. He is checking connectors for the orange hoses that run from the port engine's main fuel pump to the myriad tanks in the airframe. (US Navy)

RIGHT Details of an F110 fitted in the port engine bay of a VF-213 F-14D are revealed during a routine line check on the ramp at NAS Oceana. Four large doors could be opened outward to allow an engine to be inspected, the smaller panels at the front of the bay being nicknamed the 'daily doors', as they were opened regularly at the start of the day's flying. (Danny Coremans)

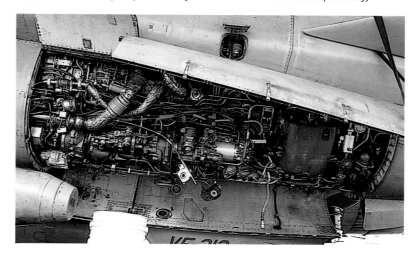

to the TF30's maximum thrust of 20,900lb and a thrust-to-weight ratio of 5.26-to-1. The General Electric engine provided dependable and stable operations in all flight aspects, with the additional bonus of an average of 30% fuel savings, corresponding to a substantial increase in flight reach.

Thanks to General Electric adopting modular concept principles when it came to construction of the F110, from a maintenance standpoint, major internal repairs could be made more efficiently. Unlike the TF30, the F110 had an afterburner system that was designed as an integral part of the engine. The computer that ran the afterburner fuel control was a separate component from its metering section, so replacement of a failed computer was completed in just minutes, compared to the almost 24 hours that it took to change out the TF30's afterburner fuel control assembly. Furthermore, through technological advances in the design of electrical connector and fluid line fittings, the F110 required less safety-wire applications than the TF30. In general, overall access to components was considerably more maintenance friendly with the newer engine.

Being a jet engine mechanic, my recollections about the other systems on the aircraft are a little less detailed. As the aircraft aged, the hydraulic systems tended to leak

more often, and the airframes shop always complained about the difficulties of changing certain components and the trouble it had with rigging the flap/slat system. The electricians were constantly busy with wiring issues, which only multiplied with the ageing of the aircraft. At one point, there were major rewiring modifications that stemmed from the original use of Capstan wire in the manufacturing process that proved to be sub-optimal with age. The avionics shop stayed busy because, quite frankly, the sensitive avionics took a beating under the everyday shock stresses associated with catapult launchings and arrested landings.

The lifespan of any airplane is greatly impacted by the physical stresses that the airframe is subjected to in its operation, and by the environment in which it operates. Any fighter jet undergoes regular and frequent high-g manoeuvring that imposes tremendous structural stresses on the airframe and its flight control surfaces. The engines are subjected to frequent rapid accelerations and decelerations, which translate into more wear and tear on the motors' internal components. Add the stresses of carrier catapult shots and arrested landings on an unstable pitching flight deck in a salt-water environment, and it is easy to see that age will take its toll. As the Tomcats got older, the maintenance-hours-to-flight-hours ratio grew exponentially.

When the production lines ended at Grumman, the replacement parts availability and the supply chain started to slow, which caused repair delays on the flight decks and flightlines. We had to start cannibalising jets in order to fix enough F-14s to meet the demands of the flight schedule. Parts cannibalisation is the process of taking good parts off of one broken airplane to replace a bad part on another airplane in order to return the latter to an airworthy flight status. The necessity of removing parts from one airplane to fix another added significantly to the maintenance hours needed for repairs. The growing maintenance-hours-to-flight-hours ratio [60 hours of maintenance for every hour of flying by 2005, compared to 20 hours for the legacy F/A-18A/C and 10–15 for the F/A-18E/F], and the associated costs involved, ultimately led to the decision by the Department of the Navy to retire the Tomcat some four years early in 2006.

RIGHT Each of the F-14's engines was mounted in its own nacelle so that a fire with one powerplant would not immediately affect the other engine. The engine bays (this is the starboard bay, looking forward) were painted gloss white so that any oil leaks or areas of heat build-up could be quickly located.
(Danny Coremans)

Improving the breed

After years of struggling with underpowered and often unreliable engines, the Tomcat was finally able to realise its full operational potential from the late 1980s with the advent of the F110 in the F-14A+, followed by the definitive F-14D – dubbed the 'Super Tomcat'.

As previously detailed, the F-14A was only meant to be an interim version of the aircraft constructed in limited numbers (36 airframes) so as to introduce the jet to front-line service. The bulk of the 700+ aircraft on order for the US Navy were supposed to be built as F-14Bs, fitted with more powerful F401 engines, and F-14Cs, which would have had the new engines and a revised digital avionics suite that could have turned the jet into an all-weather air-to-ground attack platform. Chronic budget overruns saw both variants cancelled very early on in the programme, leaving the US Navy equipped exclusively with the TF30-powered F-14A.

There was very little money available to update the Tomcat during the first decade of its fleet service, and by 1982 the jet was beginning to lag behind its contemporaries in the West (and, to a lesser degree, in the Soviet Bloc) in four key areas. First and foremost, the TF30 engine was still causing the fleet major problems both in terms of reliability and overall performance. The maintainability of the jet, and its systems (specifically its dated, valve-driven fire control system), was also poor. The AN/AWG-9 and AIM-54 had also by now become more susceptible to jamming by improved Soviet ECM expertise. Finally, the Tomcat lacked the high-speed multiplex digital databuses present in aircraft such as the F-15C, F-16 and F/A-18. The latter would facilitate the running of a modern 'glass cockpit' complete with multi-function displays, high-speed/high-capacity computers, FBW

flight controls and a Head-up Display (HUD). All these improvements would feature in the F-14D, for which Grumman received an $864 million contract in the summer of 1984.

Three years prior to this, in July 1981, the company had resumed flight operations with the original F-14B prototype that was now fitted with General Electric F101-DFE engines. Picked by the USAF as the powerplant of choice for its new B-1B bomber, as well as the latest variants of the F-15 and F-16 that were under development, the new engine (redesignated

LEFT The original F-14B (BuNo 157986), which had briefly flown with Pratt & Whitney F401 engines fitted in 1971, was removed from storage ten years later to serve again as an engine testbed for the General Electric F101-DFE. This powerplant, which evolved into the F110-GE-400, was eventually adopted by the US Navy for the F-14A+ (redesignated the F-14B in May 1991) and the F-14D Super Tomcat. *(Grumman via David F. Brown)*

BELOW The 38th, and last, new-build F-14A+ (BuNo 163411) is manned by a Grumman test flight crew at Calverton in late 1989 prior to handover to the US Navy's acceptance team. Tim Lent, seen here in the jeans and grey hooded top, was the plane captain for this aircraft – his father had been the plane captain for the very first F-14A delivered by Grumman 18 years earlier. *(Tim Lent)*

The F-14D patch worn by crews that flew the jet emphasised the more 'muscular' nature of their mount over the original A-model Tomcat. *(Tony Holmes collection)*

RIGHT The front cockpit of the F-14B closely resembled that of the original A-model, with a mix of conventional dials and gauges grouped around two Tactical Information Displays (TIDs). The bottom screen was partially obscured by the control column, which could require 60–80lb of pull from the pilot when the jet was being manoeuvred under heavy loads. *(Danny Coremans)*

the F110 in October 1982) was de-rated from 29,000lb of thrust to 26,950lb for installation in the F-14. The Tomcat's mission performance was revolutionised thanks to the F110's impressive levels of thrust.

In February 1984 the US Navy announced that it had instructed Grumman to install F110s in new production aircraft from 1988 onward. With engine testing complete by early 1987, Grumman duly commenced fitting F110s into airframes on the Calverton line. The first of 38

ABOVE A key difference between the A- and B-model front cockpits was the Head-Up Display (HUD). In the F-14A, critical information had been projected directly on to the front windscreen, but with the B-model a conventional HUD was fitted. The latter displayed data artificially focused at infinity so that the pilot did not need to refocus his eyes when looking out of the cockpit for a distant target. *(Danny Coremans)*

BELOW This mock-up of the F-14D front cockpit was built by Grumman as a briefing tool for engineers discussing the layout of the new jet with the US Navy in the late 1980s. Plenty of conventional analogue dials and gauges are in evidence, as are digital avionics in the form of two multifunction PTIDs framed by push-button functionality keys. The D-model was also equipped with a Kaiser Aerospace AN/AVG-12 HUD. *(Grumman)*

BELOW A trio of F-14Bs from VF-102 'Diamondbacks' hold formation behind a KC-135 as they head west from NAS Oceana to NAS Fallon, Nevada, for air wing work-ups with CVW-1 in early 1995. The unit had commenced its transition from the F-14A to the B-model Tomcat in June 1994, and it would remain equipped with the aircraft until it switched to the F/A-18F Super Hornet from March 2002. *(Rick Llinares)*

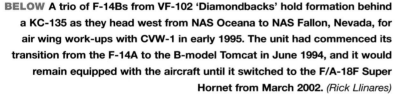

ABOVE The old 'fishbowl' TID in the rear cockpit of the F-14A/B was replaced by a new 8 x 8in Programmable Target Information Display (PTID) in the D-model Tomcat, which presented both radar and, crucially, LANTIRN data. 'With the Tomcat [thanks to LANTIRN and the PTID] you were putting the bomb into the third window from the left, from miles away,' recalled Rear Admiral Jay 'Spook' Yakeley. *(Erik Hildebrandt)*

ABOVE The front cockpit of the F-14D once it reached the front line looked remarkably similar to the Grumman mock-up. It merged the old with the new – multifunction PTIDs sat rather uncomfortably alongside good old-fashioned 'steam' gauges and dials, and systems integration between the front and back seats even in the D-model was virtually non-existent – just as it had been in the F-14A/B. *(Danny Coremans)*

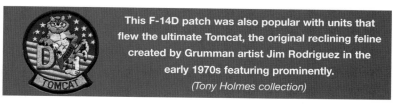

This F-14D patch was also popular with units that flew the ultimate Tomcat, the original reclining feline created by Grumman artist Jim Rodriguez in the early 1970s featuring prominently.
(Tony Holmes collection)

BELOW This view of an F-14D cockpit clearly shows the size of the PTID screen (bottom). Above it is the Detail Data Display and to the right is the Multiple Display Indicator. The Hand Control Unit can be partially seen at the bottom of the photograph in front of the PTID. Another key addition to the D-model's rear cockpit was the Sensor Slaving Panel (SSP) atop the instrument panel. *(Danny Coremans)*

new-build F-14A+s was delivered to the NATC in November 1987, this aircraft featuring minor avionics and airframe changes as well. Perhaps the most significant of these was the installation of the new Direct Lift Control/Approach Power Control system, which made the Tomcat a much safer aircraft to fly when performing ACM or when 'low and slow' around the boat on recovery. The aircraft's radar warning receiver (RWR) equipment was also improved and its radar fire control system upgraded.

Aside from the new-build F-14A+s (redesignated F-14Bs in May 1991), a total of 47 F-14As were also returned to Grumman from the fleet for upgrading. Following flight-testing at Patuxent River and Point Mugu, the first examples were issued to VF-101 at Oceana in April 1988 – all units equipped with the F-14A+ were trained by this squadron. By then flight testing of the F-14D was well under way, the prototype aircraft having completed its first hop from Calverton on 8 December 1987. Like the F-14A+, the D-model was powered by two F110-GE-400s that allowed the aircraft to launch from a carrier deck in dry power, rather

ABOVE The key external feature of the F-14D was the AAS-42 IRST mounted in a distinctive dual chin pod alongside the Northrop AAX-1 TCS beneath the radome of the jet. *(Danny Coremans)*

ABOVE Among the additions introduced to the rear cockpit of the F-14 with its conversion to a precision bomber was the Precision Strike Processor. Installed into the port console of the RIO's station in place of the TARPS control panel, the processor hosted cards that allowed the LANTIRN pod to listen in on the Tomcat's existing inertial navigation system alignment and the RIO's computer address panel actions. *(Danny Coremans)*

CENTRE The diagram for the F-14D front cockpit published in NAVAIR 01-F14AAD-1 publication *NATOPS Flight Manual Navy Model F-14D Aircraft*, dated 1 February 1997. *(US Navy)*

RIGHT The diagram for the F-14D rear cockpit published in NAVAIR 01-F14AAD-1 publication *NATOPS Flight Manual Navy Model F-14D Aircraft*, dated 1 February 1997. *(US Navy)*

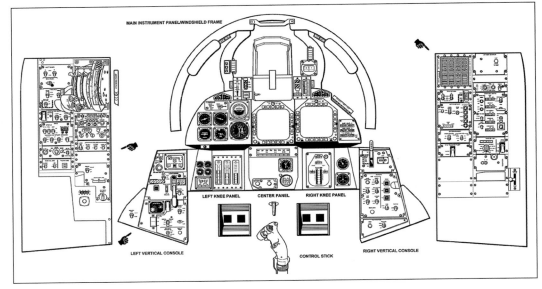

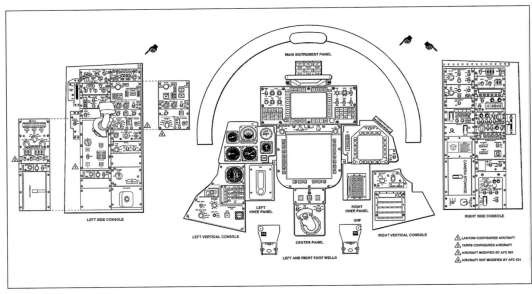

than in fuel-draining reheat as had usually been the case with the F-14A.

The airframe changes that came on line with the F-14A+ were also present in the D-model jet. However, the latter machine's avionics were appreciably different. At the heart of the improvements was the AN/APG-71 radar, which was broadly based on the AN/AWG-9 but with digital processing and night vision goggles-capable displays. A development of the AN/APG-70 radar fitted in the USAF's F-15E Strike Eagle, the new system gave the F-14D improved detection and tracking range of aerial targets, thus allowing the jet to fire its AIM-54s at a greater distance from the contact. The D-model was also equipped with a Mil-Std 1553 databus and dual AYK-14 computers, which helped run the jet's digitised cockpit and HUD, new RWR and improved secure communications equipment in the form of the Joint Tactical Information Distribution System. Externally, the aircraft boasted an AAS-42 Infrared Search and Track Set (ISRT) mounted in a distinctive dual chin pod alongside the Northrop AAX-1 Television Camera Sight (TCS) beneath the radome of the F-14. The latter, which allowed crews to positively identify contacts at distances of up to 9 miles, had been fitted as standard to all F-14A/Bs acquired by the US Navy.

The improved avionics were certainly welcomed by Tomcat crews in the front line, but that was not the real driving force behind the D-model jet according to Rear Admiral Paul T. Gillcrist: 'Although the F-14D programme was advertised as a threefold improvement in engines, avionics and radar, the hidden agenda was really to fix the engines at all costs.'

The first production F-14D was delivered to the NATC in May 1990 and the second airframe was sent to VX-4 at Point Mugu the following month. A total of 127 F-14Ds were originally scheduled for production, with a further 400+ A-models being upgraded to this standard by Grumman. However, with the end of the Cold War and the subsequent disbandment of 11 fleet Tomcat squadrons, these production numbers were slashed by Congress to the point where just 59 F-14Ds were built – 4 converted test aircraft, 37 brand new jets and 18 A-model upgrades. The last new-build F-14D (and the last brand new Tomcat) was accepted by the US Navy on 10 July 1992.

ABOVE Capt Bill Sizemore, CAG of CVW-8, peers through the Kaiser Aerospace AN/AVG-12 HUD of VF-213 F-14D 'Blacklion 207' (BuNo 161166) as he positions the jet behind a C-2A of VRC-40 Det 1 during an OIF III mission on 2 February 2006. Flying almost 500 hours during the F-14's last combat deployment, BuNo 161166 fired 163 rounds during a strafing pass in Baghdad on 17 November 2005. *(Richard Cooper)*

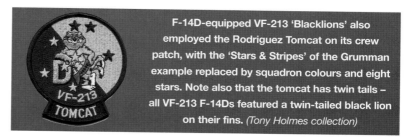

F-14D-equipped VF-213 'Blacklions' also employed the Rodriguez Tomcat on its crew patch, with the 'Stars & Stripes' of the Grumman example replaced by squadron colours and eight stars. Note also that the tomcat has twin tails – all VF-213 F-14Ds featured a twin-tailed black lion on their fins. *(Tony Holmes collection)*

BELOW The pilot of F-14D BuNo 164599 performs a crisp break to starboard away from F-14D BuNo 164604 during a training flight from NAS Point Mugu. Both jets spent their time in the test and evaluation role, initially with VX-4 and then with VX-9 Det Point Mugu following the former unit's disestablishment in September 1994. *(Ted Carlson)*

Chapter Three

The Tomcat in service

The Tomcat endured a somewhat chequered start to its service career with the US Navy due to the unreliability of its engines and complex avionics and weapons systems, swingeing defence budget cuts of the 1970s and low morale in the fleet.

OPPOSITE *Theodore Roosevelt*'s Mini-Boss joins the 'Shooter' (catapult officer) for waist catapult three as they jointly give the signal to launch VF-31's 'Bandwagon 101' (BuNo 164603) during CVN-71's JTFEX in the WestLant in July 2005. In overall charge of the flight deck, the Air Boss and his Mini-Boss deputy are Naval Aviators who are also qualified as catapult officers. *(US Navy)*

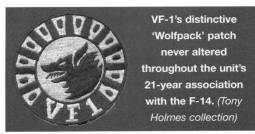

ABOVE This aircraft (BuNo 158617) was the very first Tomcat to be assigned to VF-124 'Gunfighters' when it was temporarily loaned to the unit in October 1972 so that would-be F-14 instructors could gain experience on the new fleet fighter. Finally struck off charge in October 2003, the aircraft has been preserved in Allenton, Pennsylvania, by the Veterans of Foreign Wars Post 7293. *(US Navy via Angelo Romano)*

Cold War fleet service

Despite being the most complex fighter aircraft ever to operate from a carrier flight deck, and plagued by financial wrangling and cost overruns, the F-14 attained service entry on 8 October 1972 – just 21 months after the Tomcat had made its maiden flight. The first production machine had flown in May of that year, and five months later VF-124 took delivery of its first Tomcat at NAS Miramar. This signalled a high point in the jet's development, as it

showed that the F-14 was progressing from being an aircraft undergoing testing to a fighter capable of performing its designated mission.

VF-124 was not an operational fighter unit, however. It was a Fleet Replacement Squadron (FRS) charged with providing tuition in all aspects of the aircraft; it was assigned for the air- and groundcrew who would ultimately operate the jet at sea. Staffed by seasoned Naval Aviators and RIOs drawn from the fighter community on both coasts, the unit's first job was to train the instructors who would in turn be tasked with drawing up a formal syllabus for the future tuition of front-line aircrew and maintainers. VF-124 also had to manage the transition process for fleet units that would be swapping their F-4 Phantom IIs or F-8 Crusaders for F-14s.

The flow of aircraft to Miramar from Calverton was slow to start with, and it was not until the spring of 1973 that the unit started training crews that were destined to join the Pacific Fleet's first F-14-equipped squadrons within its Fighter Airborne Early Warning Wings Pacific (FitAEWWingPac). The first two squadrons slated to introduce the jet to seagoing service were VF-1 and VF-2, which had been established specifically to fly the Tomcat at Miramar on 14 October 1972. By July 1973 both units had made sufficient progress in transitioning on to the jet with VF-124 to allow them to receive their own F-14As directly from Grumman. It would take until March 1974 for

LEFT The first two front-line units to receive the Tomcat were VF-1 'Wolfpack' and VF-2 'Bounty Hunters', both of which were commissioned specially to fly the Tomcat at Miramar on 14 October 1972. F-14A BuNo 158993 is seen here simulating a carrier approach for the benefit of the photographer during VF-1's pre-cruise work-ups. *(Robert L. Lawson via Tailhook)*

LEFT A section of VF-1 F-14As formate with two F-106As from Air Defense Command's 84th Fighter-Interceptor Squadron/26th Air Division after an ACM session in the southern California operations area. Below them is San Diego (right) and Coronado Island (left), with the latter being home to NAS North Island. The Delta Dart was regularly employed by Miramar-based fighter units as a MiG-21 simulator during training. *(US Navy)*

VF-1 and VF-2 to attain full unit strength of 12 jets apiece, however.

Assigned to Carrier Air Wing (CVW) 14, which was embarked in *Enterprise* at the time, both units completed their carrier qualifications with the aircraft in the spring of 1974 and then deployed on board the vessel for its WestPac on 17 September that same year. The cruise, which lasted until 20 May 1975, was relatively successful for the Tomcat units, as they got to expend live examples of all three missile types in the jet's inventory during training exercises, as well as flying CAPs over Saigon during the final stages of the US evacuation from South Vietnam, codenamed Operation Frequent Wind. Less successful was the fact that VF-1 lost two F-14s to engine fan blade failure, which in turn started uncontrollable fires, within the

space of 12 days in early January 1975. Both jets crashed into the South China Sea, but the crews were recovered safely.

Despite these losses, and the units being forced to make around 100 engine changes each during the course of the cruise because of the TF30's chronic unreliability, VF-1 and VF-2 returned to Miramar with 3,000 flying hours under their belts. And, overall, the deployment was described by Rear Admiral Leonard A. Snead, Commander FitAEWWingPac, as being 'the

BELOW VF-14 'Tophatters' and sister-squadron VF-32 'Swordsmen' were the first Atlantic Fleet fighter units to transition to the F-14A. They undertook their conversion with VF-124 at Miramar, where this aircraft (BuNo 159017) was photographed in May 1975. Delivered new to VF-124 in June 1974 it served as VF-14's 'Tophatter 105' before flying with VF-101, VF-11 and VF-102. It was scrapped in 1994. *(Angelo Romano)*

The 'High Hat' insignia has adorned carrier-based aircraft since the early 1920s, VF-14 having flown 23 different types of aircraft, had its designation changed 14 times (it is presently VFA-14, equipped with the F/A-18E) and been embarked in 20 different aircraft carriers (and several battleships) since its inception in 1919. *(Tony Holmes collection)*

ABOVE VF-32's storeless 'Gypsy 211' (BuNo 159025) is shot off *John F. Kennedy*'s waist catapult four during the Tomcat's maiden Mediterranean cruise in the autumn of 1975. Retired in September 1994 after service with VF-101, VF-11 and, finally, Reserve-manned VF-302 and VF-202, this aircraft has been an exhibit on board USS *Yorktown* (CVS-10) in South Carolina for many years. *(Angelo Romano)*

BELOW Recently returned to Oceana following VF-143's conversion to the F-14A at Miramar with VF-124's 'Tomcat School', 'Dog 104' (BuNo 159444) has its (compressed) nose gear checked on the ramp in 1975. Note the glowing anti-collision lights beneath the nose and on the port fin tip, which indicates that the aircraft's systems have been powered up. *(via David F. Brown)*

most singularly successful fleet introduction of a sophisticated aircraft the Navy has ever had'.

By the time these units returned to Miramar, the first two Atlantic Fleet squadrons – VF-14 and VF-32 – were nearing readiness for their operational debut. In order to speed up the Tomcat's introduction to service, the US Navy had decided to transition the first four east coast fighter squadrons slated to receive the F-14 with VF-124 at Miramar. In late 1975, former Atlantic Fleet F-4 FRS VF-101 received its first Tomcats. The unit operated both fighter types until August 1977, when VF-101 passed the last of its Phantom IIs on to VF-171 and focused exclusively on Tomcat training in support of east coast fighter squadrons.

Formerly equipped with F-4Js, VF-14 and VF-32 returned home to NAS Oceana from California in the late summer of 1974. After a further nine months of intensive training with the Tomcat, they joined up with the rest of CVW-1 aboard USS *John F. Kennedy* (CV-67) and departed Norfolk, Virginia, on 28 June 1975. The carrier headed across the Atlantic for a seven-month deployment that set the tone for future operations for Oceana-based Tomcat units during the Cold War. CV-67 spent much of its time in the eastern Mediterranean, and also exercised extensively with NATO forces.

Atlantic Fleet units VF-142 and VF-143 followed VF-14 and VF-32 through Miramar's 'Tomcat School' during the latter half of 1974, swapping their F-4Js for F-14As. Both squadrons would have to wait until April 1976, however, before they headed to the Mediterranean with CVW-6 on board *America*. The cruise highlight came in late July when Tomcats from both units provided CAP for US Marine Corps helicopters tasked with evacuating more than 300 US civilians from the

VF-143 crews wore both the official 'Fighting 143' patch, which exclusively featured the unit's black chimera – jokingly referred to as a 'pukin' dog' by naval aviators and NFOs since the early 1960s – and the Latin inscription 'sans reproache' (beyond reproach), and this one, combining the 'dog' with a Grumman tomcat. *(Tony Holmes collection)*

The official patch of VF-114 features a warrior riding a Pegasus topped by the Greek script 'First to Attack'. A similar emblem was created by SBD Dauntless-equipped VS-11/VB-21 of Carrier Air Group 11 in October 1942, and VF-114 could trace its convoluted lineage back to this unit via VBF-119 of January 1945. It did not become VF-114 until February 1950, however. (Tony Holmes collection)

ABOVE BuNo 159862 was the first F-14A assigned to VF-114 'Aardvarks' on 30 September 1976. It is seen here departing Miramar, having blown both main gear tyres while performing a no-flaps take-off at the start of its display routine at the base airshow on 24 October 1976. (Robert L. Lawson via Tailhook)

Lebanese capital Beirut after the outbreak of a bloody civil war.

Having completed the transition of the first four Atlantic Fleet Tomcat units, VF-124 switched its attention back to FitAEWWingPac and conversion of the last two front-line F-8 squadrons in the US Navy. VF-24 and VF-211 had flown the Crusader since 1959, and having completed their ninth cruise with the jet as part of CVW-21, which then disbanded, in October 1975, they commenced their transition to the F-14A just weeks later. Both squadrons were duly reassigned to CVW-9 and undertook their first WestPac embarked in *Constellation* in April 1977. VF-114 and VF-213 were the next two west coast fighter squadrons to transition to the F-14A, the latter replacing the F-4J from the spring of 1976. Both units subsequently embarked in USS *Kitty Hawk* (CV-63) with the rest of CVW-11 for their first WestPac in October 1977, the vessel replacing CV-64 on deployment.

The year 1977 proved to be a busy one for Grumman and the US Navy, and it ended with VF-41 and VF-84 setting out on their first cruise with the Atlantic Fleet in December after they had become the first units to complete their transition with VF-101 at Oceana. The latter unit had started both squadrons' conversion from the F-4N to F-14A in April 1976, VF-101 initially receiving considerable help from VF-124. Following this flurry of transitions, both FRSs would enjoy a brief respite from converting Phantom II units to Tomcats until VF-124 welcomed VF-51 and VF-111 to the classroom in early 1978. Part of CVW-15, which was newly assigned to CV-63 following an almost 20-year association with the smaller USS *Coral Sea* (CV-43), they eventually commenced their first WestPac with the F-14A in May 1979.

The *B.C.* comic strip created by cartoonist Johnny Hart in the late 1950s featured an anteater or aardvark named 'ZOT' after the noise he made when eating his prey. In 1961 VF-114 began transitioning to the Phantom II, which crews believed resembled 'ZOT'. This was duly adopted as an unofficial insignia in 1963 when the unit also changed its name from 'Executioners' to 'Aardvarks'.

(Tony Holmes collection)

BELOW Fleet Replacement Squadron VF-101 'Grim Reapers' was the Tomcat training unit for the Atlantic Fleet. The squadron initially operated F-14s alongside its large fleet of F-4s from Oceana, but in August 1977 VF-101 passed the last of its Phantom IIs on to VF-171 and focused exclusively on Tomcat training. This unidentified aircraft was one of more than 20 F-14As assigned to the 'Grim Reapers' in 1979. (US Navy)

Most deployments during the latter half of the 1970s followed a predictable pattern, with carriers typically spending around six months on cruise in the Pacific or Mediterranean. During this time, Tomcat units could expect to exercise with foreign air arms, as well as spending countless hours on CAP providing protection for the carrier battle group. One of the missions F-14 crews soon became familiar with was 'Bear' hunting. Soviet Antonov, Ilyushin and Tupolev long-range reconnaissance aircraft would routinely probe the Tomcat CAPs in an effort to get close to their carriers so as to take photographs and collect electronic signals data. Among the many Naval Aviators and RIOs to intercept these aircraft during this period was Lt John Skogsberg of VF-14, who recalled:

When the Soviet reconnaissance aircraft were able to find the carrier, they could get pretty much as close as they wanted. Short of ramming them or shooting them down, there was no practical way for us to keep them away. Our goals were to have them continuously escorted any time they were within about 200 miles of the ship – sometimes much further – and to try to always, as the escort, be in every picture they might take of the carrier. In the main, the Tu-95/142 'Bear' and Tu-16 'Badger' crews played nice, but there were stories of Il-38 'Mays' getting very low and slow to try to give the escorts problems.

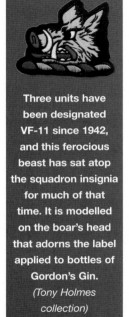

Three units have been designated VF-11 since 1942, and this ferocious beast has sat atop the squadron insignia for much of that time. It is modelled on the boar's head that adorns the label applied to bottles of Gordon's Gin. *(Tony Holmes collection)*

ABOVE Two F-14A crews from VF-11 'Red Rippers' close up with their formation leader during *John F. Kennedy*'s epic 1983–84 combat cruise to the Mediterranean. Both 'Ripper 104' (BuNo 161166) and 'Ripper 110' (BuNo 159434) are armed with live AIM-9L and AIM-9M missiles, while the former has also been firing its 20mm M61A1 Vulcan cannon during this mission. *(US Navy via Peter Mersky)*

BELOW Chained to the deck of *Nimitz*, VF-41's 'Fast Eagle 107' (BuNo 160390) boasts a single Su-22 kill marking. This aircraft, flown by Lts Larry Muczynski and Dave Anderson, downed the second of two Libyan Su-22 credited to VF-41 on 19 August 1981. The jet was lost on 25 October 1994 while assigned to VF-213 when its pilot, Lt Kara Hultgreen, aborted her landing on approach to *Abraham Lincoln*. Hultgreen was killed, but RIO, Lt Matthew Klemish, safely ejected. *(Angelo Romano)*

With the overthrow of the Shah of Iran in 1979, the US Navy found itself patrolling the narrow waters of the NAG. Carriers from both the Pacific and Atlantic Fleets would take it in turns sailing in the Gulf of Oman Naval Zone of Operations. The invasion of Iran by Iraq in September 1980 further heightened tensions in this oil-rich region, and Tomcat units were kept busy patrolling the airspace overhead carrier battle groups operating in theatre. Indeed, US Navy Tomcats would remain a familiar sight in the skies over the NAG for the next 27 years.

Despite the US Navy's operational focus having shifted to the Middle East, Atlantic Fleet carriers continued to routinely patrol in the eastern Mediterranean while assigned to the Sixth Fleet. And it was here on 19 August

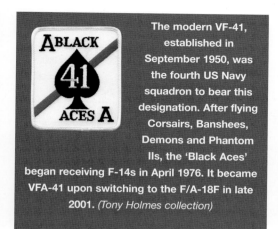

ABOVE VF-41's quartet of victorious Naval Aviators and NFOs pose for an official photograph in the squadron ready room on board *Nimitz* shortly after downing two Libyan Su-22s on 19 August 1981. Leading the section was squadron CO Cdr Hank Kleeman (standing second from left), with his RIO Lt Dave Venlet. Flying the 'Dash Two' Tomcat was Lt Larry Muczynski (second from right) and RIO Lt(jg) Jim Anderson. *(US Navy)*

1981 that the Tomcat unexpectedly won its battle spurs in its intended role as a fighter. USS *Nimitz* (CVN-68), with CVW-8 embarked, was conducting a two-day missile launching exercise against drone targets operating in international waters off the coast of Libya. The government of the latter country claimed that much of the range area in which the drones were flying was its territorial waters. The US government refuted this, stating that it was only prepared to recognise the traditional 3-mile limit.

The first day of the exercise (18 August) had seen close to 50 incursions into the missile-firing zone by Libyan Arab Republic Air Force (LARAF) aircraft, which ended with ACM between the latter and F-14s from VF-41 and VF-84, as well as F-4Js from USS *Forrestal* (CV-59). On the morning of the 19th two Sukhoi Su-22M 'Fitter-J' fighters took on a pair of Tomcats from VF-41, and the pilot of one of the LARAF jets made the mistake of launching a single 'Atoll' heat-seeking missile at the F-14s as all four aircraft converged on each other. The weapon failed to guide, however, since it had been launched outside its operational envelope. Following the strict rules of engagement (RoE) observed by US Navy aircrew at that time, which stated that they could only engage the enemy if first fired upon, the crews in the VF-41 jets each shot a 'Fitter' down with a single AIM-9L.

On a more mundane note, VF-11 and VF-31 commenced their first Tomcat deployment in January 1982 following their transition from the F-4J, the units joining CVW-3 on board *John F. Kennedy*. In December of that same year VF-33 and VF-102 also embarked on their first Mediterranean cruise with CVW-1 in USS *America* (CV-66).

Tomcats operating with the Atlantic Fleet would see more combat in 1983, although this

BELOW VF-41's sister-squadron in CVW-8 for more than a decade was VF-84 'Jolly Rogers'. Following their transition from the F-4J to the F-14A in 1976–77, VF-41 and VF-84 undertook their inaugural Mediterranean deployment with CVW-8 embarked in *Nimitz* from December 1977. F-14As BuNos 161138 ('Victory 221') and 161141 ('Victory 223') provide close escort for an E-2C from VAW-124 'Bear Aces' during NATO exercise Teamwork 80 in September 1980. *(US Navy)*

RIGHT This unique formation shot was taken at the end of Exercise Bright Star 83. Filling the slot position in amongst the Egyptian Air Force exotica that includes an F-4E, a Mirage 5SDE, a brand new F-16A, a MiG-21MF and a Shenyang F-6, is an F-14A from VF-142, embarked in USS *Dwight D. Eisenhower* (CVW-69), The remaining CVW-7 jets in this group are an A-6E from VA-65 and an A-7E from VA-66. *(US Navy)*

ABOVE Supplied new to VX-4 by Grumman in June 1979, F-14A BuNo 160696 was the 315th Tomcat delivered to the US Navy. Photographed banking sharply away from the camera aircraft with its glove vanes fully extended, the F-14 is seen here during the flight testing of the Tactical Air Reconnaissance Pod System (TARPS) prior to it being cleared for fleet use. *(Grumman)*

LEFT This photograph of the French helicopter cruiser *Jeanne d'Arc* under way in the Mediterranean was taken in early 1994 by a TARPS-equipped F-14B of VF-103 using the pod's KA-99 panoramic camera, which rotated from horizon to horizon and could be used for side oblique photography. The Tomcat was being crewed by pilot Lt Moore and RIO Cdr Steven 'Snotty' Schlientz, CO of VF-103. *(via David F. Brown)*

time their primary weapon was the Tactical Air Reconnaissance Pod System (TARPS) rather than an air-to-air missile. With the retirement of the Vietnam-era RA-5C Vigilante and RF-8G Crusader from front line service in 1980–81, the US Navy needed a new carrier-based photo-reconnaissance platform. With its long range and high speed, the F-14 was chosen for the task. Development of TARPS had commenced in April 1976, with the 17.29ft-long pod housing two cameras and an infrared reconnaissance sensor optimised for use at low-to-medium altitudes. Initially, just 50 F-14As had their rear right Phoenix station wired for TARPS operation, these aircraft then being spread among the front-line force. Only one squadron in an air wing would be assigned the TARPS mission, and the first pods (weighing in at a hefty 1,760lb) were used operationally by VF-84 in late 1981.

By the time VF-32 was tasked with flying operational TARPS missions over Grenada in October 1983 and Lebanon two months later, the unit was highly proficient with the system. Embarked in USS *Independence* (CV-62) as part of CVW-6, it often relied on VF-14 to CAP these potentially hazardous flights. In Grenada, the TARPS imagery provided the US Marines Corps and US Army Rangers with intelligence on troop movements and gun emplacements ahead of the invasion of the Caribbean island, codenamed Operation Urgent Fury. In Lebanon, VF-32 flew more than 40 TARPS missions over Druse and Syrian artillery positions, as well as carrying out a bomb damage assessment mission following the ill-fated Alpha Strike on 4 December. The latter had been hastily arranged after a TARPS

ABOVE LEFT Naval Aviators from VF-31 'Tomcatters' practise their mirror formation manoeuvre during the unit's Mediterranean/Indian Ocean cruise embarked in *John F. Kennedy* in early 1982. Both F-14As (BuNos 159009, closest to the camera, and 159437) are armed with live AIM-9M and AIM-7M missiles. *(US Navy via Peter Mersky)*

ABOVE Lt Paul Nickell of VF-24 poses in front of F-14A BuNo 159621 on the Miramar flightline in 1983. Typical of the Naval Aviators and NFOs that manned the F-14 units during the final decade of the Cold War, Nickell completed two WestPac/Indian Ocean deployments during his time with VF-24 (September 1982 to December 1985) after spending a little over a year learning to fly the Tomcat with VF-124. *(Paul Nickell)*

BELOW A four-ship of KC-130s from VMGR-352 provide fuel for four F-14s from VF-1 and VF-111 and a lone F-4N from VMFA-531. Leading the formation, photographed in early 1982 over hilly terrain in central California, is KC-130F BuNo 147572, which was delivered to the US Marine Corps in 1962. As this shot clearly demonstrates, the F-14 had no problem refuelling from a KC-130. *(Frank B. Mormillo)*

ABOVE Tomcat units typically numbered close to 200 men during the Cold War cruises of the 1970s and 1980s, and this group photograph shows the personnel assigned to VF-1 during its 1989 WestPac/Indian Ocean deployment. In the front row, flanking VF-1's master chief, are the unit's XO, Cdr George Moe (left), and CO, Cdr Ron McElraft (right). *(Neil Jennings)*

RIGHT Delivered new to VF-124 in January 1986, BuNo 162594 was later assigned to VF-111 'Sundowners' and served as its 'CAG bird'. Aside from the unit's trademark sharksmouth, the aeroplane also features RR RECCE RALLY and BOOLA BOOLA stencilling just aft of the modex 200. VF-111, as CVW-15's TARPS unit, had won the 1990 Recce Rally competition open to all US Navy tactical aerial reconnaissance units assigned to the Pacific Fleet. *(Tom Twomey)*

RIGHT BuNo 162594 had joined VF-111 from VF-124 in 1988 and, as previously noted, it eventually became the unit's 'CAG jet'. It flew as 'Sundowner 200' until 28 September 1992. It then spent 18 months in maintenance before returning to fleet service with Japan-based VF-21 in early 1994. The aircraft transferred to CVW-5's VF-154 'Black Knights' in January 1996 before joining VF-101 shortly thereafter. *(Tom Twomey)*

LEFT VF-51's 'Eagle 114' (BuNo 162610) cruises over scattered cloud in the eastern Pacific in early April 1991 at the start of CVW-15's WestPac/Indian Ocean deployment embarked in *Kitty Hawk*. Assigned new to VF-1 in 1987, this aircraft had become 'Eagle 101' by the time VF-51 next headed out on cruise in November 1992, and it remained as the CO's aircraft through to the 'Screaming Eagles" disestablishment on 31 March 1995. *(US Navy)*

The oldest fighter squadron in continuous service with the Pacific Fleet, VF-51 could trace its lineage back to 1927 when its 'Screaming Eagles' insignia adorned Curtiss F6C-4 biplane fighters of VF-3S 'Striking Eagles'. Following several redesignations during and immediately after the Second World War, the 'Screaming Eagles' became VF-51 in August 1948. The unit retained this striking insignia through to its disestablishment in March 1995. *(Tony Holmes collection)*

AN/AWG-9 radar. The VF-32 crews duly performed avoidance manoeuvres no fewer than four times in an attempt to avert a confrontation, but on each occasion the LARAF aircraft matched their turns. When the jets were just 13 miles apart, a fighter controller on board *John F. Kennedy* gave the Tomcat crews permission to engage the MiG-23s, and two Sparrows were launched at the lead jet – it was quickly shot down. The second aircraft was destroyed by a Sidewinder after a third Sparrow had malfunctioned.

BELOW Seen returning to Oceana on 29 January 1989 at the end of VF-32's eventful 1988–89 Mediterranean cruise with CVW-3 embarked in *John F. Kennedy*, this Tomcat (BuNo 159237) was one of two F-14As from the unit credited with downing a pair of Libyan MiG-23s some 25 days earlier. *(David F. Brown)*

TOMCATS-4 LIBYA-0

This bumper sticker was hastily produced and widely distributed at NAS Oceana following the Libyan MiG-23 shootdown by VF-32 on 29 January 1989. The score reflected the Tomcat's accumulated success over the LARAF in the 1980s; Atlantic Fleet F-14 units emerged victorious from two engagements over the Mediterranean. *(Peter Mersky collection)*

'Bear' and 'Badger' hunting

Close encounters between probing Soviet long-range Antonov, Ilyushin and Tupolev reconnaissance aircraft and Tomcat crews flying CAPs for carrier battle groups operating in the northern hemisphere were relatively commonplace during the Cold War years. F-14 crews worked hard to keep the snooping 'Bears', 'Badgers' and 'Mays', as well as the occasional 'Flogger', away from the fleet, as Tomcat pilot Jon 'Hooter' Schreiber relates:

So you have your Wings of Gold, you have finished the RAG (or FRS, depending on your year group), SERE school has taught you the pleasures of water boarding and you are now in the Fleet. 'Man-o-Manischevitz', this is going to be exciting and important – am I ready to become a warrior? Do I need to buy a personal weapon? Hmmm . . . choices, choices – .357 go to heaven? 9mm? Hollow point of course. When do we leave on cruise? These are the things that might have gone through the minds of thousands of Naval Aviators since about 1911.

Back in the day, 1987-ish, when the Cold War was still a thing and Ronald Reagan was President, I made a cruise with the 'Bounty Hunters' of VF-2 in the F-14A. I had finished the syllabus at VF-124, the west coast F-14

RAG, on 8 May 1987. Less than four weeks later I had my day and night minimums to be qualified to land on *Ranger*. Mind you, I was not a 'nugget' [new guy]. I had already done a tour in F-4N Phantom IIs with VF-154 and had more than 300 traps on USS *Coral Sea* (CV-43), so I was quite familiar with the routine of carrier deployments. I clearly recall my excitement as a lieutenant (junior grade) going to sea for the first time to conduct real-world operations, planning Alpha Strikes, flying during Cyclic Ops and Flex Deck, executing Vector Logic (very hard to do in an F-4N, by the way!) and, of course, enjoying exotic port calls and 'Cubi Dogs'.

Once on cruise, I was introduced to the excitement of the combat air patrol, AKA the CAP, AKA drilling holes in the sky, Tanker Posit and Max Conserve. That's right, a lot of Naval Aviation is flying cool airplanes in a pretty boring manner just waiting for something to happen, and, fortunately, not too much did happen.

What did happen, back in the waning days of the Cold War, were 'Escort Missions'. The term 'Escort Missions' does not evoke the kind of sweaty palm-inducing awe that a radio call like '"Bullet 201", your bogey is 350 at 40 from Bullseye. Warning red, Weapons free' does. Although I must say that given the threat back then, 'Escort' was a damn important element of keeping the 'Ruskies' at bay. In this chapter I will cover the Concept of Operations used during my participation in the Cold War flying the F-14A.

BELOW As the fleet's premier air defence fighter, the F-14 was called on to fly interception missions against probing Soviet long-range bombers and maritime patrol aircraft from the very start of its front-line service. Devoid of external tanks but equipped with an AIM-54A and AIM-7F, VF-51's 'Eagle 113' (BuNo 160687) flies in formation with a Soviet Naval Aviation Tu-95RT 'Bear-D' near the Philippines on 15 October 1979.
(US Navy)

After the work-ups and a short 'pineapple cruise', where we trained around the Hawaiian Islands for about a month, we would send our equipment and most of the squadron personnel to wherever the ship was docked – often at NAS North Island, in San Diego. We would load our equipment and people dockside and then fly the planes from Miramar to the ship once it had sailed a few hundred miles west of California. The transition from shore-based to ship-based was considerably more complicated than the above suggests, but that is an entirely different story.

Once the Air Wing was aboard with all the planes and people, our Point of Intended Movement (PIM) would start going south and west towards Hawaii. Over the week or two it took to get near Hawaii, we would complete critical training and maintenance and ensure we were in the cyclic ops mind-set. Cyclic ops is a launch and recovery strategy wherein aircraft in groups would launch to conduct force protection in 1 hour and 45 minute 'cycles'. If you were lucky there might be a shore detachment to Oahu and some ACM with the Marines flying from MCAS [Marine Corps Air Station] Kaneohe Bay. This lasted for only a few days or a week at most, and then 'westward-ho'.

Literally, it was like the flick of a switch once your PIM extended past Hawaii by more than about 100 miles, for that was when the Alert posture was established. So what was the Alert posture? Normally, it meant one of two schemes – continuous or non-cyclic ops. The most stringent scheme was the continuous or 24-hour Alert even during ongoing cyclic ops. The latter normally had at least four fighters flying during each 1 hour and 45 minute cycle. Typically, cyclic ops generally lasted from dawn to about five hours after local sunset. The second scheme would only stand up the Alerts after cyclic ops had ended for the night. The first scheme of continuous Alerts was pretty tiring for most of the air wing and those members of the ship's company involved in launch and recovery operations. It also meant more planes on the flight deck, although the number required was mitigated somewhat by the spare fighters for each launch being redesignated as the Alert 5 aircraft after the launch was complete.

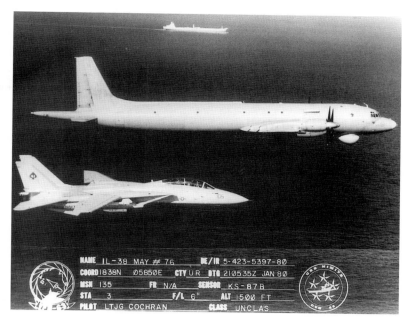

Although tiring, the continuous Alert posture ensured that any inbound aircraft that were carrying air-to-surface missiles – typically 'Kelt', 'Kitchen', 'Kingfish', 'Kangaroo', etc. – could be intercepted at a pre-launch distance. This was generally between 100 and 350 nautical miles, depending on the missile. This was important, as we were always taught that it was easier and safer to kill the 'Archer' than to try to kill the 'Arrow'.

In the second scheme, cyclic ops would cease after the second or third night recovery about 3.5–5 hours after sunset. Essentially, we had 'airborne Alerts' during our cyclic operations, which meant that if something was coming inbound, two of the fighters and a tanker could head that way and escort any aircraft that might want to overfly the battle group.

In either scheme, during cyclic ops the fighters would fly a pretty predictable profile. Launch, tank, vector to a CAP station 200–300 nautical miles along the threat axis and then CAP. A CAP is nothing more than a holding pattern flying at maximum conserve angle-of-attack, with your primary mission being to get radar contact, as far away as possible, of anything heading towards the carrier battle group.

In respect to the 'as far away as possible' strategy, Tomcat crews embarked in *Ranger* during the 1987 cruise proposed and demonstrated a new tactic that allowed the jet to keep its radar looking out at the threat axis

ABOVE Tu-16Rs were also frequently encountered during the height of the Cold War, with aircraft featuring SRS-3 Elint pods beneath their wings (as seen here). Flying from Cam Ranh Bay in Vietnam, these aircraft were searching for the *Kitty Hawk* battle group when they were intercepted by a pair of VF-1 jets on CAP during the spring of 1984. 'Wichita 106' (BuNo 161294) is armed with an AIM-54C and an AIM-7M.
(C.J. Heatley)

for longer periods. Called 'TankSaw', the tactic involved tankers and fighters heading outbound as far as they could in the direction of the CAP station before the F-14 needed to be refuelled. The tanker then would give the fighter as much fuel as possible, before turning back to the ship. During the fuelling operation the fighter had to turn off its radar, potentially leaving the carrier battle group exposed to a sneak attack. However, thanks to the long initial outbound leg flown when employing the 'TankSaw' tactic, there had been time for another fighter from the subsequent launch to provide radar coverage of the threat axis while the first Tomcat was refuelling.

With its tanks topped off, the first fighter would detach from the tanker, fire up the AN/AWG-9 radar again and continue outbound, leaving the second F-14 to refuel. The first jet would eventually turn around when it had gone as far as it could following its inflight refuelling (about 600–800 miles as I recall). The crew of each F-14 would then return to the vicinity of the ship either to top off their tanks and head back outbound or to land. It was a pretty complex scenario that I only participated in once. 'TankSaw' certainly gave us an enhanced long-range detection capability.

We did not always use our radar when we flew our CAP missions, occasionally conducting operations while observing Emissions Controlled (EMCON) conditions. With EMCON, the radar was left in standby, and woe be unto the aircrew that transmitted without a damn good

reason. An example of a damn good reason would be if you received a radio call from an AWACS or E-2 – 'The Voice from the Sky' – which would be in some sort of code. You would not acknowledge the transmission, but you would just start heading in the direction that the voice told you to go, with your radar still in standby until the voice told you to illuminate. The objective, of course, was to surprise the interloper and give them as little time as possible to figure out what was going on. By employing EMCON, the carrier battle group's position would almost certainly not be compromised.

I recall that on one EMCON day our Skipper had an airborne emergency and turned on his radar just to get one sweep of the ship to ensure he was able to get back. Then he turned the radar to standby. They got back to the ship fine, but the Skipper and his pilot were subjected to a rather one-way discussion that involved great furrowing of brows and the gnashing of teeth on the part of some very senior people. Personally, I thought that the Skipper had done the right thing.

Station keeping in EMCON could be a challenge. The ship's TACAN [Tactical Air Navigation system] was turned off, and we did not have a Global Positioning System back then – it certainly would have been great to have had such a capability. If you were able to get a good Inertial Navigation System (INS) alignment it wasn't too bad, but if you had to use 'Ded'

Reckoning (yes, I use the old school spelling for Deduced Reckoning) it was a completely different story. Once, in a Phantom II which had no INS, my RIO and I determined that over the course of our flight we ended up about 300 miles away from where we were supposed to be – winds can be tricky.

Okay, so back to the CAP. Let's say everything went well on your launch, tank and flight, and you are established at your CAP station. After a few orbits around your CAP station you get an interesting radar contact or are given a vector for an intercept. Then off you go. Generally speaking, the intercept of your typical 'Bear', 'May', 'Cub' or 'Badger' was pretty standard, consisting of a series of manoeuvres to keep the contact in a weapons envelope as you joined on it via a stern conversion. The objective of a stern conversion was to achieve target solution geometry for each of the weapons that you were carrying – from Phoenix to Sparrow to Sidewinder to guns to Minolta. With the Phoenix, that meant you had a kill solution nearly 100 miles away from visually acquiring the target. The pilot and RIO would work closely together to ensure the geometry would be optimised at every stage of the intercept.

Let me segue here for a moment to describe a technical detail that is key to keeping the geometry optimised. The key to a good intercept was maintaining proper aspect angle, which was a major factor in obtaining a kill solution for any given stand-off weapon. Aspect angle is the direction in which the bogey would have to look to see you. This is derived through the use of the relative positions of the bogey and the fighter and mechanically calculated using the acronym 'RBA', which means Reciprocal, Bearing, Aspect. Reciprocal is worked out by calculating the reciprocal of the bogey's heading – if the bogey is heading on a 180-degree heading to you, the reciprocal is 360 degrees. The bogey's heading can be given to you from someone else, or you can determine what it is when you lock him up with your radar.

Bearing is the direction from the fighter to the bogey, so if the bearing is 030, which is 30 degrees right of 360 degrees, this results in 30 degrees right aspect. So the bogey would have

to look 30 degrees right of his nose to see you in his 'one o'clock' position.

With a long-range Phoenix shot, a low aspect angle of less than 10 degrees was best. The Sparrow envelope was somewhat shorter in range, and higher aspect angles were okay, although you did not want to have more than about 35 degrees of aspect for a maximum range launch with this weapon. The Sidewinder's envelope was smaller still, and the AIM-9s we carried in 1987 had some good 360-degree aspect angle capability when inside of visual range. Of course, if you were going to shoot the bogey with the gun, aspect angle did not matter too much. You would simply point and shoot, just like you would with your camera, but you had to be pretty close to do that.

Assuming you did not receive a 'warning, red weapons free' call (which indicated that your bogey was confirmed to be a bad hombre and you could shoot whenever you wanted), your goal was to end up flying formation on the bogey while he motored around near the battle group. Some RoEs were to position yourself between the bogey and the ship of interest so as to block would-be picture takers from having a clear view of the ship.

That is the nuts and bolts of a normal escort from a CAP station. From an Alert launch, the basics of the intercept and escort remain the same but how you get there is a whole lot different.

There are at least three levels of Alert –

ABOVE Lt Jon 'Hooter' Schreiber poses with 'Bullet 202' (BuNo 162598) at Miramar following VF-2's return from its 1987 WestPac/ Indian Ocean cruise on board *Ranger*. This was his second such deployment, having previously completed one with F-4N-equipped VF-154 in 1983. *(Jon Schreiber)*

ABOVE Lt Jon 'Hooter' Schreiber commences the debriefing of a recent Alert 5 interception mission in VF-2's ready room on board *Ranger* during his 1987 cruise. Such encounters were painstakingly analysed by the Naval Aviators and NFOs involved, usually in the company of the squadron's Intelligence Officer, so that any unusual features or activities of the Soviet aircraft could be documented and then disseminated to other fighter units in the fleet. *(Jon Schreiber)*

some people do. Aircrew are assigned 2 hours of Alert time. So if you are assigned as an Alert 30 at 0200 hrs, you will become the Alert 15 at 0400 hrs and the Alert 5 at 0600 hrs.

The 30-minute Alert aircrew needs to be available to be airborne within 30 minutes. Mechanically, that means if something is inbound you need to be able to wake up or quit whatever you might be doing, don your flight gear, get an updated weather and threat briefing, pre-flight your airplane and take off within 30 minutes.

The 15-minute Alert means you are in your flight gear and you are in the ready room just below the flight deck. If the Alert 5 is launched, you are expected to run to the flight deck, with current weather and threat info, quickly man-up and start your jet, go through your pre-take-off checks and standby with engines turning.

The 5-minute Alert crew is actually strapped into the airplane and is usually sitting very near the catapult with a huffer (gas tubine-equipped engine start cart – that's right, we did not have an APU in the F-14) and electrical power connected. The Alert 5 crew should have started the jet when they took over the watch, checking out all the systems and then shutting down to await the call 'Launch the Alert Five!' to be announced over the 1MC [1Main Circuit – the shipboard public address circuit]. If this occurs during cyclic ops, then it is normally just one or two fighters that get launched. If the call

30 minutes, 15 minutes and 5 minutes. If you are familiar with baseball, the alerts are similar to 'in the hole', 'on-deck' and 'at bat'. Some folks call the next alert 30 aircrew in line to be the alert 60. I don't like that terminology, but

RIGHT The Alert 5 crew of VF-24's 'Rage 205' (BuNo 159625) chat with the jet's plane captain and two safety inspectors while manning their aircraft on board *Ranger* during its 1983–84 WestPac/Indian Ocean deployment. Note that the Tomcat is not chained down to the flight deck and the tow bar has also been removed from the nose gear. *(US Navy)*

is made when cyclic ops have ended, the Alert 5 launch is normally a helicopter off the deck first, then the fighters, then the tankers. It is pretty hectic, and it normally takes place in the inky blackness that characterises night carrier operations. I have gone from a deep sleep to travelling at more than 500 knots in a matter of a little over 4 minutes – it is a hell of a way to wake up.

Mind you, the deck crew has to react just as quickly, so an alert launch is a full team effort – ordies, maintenance, flight deck directors, safety crew, fire crew, final checkers, cat crew, plane captains, fuellers, etc. It is truly an amazingly well-coordinated and complex sequence of events that gets a jet off a carrier deck in less than 5 minutes.

In the process, the aircrew will be given an initial vector for the threat. That could come via a piece of paper that you are handed, a 1MC announcement or a chalk board with something like '350 @ 200 25K' written on it – translated, that means 'head 350 degrees, the bogey is currently 200 nautical miles away at 25,000ft'. If you are not in EMCON you will get the initial vector on the catapult over the radio, assuming you have remembered to turn it on. I mean 'holy cow', I just woke up and had a whole bunch of stuff to do. Shortly after launch, literally a few seconds after leaving the catapult, you will turn on to the threat heading and proceed expeditiously to the bogey. Once you are on

ABOVE Lt Jon 'Hooter' Schreiber paired up with veteran RIO and former Topgun instructor Lt Cdr Dave 'Bio' Baranek during the *Ranger* cruise in 1987, and the pair spent countless hours like this on deployment – manning the Alert 5 jet beneath the broiling summer sun while CV-61 operated in the Pacific or Indian oceans. Here, both men have donned suitable headgear to protect them from the sun's rays. *(Jon Schreiber)*

your way, the intercept and escort are pretty much the same as previously discussed when vectored on to a bogey from a CAP station – fly optimum geometry, join up and hang on.

In many cases the bogey turned away before getting to the battle group. Indeed, I

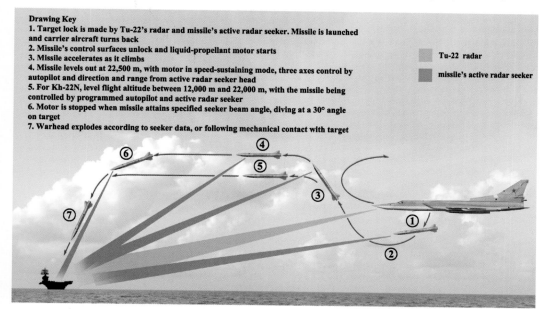

Drawing Key
1. Target lock is made by Tu-22's radar and missile's active radar seeker. Missile is launched and carrier aircraft turns back
2. Missile's control surfaces unlock and liquid-propellant motor starts
3. Missile accelerates as it climbs
4. Missile levels out at 22,500 m, with motor in speed-sustaining mode, three axes control by autopilot and direction and range from active radar seeker head
5. For Kh-22N, level flight altitude between 12,000 m and 22,000 m, with the missile being controlled by programmed autopilot and active radar seeker
6. Motor is stopped when missile attains specified seeker beam angle, diving at a 30° angle on target
7. Warhead explodes according to seeker data, or following mechanical contact with target

Tu-22 radar

missile's active radar seeker

LEFT A typical missile attack profile for a Soviet Tu-22. *(Artwork by Tom Cooper)*

ABOVE VF-2's 'Bullet 201' (BuNo 162596) and 'Bullet 200' (BuNo 162604) 'dirty up' for 'Bio' Baranek's camera upon returning to *Ranger* following an uneventful mission during the carrier's 1987 deployment. Both jets have their wings at mid-sweep and their tailhooks extended, and they boast identical weapon loads – a solitary AIM-54C, AIM-7M and AIM-9L each. This was a typical mission load for Alert 5 jets. *(Dave Baranek)*

VF-2's insignia pays homage to its history as the first squadron to deploy on board a US Navy carrier in 1922, the USS *Langley* (CV-1). Originally, the name of the pilot assigned to the aircraft was painted on the left side of the crest where the blue stars can be seen, but the stars were added instead once it was realised that personnel names changed too frequently to be repeatedly applied. *(Tony Holmes collection)*

only saw one 'Bear' fly by the ship in the three cruises that I made. While flying a Phantom II, I escorted an Indian Il-38 'May' maritime patrol aircraft (the Soviet equivalent of a P-3 Orion) that flew past the ship. During my time flying the F-14, I escorted an An-12 'Cub' transport, but it did not fly by the ship. Neither the Il-38 nor the An-12 were considered terribly threatening. I was once vectored on to a couple of Tu-16 'Badgers', but the weather was so bad we never saw them.

Once an Alert 5 launches, the Alert 15 crew becomes the Alert 5 and the Alert 30 crew becomes the Alert 15, and another crew will be woken up to become the new Alert 30. This occurs daily for months at a time, and can be mind-numbingly boring. So how do we manage to keep our spirits up? Sure we got to fly the F-14, go fast, go high and go far, but what's the fun in that. You've got to add some 'colour'.

'Colour' gets added all along the way by wearing odd hats or sunglasses while in the

Alert 5 Tomcat. You can add 'colour' by the way you turn to the threat after launch, or how you interact with the threat aircrew and even how you return to the ship. This is all serious stuff, but you can also have fun with it.

As an example of how to 'colourise' your turn to the threat, I offer this short sea story.

One of our new guys was a pretty good and aggressive pilot. When he got scheduled for his first Alert 5, he asked a few of us old salts about the protocol for turning after launch. When all of us told him to turn 'immediately' to the specified heading, he took us at our words. To us, 'immediately' meant after the ship was behind you. He was launched from the waist catapult from *Ranger*, which meant there was still a couple of hundred feet of boat on your right as you left the catapult. This particular pilot must have been putting in his turn as he was trundling

The distinctive shape of the Tomcat in planform with its wings fully swept was a popular addition to numerous squadron patches that typically adorned the shoulders of F-14 naval aviators and NFOs. This was the version worn by the 'Bullets' of VF-2, with the yellow Tomcat adorning the unit's well-known 'Langley Stripe'. *(Tony Holmes collection)*

down the cat track, for he did a 'pylon turn' to the right around the bow at flight deck level! I don't think there was more than 100ft between his boot laces, which we could see, and the bow when he went past in a 90-degree angle of bank. The Air Boss was looking down at him from the tower. He got to meet both the Air Wing Commander and the Captain of the ship upon his return, and again there was furrowing of brow and gnashing of teeth.

'Colour' in terms of coming back to the ship after a good escort was provided by high-speed breaks over the 'island' or fan breaks at the 'round down' (which is at the aft end of the landing area), although these were only counted as real 'colour' if your landing was graded as an OK or better.

There are myriad stories of how to interact with the bogey's aircrew, and I have seen photographs showing various hand gestures and displays of popular men's magazines from both the bogey's aircrew and their US Navy counterparts. I have heard apocryphal tales of beverage displays, written communications and 'skilful' flying manoeuvres while alongside said bogey. I will state for the record that no shenanigans occurred on either of my two escorts.

The big airplane intercepts and escorts, though terribly important, were fairly mundane in their execution, as would be expected of large aircraft with, allegedly, nuclear weapons on board. I must say though that the 'Bear' I saw come by our ship was a little less mundane.

ABOVE This self-portrait of 'Bio' Baranek was taken seconds after he had ridden *Ranger*'s waist catapult four at the start of an Alert 5 mission in 1987. Visible on bow catapult one is Baranek's wingman, moments away from launch. Chained down over bow catapult two are A-6Es from VA-145 and VMA(AW)-121 while an EA-3B Skywarrior of VQ-1 can be seen to the left of the Tomcat under tension. *(Dave Baranek)*

He was really low – like at, or below, flight deck level. I think the Russian pilot had been sampling the alcohol-based coolant in the aircraft's radar system.

BELOW Indian Navy Il-38s and Tu-142s were frequently encountered by F-14 crews throughout the 1980s, especially when their carrier was sailing to or from the Persian Gulf via the Indian Ocean and the Bay of Bengal. This Tu-142ME 'Bear-F Mod 3' of Indian Naval Air Squadron 312 flying from Goa was photographed in formation with VF-111 F-14A BuNo 160676 in July 1988. *(US Navy)*

ABOVE The pilot of VF-1's 'Wichita 103' (BuNo 162603) carefully matches his angle of bank with the Tu-95RT 'Bear-D' that he is shadowing following an Alert 5 launch from *Ranger* in 1989. This version of the Tu-95 was the most frequently intercepted by Western air arms. When flying in such close proximity to a 'Bear', Tomcat crews would be almost deafened by the growl from the Tu-95's 32 thrashing blades. *(US Navy)*

correct Return to Base procedures. Here are a couple of stories along those lines.

We were deployed in the Gulf of Oman (GOO) supporting Operation Ernest Will – the US Navy mission to provide naval and air cover for tankers transiting through the Strait of Hormuz. The Iranians had 'Silkworm' anti-ship missiles deployed at various locations along their coastline, most notably the Al-Faw Peninsula, from where several missiles struck various tankers and a fuelling station in Kuwait in 1987. The 'Silkworm', which is about the size of an A-4 Skyhawk, cruises at Mach 0.8–0.9 at an altitude of about 20m, depending on the variant. We had intel that there were also 'Silkworms' in Bandar Abbas, Jask and Chabahar, on the western and southern coasts of Iran.

We manned regular CAP stations between the battle group and those coastal cities.

One rather hazy, but otherwise clear day, a low-flying, non-squawking, high subsonic (Mach 0.8–0.9) target was spotted 'feet wet' [over open water] near Jask. One of our F-14s was vectored from its CAP station toward that target with 'warning red, weapons free' clearance. The pilot and RIO 'romanced' their AN/AWG-9 radar and got a good lock on a target at an altitude of about 50ft, heading straight for the battle group. They had a Sparrow missile selected and were approaching the maximum range kill envelope, being prepared to fire. However, the picture they saw in the TCS looked odd, so the crew waited a bit longer so as to get a better view of the target.

As it turned out, the 'target' was a French Navy F-8 Crusader. Because he was so low

RIGHT This fully-armed MiG-23MLD was one of several 'Floggers' intercepted by VF-1 and VF-2 crews during CVW-2's WestPac/Indian Ocean cruise in 1987. Flying from Cam Ranh Bay, 'Bort 03' features a camouflage pattern based on the scheme applied to exported MiG-23MS/BNs in the 1970s. Soviet owned and operated 'Floggers' based in Vietnam would usually be scrambled to intercept EP-3E Orion ELINT aircraft flying missions over the Gulf of Tonkin or the South China Sea. *(Tom Cooper collection)*

To be clear, not all intercepts were of Russian aircraft. As I wrote earlier, one of my intercepts and escorts was of an Indian Navy Il-38, which was the Russian-built equivalent of the P-3 Orion. Sometimes, we would intercept airliners that were not 'squawking' [sending out a response via a transponder following a radio-frequency 'interrogation' either from another aircraft or air traffic control] and sometimes allied nations flying smaller aircraft had to be intercepted because they were not following the

he did not have radio contact with any of the friendlies and had turned off his transponder when he went feet dry [flew inland from the sea]. When he was done doing whatever he was doing, he went feet wet near Jask and was returning to the French aircraft carrier *Foch*, which was in the GOO with us. Several Air Wing personnel and our pilot and RIO subsequently flew over to the *Foch* to remind our friends that they should follow the Standard Operation Procedure (SOP) that we had all been issued with for returning to the battle group along the threat axis. That SOP had a serpentine flight profile in order to not look like a 'Silkworm' missile. This particular French pilot was nonplussed to find out that he was about a minute from being pain perdu.

I also had a 'warning red, weapons free' episode at about 0200 hrs one morning. Again, we were on one of our CAPs up towards Jask when we received a vector towards a non-squawking, non-talking target at about FL250 [25,000ft above sea level] travelling at a speed of about 0.7 Mach, which could have been any number of things. It was a crystal clear, moonless night, and as soon as we locked on I could see the navigation lights and flashing beacon on the target, which a normal bad guy would not have turned on. As we got closer I could see a whole lot of other lights as well. Those other lights were windows on the starboard side of an airliner full of people going somewhere to the south-east that would pass over the battle group. We broke lock and safed our weapons. We kept our lights off and joined up a few hundred feet away, reported what we were looking at and were then directed to return to our CAP station.

Of course, Alert 5s were launched against smaller tactical aircraft too, as described in the following sea story. According to my logbook, on 14 August 1987 I was flying F-14A BuNo 162594, with Cdr Jim 'Thumb-Dog' Dodge as my RIO – he was CO of the 'Bounty Hunters' at the time. We happened to be sailing in the South China Sea off the coast of Vietnam, near Cam Ranh Bay. On this particular day I was in one of the Alert 5 aircraft. The Skipper and I were positioned on Cat 3 when the call came to launch the Alert 5. We started our Tomcat, went through our checks and were airborne in less

than 5 minutes. We were told that there was a MiG-23 'Flogger' [one of a number of Soviet air force aircraft then flying from the former USAF base at Cam Ranh – the facility was leased by the USSR from 1979 to 1989, the aircraft supporting Soviet naval vessels based at the nearby port] headed towards the ship. I was excited to be actually launching on a threat, but not overly so. Basically, I thought 'this should be fun'.

Since we were operating under normal peacetime RoE, our only mission was to keep the bogey from flying near the ship unescorted. We would not shoot it down if it decided to fly over the ship, unless it did something very provocative. As I recall, our RoE was along the lines of don't shoot first! When we launched we were only about 100 miles east of Cam Ranh Bay, which meant I would be pretty heavy at the merge unless I dumped fuel. Being heavy at the merge would limit my manoeuvrability by about 1.5gs, but that would not be a problem unless things spiralled out of control. The Skipper got a radar lock very shortly after we vectored west, and I could see a black dot in the HUD diamond at about 20 miles. We went through our intercept checklist and talked about our game plan on the way in. At the speed we were closing we would be at the merge in a little over a minute.

During this brief moment of relaxation, I recall taking in the view. A thin overcast made the ocean appear grey rather than blue. There was little natural wind so the ocean almost blended into the sky to the north and the south. To the west, through my HUD, I could make out the verdant mountains of Vietnam breaking the monotony of grey sea and grey sky. The overcast was actually a nice environmental element that would take sun glare and sea glint out of the engagement calculus.

We were at about 5,000ft when we went head-to-head, passing closely port-to-port (left side of each aircraft). The 'Flogger' reversed to the right and went obliquely nose up. I continued to the left and pulled a little more vertically to get an altitude advantage, hoping to pull in behind the 'Flogger'. After about 180 degrees of turn I passed about 1,000ft above the bogey a little aft of his wing line. This was going well. The 'Flogger' pilot reversed again

and I continued to roll through about three-quarters of an aileron roll and pulled back into him now in a right-hand turn. The 'Flogger' pulled a little more nose high and we ended up in an oblique scissors – not a pure vertical fight but not a slow-speed flat scissors either. It was more of a corkscrew to the south-west. We had a little advantage, but I suspect the 'Flogger' pilot says the same thing when he tells his side of the story.

This continued for a couple of turns, after which the bogey just kind of stopped playing. He levelled off and pointed back towards the mainland. The Skipper and I rolled out and tried to join up as the 'Flogger' appeared to be heading back to base. We had a good TCS picture of the plane as we got closer. We made sure we were not going to violate the 12-mile airspace limit surrounding the coast of Vietnam and cause some sort of political incident. We double-checked our position with the E-2C Hawkeye and the ship, both of which were keeping us aware of our geographic location and other potential threats in the area of operation. Another Alert 5 was escorting a different MiG-23 several miles north of us in the area near an EP-3 that was flying an ELINT [electronic intelligence] mission.

As we got closer to the 'Flogger', we wanted to join up and snap a few photos. We thought that the pilot would be willing and photogenic. He had other plans, however. He began modulating his thrust from 'burner to idle, deploying and retracting his speed brakes and flapping his wing spoilers and elevons up and down like he was sending us semaphore signals. Perhaps, if I had ever learned to read semaphore, I might have understood that he

was saying 'DON'T JOIN UP ON ME, YANKEE WAR DOG'. This went on for a while until we got close to the 12-mile limit and had to break off, which I did by turning south-south-east and heading back to international airspace.

My Skipper reminded me not to let the 'Flogger' get behind us. We kept sight of it until he turned back to the right, which would have put him at our 'six' [tail]. We came back hard right to keep him in sight and to put our nose on the MiG-23. The E-2C said he was outbound towards the ship again. As we closed on the MiG-23, he turned into us and we went through the same 'dance' – head-on pass, rolling scissors, jink-and-jive jaunt back towards the beach. I would then break it off, and the MiG duly headed back in the direction of the ship, and we would have to re-engage. It was a 'Groundhog Day' sort of flight. On the third and final engagement we were finally able to join up briefly, where upon I saw that this 'Vietnamese' pilot was anything but Vietnamese. He was stuffed into the cockpit. I am guessing he was about 6ft 2in, weighed 220lb and had red hair and a relief pitcher moustache. Indeed, he was quite photogenic.

The Tomcat was an excellent tool during the Cold War. It had decent loiter time, a great radar, some really sweet stand-off weapons and a crew of two steely-eyed warriors capable of opening a 'can of whoop ass' on all comers. It was as capable in the long-range intercept role as it was in the turning dogfight, with kill envelopes from 500ft to 100 miles. As the patch says, 'Anytime baby!' I am proud to call myself a Tomcat pilot, and I am honoured to have been able to fly and work with some truly great people.

LEFT VF-143 was
one of four Tomcat
squadrons that
provided protection for
vulnerable Gulf states
after the Iraqi invasion
of Kuwait in August
1990. Committed to
Desert Shield patrols
for a month at the end
of its six-month-long
Mediterranean/Persian
Gulf deployment, VF-143
(and its sister-squadron
VF-142) flew fully armed
jets on standing patrols
over Saudi Arabia from
their carrier, *Dwight D.
Eisenhower*, in the Red
Sea. *(US Navy)*

Operation Desert Storm

Although the campaign to remove Iraqi
troops from Kuwait – codenamed
Operation Desert Storm – was an overwhelming
success for the hastily formed Western
Coalition, the Tomcat was usurped in its primary
role as an air-superiority fighter by the USAF's
F-15C Eagle. Indeed, the latter aircraft claimed
34 aerial victories to the F-14's 1. The sidelining
of the Tomcat in Desert Storm would have a
profound effect on the aircraft's future career
with the US Navy.

On 2 August 1990 Iraqi forces invaded
neighbouring Kuwait, catching the Western
world by surprise. When President George
H.W. Bush announced the commencement
of Operation Desert Shield four days later, the
nearest American air power to the threatened
Gulf states was USS *Independence* (CV-62),
with VF-21 and VF-154 on board as part of
CVW-14. The purpose of Desert Shield was to
deter Iraqi leader President Saddam Hussein
from ordering his victorious army into Saudi
Arabia. USS *Dwight D. Eisenhower* (CVN-69)
bolstered the US naval presence in the region
on 8 August when it steamed from the eastern
Mediterranean through the Suez Canal into the
Red Sea. Its embarked air wing – CVW-7 –
included VF-142 and VF-143, which were giving
the F-14A+ its operational debut.

By the time these two vessels were replaced
in theatre by five carriers hastily despatched
from the USA and one from Japan (without
any Tomcats embarked), more than 500,000
American and Coalition troops had been
committed to Desert Shield. Despite this
overwhelming force massing on the borders of

Iraq and occupied Kuwait, Saddam Hussein
refused to withdraw his troops from the latter
country and Operation Desert Storm was
launched on 17 January 1991.

A total of 99 Tomcats would see action
during this one-sided conflict, with the F-14As
of VF-14 and VF-32 embarked in *John F.
Kennedy*, the F-14A+s of VF-74 and VF-103
on board *Saratoga* and the F-14As from VF-33
and VF-102 on board *America* all operating
from the Red Sea. The latter carrier moved
into the NAG in early February prior to the start
of the ground war. *Ranger*, with the F-14As
of VF-1 and VF-2 on board, and *Theodore
Roosevelt*, with the F-14As of VF-41 and VF-84
embarked, had been operating in the NAG
from the start of the conflict.

Tomcat units would fly mainly strike
escort, CAP and TARPS missions during
the war. Typically, the CAP missions lasted
5–7 hours with inflight refuelling, while most
strike escort sorties averaged just 3 hours in
duration. The F-14's standard mission load-out
during the conflict consisted of two AIM-54C
Phoenix and two AIM-7F Sparrow missiles
under the fuselage, two more AIM-7s and
two AIM-9Ls on the wing glove pylons and
two external fuel tanks on the under-nacelle

This patch was
made specifically
for the squadrons
assigned to CVW-1
embarked in
America for Desert
Storm, including
VF-33 and VF-102.
*(Tony Holmes
collection)*

All of the carriers involved in Desert Storm
had special patches created to mark their
participation in what had been the largest
gathering of US naval air power since the
Second World War. This particular offering from
America and CVW-1 was quite subdued when
compared with others seen post-conflict.

(Tony Holmes collection)

LEFT Once *America* had taken up station in the NAG, VF-33 switched from flying strike escorts and MiGCAPs to the far more mundane fleet air defence role. This F-14A was photographed flying just such a sortie in late February 1991, fully armed with a mix of short-, medium- and long-range air-to-air missiles. This load-out was common among non-TARPS configured Tomcats in Desert Storm. *(US Navy)*

CENTRE VF-41's 'CAG bird' (BuNo 162703) has been chained down to the flight deck over *Theodore Roosevelt*'s fantail during the carrier's express crossing of the Atlantic in early January 1991. The aircraft's near-spotless appearance reflects the fact that CVW-8 had only been embarked on board CVN-72 a matter of days when this photograph was taken. The carrier reached the Red Sea shortly after hostilities had started and CVW-8 commenced flying combat sorties straightaway. *(Rick Morgan)*

hardpoints. TARPS-configured jets replaced the two under-fuselage AIM-7s with the reconnaissance pod.

The high hopes that the fighter community had of adding to the jet's victory haul were stymied by the IrAF's (Iraqi Air Force's) non-appearance in its patrol sectors. Up until the invasion of Kuwait, when the F-14 units were allocated a single CAP station over Iraq, the Tomcats had been tasked with performing defensive CAPs for the carrier battlegroups in the Red Sea and the NAG. When the jets did venture over enemy territory while escorting strike mission, the IrAF refused to engage them.

Some Tomcat crews believed that the Iraqi pilots chose to flee whenever they picked up

LEFT In Desert Shield/Storm RAF tankers proved popular with Tomcat crews as their wing-mounted drogues were less likely to knock off the doors fitted to the F-14's refuelling probes than those employed by the KC-135s in particular. Here, 101 Squadron's VC10 K2 ZA140 has trailed its starboard wing hose and drogue for EA-6B 'Zapper 620' (BuNo 163400) of VAQ-130 and its escort, F-14A 'Camelot 104' (BuNo 160396) from VF-14. *(Dave Parsons)*

ABOVE Tomcat units relied both on strategic tankers – here, represented by a 93rd Air Refueling Squadron (ARS) KC-135R – and tactical tankers like VA-75 KA-6D BuNo 151579, which is topping off its fuel before pressing in over the coast with US Navy strike aircraft from CVW-3. Keeping a close eye on proceedings are the crew of 'Gypsy 204' (BuNo 160397) from VF-32, armed with Phoenix, Sparrow and Sidewinder missiles. *(Dave Parsons)*

ABOVE VF-14's 'Camelot 114' (BuNo unknown) takes on fuel from a 190th ARG (Kansas Air National Guard) KC-135E towards the end of Desert Storm. The ubiquitous USAF tanker was dubbed the 'Iron Maiden' by Tomcat crews due to the unforgiving nature of the basket (and the steel 'knuckle' fitting that attached the basket to the hose) fitted to the Stratotanker. The latter inflicted much damage to F-14 probe fairings. *(US Navy)*

emissions from the F-14s' AN/AWG-9 radar. 'It was obvious that the Iraqis did not want to fight, and they were running from us, or we were shooting them out of the sky,' stated Dave Parsons, who flew missions as a RIO with VF-32 during Desert Storm. 'They wouldn't go anywhere near an F-14. That's a big part of the reason why the F-14s didn't get any kills against fixed-wing aircraft.'

LEFT VF-41's 'Fast Eagle 100' breaks into the landing pattern overhead *Theodore Roosevelt* on 26 February 1991 at the end of yet another quiet CAP over the Red Sea. The fighter is armed with four AIM-7Ms and a similar number of AIM-9Ms, the AIM-54Cs having been left on board ship due to the weight penalty associated with these weapons. *(US Navy)*

There was also a feeling within the Tomcat community that USAF E-3 AWACS controllers who ran the interceptions of IrAF aircraft favoured the allocation of F-15Cs to deal with the enemy threat. Doug Denneny, who served as a RIO with VF-14 in the late 1980s, explained:

There was a lot of parochialism as to where the F-14 and F-15 fighter CAPs were placed. The Eagles got the kills because it was the USAF's

BELOW **The view through the windscreen of a VF-33 jet as it approaches the coast of Kuwait. The black rectangular shape in the pilot's eye-line is a small video camera for recording the symbology projected on to the windscreen – the F-14A did not have a modern HUD. Beneath the cockpit coaming is the Air Combat Maneuver panel, with the illuminated words in red denoting that the M61A1 is optimised for a HIGH rate of fire, the seeker head cooling for the AIM-9 is ON and missile preparation (all weapons are primed and ready to engage hostile contacts) is also ON.** *(US Navy)*

E-3 AWACS that were running the show up north. They would even call Navy guys off and then bring in Eagles for easy pickings. This could just be the ranting and raving of pissed-off Navy pilots, but from what I personally saw in OIF [Operation Iraqi Freedom], there was probably a shred of truth in these stories.

Veteran EA-6B Prowler Electronic Countermeasures Officer Rick Morgan flew with VAQ-141 during Desert Storm, and he witnessed at first hand the frustration felt by F-14 crews during the campaign

In CVW-8 and we had two very good Tomcat squadrons, VF-84 and VF-41. They all thought – and probably reasonably so – that there would be more air-to-air action than they saw, and they definitely had 'knives in their teeth' to start things out. Very soon it became apparent that MiG killing (and shooting down Mirages and other IrAF types) was probably not going to happen, so flying TARPS missions became critical, as well as the easiest path to a Strike-Flight Air Medal for the VF [fighter] guys. I shot AGM-88 High-speed Anti-Radiation Missiles [HARMs] in support of two of these missions, one as an SA-6 SAM was launching on a VF-84 TARPS bird. We either killed the site or scared the peanuts out of him as the SAM went stupid at HARM impact. They were satisfying missions from both crew's standpoints, and were certainly much more exciting from the F-14 crew's point of view.

So why so few kills? Word was the USAF (who wrote the Air Tasking Order) was taking the most lucrative CAP locations for their own F-15s and the F-14s just didn't have the opportunity. There was another story going around, apparently with some truth, that the Iraqi RWR systems were tuned for the AN/AWG-9 since it was the biggest threat system their arch enemies, the Iranians, had. As the story went, every time their gear picked up an AN/AWG-9 from a Navy Tomcat they'd run the other way – and usually right into a group of waiting USAF Eagles. In the end the F-14s only bagged a single luckless helicopter during the war.

We had another day when I saw an F-14 pilot throw his helmet across our intel center

after a flight. He'd been on North Gulf CAP and saw at least one Mirage F 1 underneath him. As I recall the story, he rolled in and was ready to shoot when the E-2 told him to hold fire as 'it's friendly'. He followed instructions and didn't pull the trigger, but came back in a lather because he was convinced it was Iraqi. We later found out it was actually a Qatari Air Force bird, supposedly on the first day they'd flown in the war – except nobody had told us of their participation! Navy discipline and a sharp E-2 crew had paid off and kept a certain 'blue-on-blue' from occurring.

In reality, Tomcats had been kept out of the aerial action because the US Navy had failed to develop the necessary systems – primarily up-to-date Identification Friend or Foe (IFF) equipment – and procedures required to

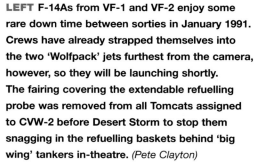

LEFT F-14As from VF-1 and VF-2 enjoy some rare down time between sorties in January 1991. Crews have already strapped themselves into the two 'Wolfpack' jets furthest from the camera, however, so they will be launching shortly. The fairing covering the extendable refuelling probe was removed from all Tomcats assigned to CVW-2 before Desert Storm to stop them snagging in the refuelling baskets behind 'big wing' tankers in-theatre. *(Pete Clayton)*

CENTRE Lt Stuart 'Meat' Broce and Cdr Ron 'Bongo' McElraft (VF-1's CO) used this jet (BuNo 162603) to achieve the only aerial victory credited to the F-14 in Desert Storm when they downed a Mil Mi-8 'Hip' helicopter with an AIM-9M on 6 February 1991 – this kill marking was added to the jet upon its return to CV-61. *(US Navy)*

BELOW The 'Wolfpack' gather in front of 'Wichita 106' (BuNo 162608) shortly after the cessation of hostilities. Mi-8 killer Lt Stuart Broce is standing immediately below the yellow rescue arrow, while his RIO on that mission, unit CO Cdr Ron McElraft, is squatting in the front row, eighth from left. To his left is CVW-2 CAG, Capt (later Rear Admiral) Jay Campbell. *(Neil Jennings)*

integrate carrier air wings as part of a joint air component command. This meant that F-14 crews were unable to solve the strict RoE that would have allowed them to autonomously engage aerial targets using only their onboard sensors. Instead, they had to rely on controlling platforms such as USAF E-3s to give them their clearance to fire. With the RoE criteria met, fighters with beyond visual range (BVR) air-to-air missiles like the AIM-7 Sparrow and AIM-54 Phoenix could fire their ordnance at long range, safe in the knowledge that no friendly aircraft in the area would be shot down instead. USAF F-15C pilots could solve all the required RoE criteria for identifying an enemy aircraft from within their own cockpits, prior to shooting it down. The F-14, conversely, lacked the IFF systems and software to meet all RoE criteria, which left its crew reliant on outside clearance to engage. The job of defeating the IrAF was therefore given to the Eagle pilots, who duly shot down 34 aircraft.

Ultimately, the F-14 performed just six intercepts, resulting in a solitary aerial kill in Desert Storm. The latter took the form of a Mil Mi-8 helicopter that was shot down by

ABOVE LEFT Suitably adorned with VF-84's chevrons, a TARPS pod is wheeled towards 'Victory 211' (BuNo 161164) – one of three Tomcats assigned to the unit that had been configured for the TARPS mission – chained down to the flight deck over the stern of *Theodore Roosevelt*. Initially, only 50 F-14As had their rear right Phoenix station wired for TARPS operation, these aircraft then being spread among the front-line force. *(US Navy)*

ABOVE CVW-17, embarked in *Saratoga*, boasted the only F-14A+-equipped units – VF-74 and VF-103 – committed to Desert Storm. VF-103 had the TARPS mission for the air wing and saw considerable action providing Coalition forces with up-to-date images of targets before and after they had been attacked. Fuelled, armed and declared mission ready, 'Devil 101' (BuNo 162919) is about to be towed forward towards *Saratoga*'s bow catapults to serve as an Alert 5 jet. *(US Navy)*

RIGHT 'Big wing' tanker support was critical to the success of Desert Storm. Proving the point, F-14A+ BuNo 162920 from VF-103 is seen taking on fuel from a 145th ARS (Ohio Air National Guard) KC-135E over the Red Sea in February 1991. This photo was taken by a KA-99 camera installed in a TARPS pod slung beneath a second F-14 from VF-103. *(US Navy)*

RIGHT Two reinforced concrete aircraft hangars at the Ahmed Al Jabir airfield in Kuwait show the results of a Coalition bombing strike during Desert Storm. The hangars, hit by laser-guided bombs, had been suspected of housing Iraqi aircraft. This photograph, also taken with a KA-99 low-altitude panoramic camera installed in a TARPS pod carried by a Tomcat, was typical of the footage shot by F-14 units during the campaign. *(US Navy)*

ABOVE RIGHT *Abraham Lincoln* was relieved in the NAG by *Dwight D. Eisenhower*, with CVW-7 embarked. This air wing flew in Desert Shield more than a year earlier and, having missed Desert Storm, it was once again required to fulfil a watching brief on Iraq. CVW-7 earned an unfortunate reputation for arriving on the scene either before the fighting had started or after it had ended, leading to it being nicknamed the 'peace air wing'. *(US Navy)*

BELOW After Desert Storm US forces supported UN peacekeepers keeping an eye on Iraqi troop movements to ensure that there was no military build-up along the defeated nation's borders with Kuwait and Saudi Arabia. Fully armed 'Aardvark 107' crewed by Lts Shane Smithson and Steve Gozzo was photographed flying past knocked-out hardened aircraft shelters at a Kuwaiti air base on a CAP mission in September 1991. *(US Navy)*

a crew from VF-1 on 6 February 1991. This victory went some way to even up the score for the Tomcat, as VF-103 had lost a jet to an SA-2 SAM on 21 January – its pilot had been rescued and the RIO captured. This aircraft had been flying a TARPS sortie, thus proving that these sorties were usually more action-packed than the traditional fighter missions flown by the Tomcat in Desert Storm. The importance of tactical reconnaissance grew as the conflict progressed, for the US Navy had quickly found that it could not rely on USAF tactical reconnaissance assets for up-to-date bomb damage assessment photographs in the wake of air strikes by carrier-based attack aircraft. TARPS-equipped F-14s also helped in the daily hunt for Iraq's mobile 'Scud' ballistic missiles.

Despite maintaining a mission-capable rate of 77%, logging a total of 4,182 sorties and completing 14,248 flight hours (more than any other US Navy fixed-wing aircraft) during the 40-day air war, the F-14 had proven largely ineffective in its primary role as an interceptor. And at this point in the jet's history, being a fighter was still virtually the only role it could perform. This would all change in the early 1990s, however, with the advent of the multi-role 'Bombcat'.

'Bombcat' evolution

The post-Desert Storm years were bleak ones for the US Navy's fighter community, with swingeing budget cuts seeing 11 fleet Tomcat units disestablished due to the aircraft's astronomical maintenance costs and single-mission capability. However, just when it looked like the F-14's ocean-going days were numbered, a reprieve came thanks to the accelerated demise of another Grumman 'Ironworks' product. The all-weather, long-range A-6 Intruder bomber was hastily chopped, again due to high maintenance costs and the supposed evaporation of its mission in the post-Cold War world.

With the Intruder on the verge of retirement, and the Tomcat seemingly following in its footsteps, the US Navy now found itself facing a shortage of tactical carrier aircraft to fulfil its global 'policing' mission. When the F-14 was developed in the late 1960s, Grumman had built the jet with the capability to drop bombs, although this mission requirement had not been specified by the US Navy. For the first two decades of its service life, the Tomcat had been operated exclusively as a fighter, with the additional photo-reconnaissance role being adopted begrudgingly by fleet squadrons in the early 1980s. Indeed, there was a bumper sticker popular in the fighter community at Miramar and Oceana throughout this time that bore the mantra 'Not a pound for air-to-ground', referring to the fact that the F-14 was an interceptor through and through. Conversely, in the early 1990s, some career attack aircrew in the A-6 Intruder and F/A-18 Hornet camps doubted that their brethren flying Tomcats had the maturity to perform the strike role. This led to the widespread belief among 'mud movers' at the time that 'Any dollar spent on a Tomcat is much better spent on a Hornet'!

ABOVE **F-14A BuNo 157990 was FSD aircraft No 11 and, as such, the jet was assigned to NAF Point Mugu in the early 1970s. It conducted trials with a variety of ordnance, including this mixed mission load-out that saw the Tomcat laden down with 14 Mk 82 500lb dummy bombs fitted with Mk 15 Snakeye tail retarders, two AIM-9 Sidewinders and two AIM-7 Sparrows, plus external tanks.** *(US Navy)*

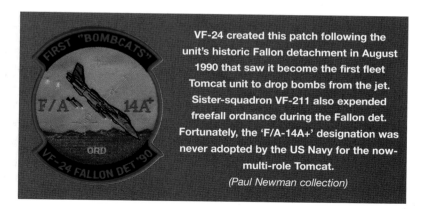

VF-24 created this patch following the unit's historic Fallon detachment in August 1990 that saw it become the first fleet Tomcat unit to drop bombs from the jet. Sister-squadron VF-211 also expended freefall ordnance during the Fallon det. Fortunately, the 'F/A-14A+' designation was never adopted by the US Navy for the now-multi-role Tomcat.

(Paul Newman collection)

RIGHT **F-14A BuNo 162602 of VF-51 prepares to roll in over Fallon's Bravo 20 range during CVW-15's three-week stay at the naval air station in January 1994. BuNo 162602 was written off on 11 July 1994 when it broke in half following a heavy landing onboard *Kitty Hawk*, the cockpit section of the jet sliding down the flight deck and over the side of the vessel.** *(Tom Twomey)*

ABOVE Lt Cdr Randy Parrish (pilot) and VF-51 CO, Cdr John Sill, release all four Mk 83 bombs from 'Eagles 102' in a diving attack on the Bravo 20 range. VF-51 dropped 50,000lb of live and inert ordnance during its Air Wing Fallon detachment in January 1994. *(Tom Twomey)*

BELOW Perfectly illustrating the evolving ground attack role adopted by the F-14 community in the wake of Desert Storm, VF-14's CAG jet (BuNo 161855) is armed with two live AIM-7Ms and AIM-9Ls on the wing glove pylons and a pair of Mk 83 general-purpose bombs fitted with BSU-85 high-drag fins on the centreline BRU-32 racks. *(US Navy via Peter B. Mersky)*

Despite F-14 crews clearly needing to embrace the precision strike mission in order to secure their very survival in the fleet, many of those flying the jet still felt that it was a fighter first and foremost. One such individual was future Weapons and Tactics and Strike Fighter Tactics Instructor James 'Puck' Howe:

When I was a young student in VF-101 in the early 1990s, the Tomcat was just starting to develop the air-to-ground capability that had been inherent in the aeroplane since its creation. Looking back, it's pretty funny, as we didn't really have any idea what we were doing. It wasn't exactly giving a loaded gun to a child, but it was close. Moreover, no one really seemed too serious or too happy about the F-14's potential to become a 'strike fighter'. We were purebred fighter pilots – stuck-up, arrogant and shameless. We sang 'You've Lost that Loving Feeling' and made it look cool. Dropping bombs was for people who didn't make the cut. But our leadership kept telling us that a single-role aircraft would not last long in a newly cost-conscious Navy. If we didn't figure out bomb dropping, and quickly, the Tomcat was going to fade unceremoniously into oblivion. Enter 'flexibility'.

Within five years the F-14 went from being a Cold War relic protecting the battle group from 'Bear' and 'Backfire' raids that were never going to happen, to being the self-escorting strike fighter of choice. The Tomcat, with its two-seat cockpit, a big payload and more fuel, greater speed and greater bring-back than the F/A-18, had become the 'Bombcat'. Much to the chagrin of our Hornet brethren, the toughest missions were now doled out to Tomcat squadrons.

Threatened with wholesale disestablishment, the fighter community looked to diversify in order to remain relevant. Seeing that the precision bombing role once performed by the A-6 was now vacant, key personnel within the east and west coast fighter wings pushed to pair the Tomcat up with some form of bolt-on targeting pod system.

Experimentation with gravity bombs hung beneath standard Tomcats had taken place just prior to Desert Storm (the first live bombs

RIGHT NF-14A BuNo 159455, assigned to the Naval Air Test Center at NAS Patuxent River, was heavily involved in the early 'Bombcat' air-to-ground capability trials at the Naval Weapons Center at China Lake in November–December 1990, undertaking 23 flights with a variety of air-to-ground ordnance. Seen here during a test drop in May 1996, the jet is fitted with FPU-1A/A external tanks modified to carry cameras for recording weapon separation. *(US Navy)*

dropped from a fleet Tomcat were expended by an F-14B from VF-211 in August 1990 on targets on a range near Yuma, Arizona). Although senior naval officers realised that the F-14 would not be a viable fighter/attack platform without some kind of precision weapons delivery capability. Little funding was available to develop such a system, so an 'off-the-shelf' pod was acquired thanks to the securing of modest financing through the lobbying of AIRLANT (Naval Air Force Atlantic) in the autumn of 1994. The equipment chosen was the combat-proven AN/AAQ-14 LANTIRN (low-altitude navigation and targeting infrared night) pod, developed for the F-15E by Martin Marietta (later Lockheed Martin).

Working with a tiny budget, the Tomcat community, ably assisted by a clutch of defence contractors, integrated the digital pod with the analogue F-14A/B, and by March 1995 a test aircraft – supplied by VF-103 – was dropping laser-guided bombs (LGBs) with the aid of the AN/AAQ-25 LANTIRN (as the US Navy designated the modified AN/AAQ-14). The results of this early evaluation were stunning, with the Tomcat crew obtaining better infrared

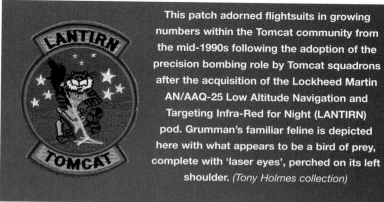

This patch adorned flightsuits in growing numbers within the Tomcat community from the mid-1990s following the adoption of the precision bombing role by Tomcat squadrons after the acquisition of the Lockheed Martin AN/AAQ-25 Low Altitude Navigation and Targeting Infra-Red for Night (LANTIRN) pod. Grumman's familiar feline is depicted here with what appears to be a bird of prey, complete with 'laser eyes', perched on its left shoulder. *(Tony Holmes collection)*

imagery, and bomb accuracy, than the similarly equipped USAF F-15E Strike Eagle and F-16C Fighting Falcon. On 14 June 1996 the first fleet-capable LANTIRN pod was delivered to VF-103 at Oceana. During the ceremony held to mark this occasion, Secretary of the Navy John H. Dalton proudly proclaimed 'The Cat is back.'

To give an unsophisticated bomber like the basic F-14 a precision targeting capability, the basic LANTIRN system was modified into US

RIGHT The Lockheed Martin AN/AAQ-25 LANTIRN pod revolutionised the F-14's combat employment in its final decade of front-line service with the US Navy. Featuring an integral GPS for position information and an inertial measurement unit for improved stabilisation and accuracy, the pod (costing $3 million) also boasted an internal computer that generated ballistics data for the various precision munitions carried by the F-14. *(Danny Coremans)*

ABOVE Belying its relative youth, heavily weathered F-14D BuNo 163418 of VF-11 prepares to receive fuel from a KC-135 during air wing work-ups in the spring of 1995. The aeroplane became the first D-model to be delivered to VF-124 in October 1990, and it was transferred to VF-11 two years later when the unit switched from the Atlantic to the Pacific Fleet and transitioned to the ultimate Tomcat variant. *(Ted Carlson)*

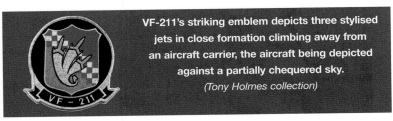

VF-211's striking emblem depicts three stylised jets in close formation climbing away from an aircraft carrier, the aircraft being depicted against a partially chequered sky.
(Tony Holmes collection)

BELOW VF-211's F-14A 'Nickel 110' (BuNo 162606) descends toward *Nimitz* in late 1997. The aircraft features a common loadout for the F-14 during the 'Fighting Checkmates" 1997–98 OSW deployment – an AIM-54C and an AM-9M on the port shoulder pylon, an AIM-7M (in the rear under-fuselage well), two Mk 7 CBUs on the forward BRU-32 racks, a LANTIRN pod on the starboard shoulder pylon and a full load of 20mm ammunition. *(Dave Baranek)*

Navy-specific LTS (LANTIRN Targeting System) configuration. Martin Marietta removed the navigation pod of the two-pod LANTIRN system and vastly improved the targeting pod for Tomcat use. The US Navy pod featured an embedded GPS and inertial measurement unit that provided it with line-of-site cueing and weapon-release ballistics. Critically, the RIO had a much larger display in his cockpit than the one presented to his equivalent Weapon Systems Officer in the F-15E, which led to better apparent magnification and target recognition.

Unlike its USAF configurations, the LTS performed all the weapon-release calculations and presented release cues that it had generated to the aircrew. It also incorporated a masking avoidance curve display and, eventually, a north orientation cue and 40,000ft-capable laser. The latter would prove extremely useful in allowing F-14 aircrew to employ LGBs above potential threat system altitudes, especially in the higher terrain of Afghanistan during Operation Enduring Freedom (OEF).

But all that lay in the future, for in June 1996 the F-14/LTS partnership remained unproven in combat. Nine months earlier, in a precursor of things to come, the Tomcat had briefly been given the chance to prove its worth in the 'mud-moving' business when, on 5 September 1995 during Operation Allied Force, two F-14As from VF-41, embarked in *Nimitz*, dropped LGBs (designated by F/A-18s) on an ammunition dump in eastern Bosnia.

Aside from brief campaigns in the Balkans (1995 and 1999) and Afghanistan (2001–02), combat operations for F-14 pilots and RIOs during the jet's final 15 years of front-line service had taken place from carriers sailing in the NAG. In the wake of Desert Storm, a No-Fly Zone had been created over southern Iraq with UN backing as Operation Southern Watch (OSW) on 26 August 1992 in order to protect Shi'ite Muslims from persecution by Saddam Hussein's regime. Joint Task Force-Southwest Asia (JTF-SWA), consisting of units from the United States, Britain, France and Saudi Arabia, was established on the same date to oversee the day-to-day running of OSW.

The Tomcat proved to be a primary asset in OSW, although not because of its ability as

RIGHT Tomcat units committed to OSW would occasionally carry out Operation Sea Dragon maritime surveillance sorties, the jet's two-man crew, its long range and the LANTIRN pod making the F-14 well suited to such missions. F-14D (BuNo 163904) from VF-31, embarked in *Abraham Lincoln* with CVW-14 in August 1998, is armed with an AIM-54C and a Mk 7 CBU that probably contains Mk 20 Rockeye bombs. *(Jim Muse)*

CENTRE Until the advent of the LANTIRN pod and precision-guided munitions, the F-14's primary mission in OSW was tactical photo-reconnaissance when configured with a TARPS pod. Weighing 1,760lb, the pod remained in use with the fleet until late 2004. This VF-102 F-14B (BuNo 163221), on an OSW mission from *George Washington* in early 1998, also carries an AN/ALQ-167(V) 'Bullwinkle' ECM jamming pod as well as AIM-7M and AIM-9M missiles. *(US Navy)*

a long-range fighter. As had been the case in Desert Storm, the F-14's TARPS capability provided JTF-SWA with the flexibility to monitor Iraqi military activity on a daily basis in good weather. Although the TARPS mission was seen as a necessary evil by a number of dyed-in-the-wool fighter crews, it nevertheless enabled the Tomcat community to make a concrete contribution to the daily enforcing of OSW. TARPS sorties also tended to be far more eventful than the typically mundane and boring CAPs that were the 'bread and butter' sorties of the F-14 units in theatre in the years prior to the arrival of LTS-equipped aircraft.

The ultimate F-14 bomber toting an LTS pod had to wait until 16 December 1998 to prove its worth in OSW. On that date the US Navy

RIGHT This photograph was taken by a VF-2 F-14D carrying a TARPS-DI pod during CVW-2 work-ups in April 1998, the Scud missiles and their transporter erector launchers being sited on one of the ranges at Nellis AFB. The TARPS-DI system was ideally suited to pinpointing mobile targets like Scuds and then transmitting photographs in digital data form via the F-14's encrypted line-of-sight UHF radio to waiting strike aircraft. *(US Navy)*

LAT: 37:41.6 LONG: 116:38.1 HEADING: 345.9
AGL ALTITUDE: 04120 TIME: 00:21:16 DATE: MON APR 20 1998
PITCH: 01.1 ROLL: 02.2
TARPS DI Image of Nellis AFB Target

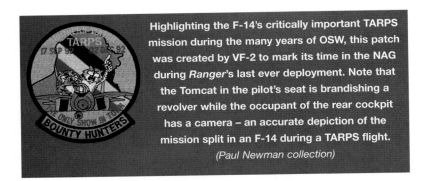

Highlighting the F-14's critically important TARPS mission during the many years of OSW, this patch was created by VF-2 to mark its time in the NAG during *Ranger*'s last ever deployment. Note that the Tomcat in the pilot's seat is brandishing a revolver while the occupant of the rear cockpit has a camera – an accurate depiction of the mission split in an F-14 during a TARPS flight.

(Paul Newman collection)

CVW-3 saw action both over Iraq and in the Balkans during its busy 1998–99 Mediterranean/NAG deployment embarked in *Enterprise*. The air wing's Tomcat unit, VF-32, was at the forefront of strikes during Operation Desert Fox, its F-14s providing precision guidance for aircraft attacking military targets deep inside Iraq.

(Paul Newman collection)

BELOW A maintainer from VF-32 takes advantage of a lull in activities between air strikes against Iraq during Operation Desert Fox to paint bomb tally symbols on an F-14B from the squadron. This photograph was taken on board *Enterprise* on 18 December 1998.
(US Navy)

spearheaded Operation Desert Fox in what proved to be a precursor for Operation Iraqi Freedom five years later. F-14Bs from VF-32, embarked in *Enterprise* as part of CVW-3, were involved in the first wave of attacks against Iraqi air defence installations, dropping self-guided GBU-12, GBU-16 and GBU-24 LGBs. The Tomcats also 'lased' for accompanying F/A-18 Hornets. Two days later, the F-14Ds of VF-213, on board USS *Carl Vinson* (CVN-70) with CVW-11, joined in the action. During the four days of Desert Fox, VF-32 alone had dropped 111,054lb of ordnance, consisting of

16 GBU-10s, 16 GBU-16s and no fewer than 26 2,000lb GBU-24 penetrator LGBs. The latter proved to be the laser-guided weapon of choice against hardened aircraft shelters, HQ bunkers and command and control buildings. Not all of the Tomcats sortied were carrying bombs, however, as both VF-32 and VF-213 also conducted a series of escort CAPs for USAF B-1Bs committed to Desert Fox from day two of the campaign.

'The Tomcat's distinct size and power made it an intimidating foe to any enemy', noted VF-32 CO Cdr Will Cooney shortly after Desert Fox had come to its conclusion. 'With the big motors in the F-14B/D, its speed and power were very impressive. Coupled with size, large ordnance load and long legs, the Tomcat could really reach out and touch the bad guys in OSW.'

The adoption of a more aggressive stance by the IrAF after this campaign almost resulted in a US Navy Tomcat claiming its first Phoenix missile kill when, on 5 January 1999, a pair of F-14Ds from VF-213 fired two AIM-54Cs at MiG-25s that had penetrated the No-Fly Zone. The Iraqi jets were already heading back north at high speed by the time the Tomcat crews got to fire their missiles at very long range. Neither hit their intended targets.

Two months later, in March, the Tomcat returned to action over the Balkans when VF-14 and VF-41 were committed to Operation Deliberate Force – NATO's campaign to free Kosovo from Serbian control. Flying venerable F-14As from USS *Theodore Roosevelt* (CVN-71), the units expended close to 800,000lb of LGBs and iron bombs. Crews from both squadrons also functioned as Forward Air Controllers (Airborne) for other assets involved in the Kosovo campaign. VF-14 CO, Cdr Ted Carter, explained how the FAC(A) mission was carried out:

We flew in sections, one aircraft serving as an escort for the other. Each F-14 usually carried four bombs, which we used for both striking a target ourselves or for marking a target for other strike aircraft. The FAC(A) is like a quarterback on a football team, seeking out and identifying targets, ushering strike aircraft to the scene, recommending

the type of ordnance for a particular target, ensuring they recognised potential terrain hazards and providing them with run-in and recovery headings.

Units committed to carrying out the OSW mission continued to counter Iraqi AAA and SAM opposition during 1999, and on 9 September, following a heightened response to its patrols, CVW-2, embarked in *Constellation*, launched Operation Gun Smoke. Some 35 of 39 AAA and SAM sites targeted for destruction were eliminated in a series of precision strikes that saw the largest expenditure of ordnance in a single day since Desert Storm. The F-14Ds of VF-2 played a leading part in the success of this campaign, and aside from dropping LGBs, the unit also got to fire a single AIM-54C against an Iraqi MiG-23. Again, this missed its target due to the weapon being fired at extreme range.

Tensions remained high over Iraq well into 2001, and on 16 February that year CVW-3, operating from USS *Harry S. Truman* (CVN-75), targeted five command, control and communications sites. Again, VF-32 found itself in the vanguard of the one-day war, dropping LGBs, lasing for fellow Hornet strikers, running TARPS missions and conducting Defensive Counter Air (DCA) sweeps in the OSW patrol area.

ABOVE VF-41 head west for CVW-8's Air Wing Fallon deployment prior to its combat-filled 1999 deployment to the Mediterranean and the NAG embarked in *Theodore Roosevelt*. Although both the 'Black Aces' and sister-squadron VF-14 were equipped with some of the oldest Tomcats in the fleet, these aeroplanes had benefited from a slew of upgrades to their avionics and flight controls. *(Ted Carlson)*

BELOW Armourers from VF-14 check the guidance vanes of a GBU-24A/B Paveway III 2,000lb LGB that they have shackled to the port BRU-32 bomb rack of a 'Tophatters' F-14A on 14 April 1999 during Operation Allied Force. First dropped from a Tomcat in combat by VF-32 and VF-213 during Desert Fox some five months earlier, the difficult to employ 'bunker-busting' GBU-24 was developed for use against well-defended, high-value targets. *(US Navy)*

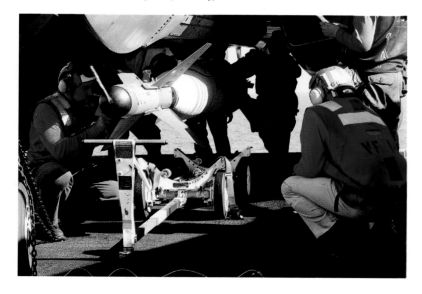

LEFT On 9 September 1999, CVW-2, embarked in *Constellation*, launched a one-day series of intensive strikes on AAA and SAM sites in southern Iraq as part of Operation Gun Smoke. F-14D-equipped VF-2 was in the vanguard of the campaign, and one of its crews also got to fire off a single AIM-54C at extreme range against an Iraqi MiG-23, but the weapon missed its target. *(Tom Twomey)*

The steady escalation of the conflict in the region was only brought to a halt, albeit temporarily, by the devastating attacks on the World Trade Center, in New York City, and the Pentagon on 11 September 2001. The subsequent declaration of the War on Terror by President George W. Bush saw US carrier battle groups under Fifth Fleet control removed from their OSW station and pushed further east into the Arabian Sea and Indian Ocean in order to support Operation Enduring Freedom in Afghanistan.

Now a truly multi-role fighter-bomber, with more mission taskings than any other aircraft then embarked in a US carrier, the venerable Tomcat was set to play a leading role in the conflicts over Afghanistan and Iraq, rather than being the bit-part player that it had been in Desert Storm. According to former RIO Dave Parsons, who, as a civilian contractor, was a key facilitator in getting the F-14 paired up with the LTS:

It is perhaps the ultimate irony that the Tomcat, designed to be the supreme air superiority machine, left a much larger combat legacy as a precision strike fighter. This was a role it was never envisioned to perform, and the jet very nearly missed the opportunity altogether to prove itself as a precision bomber.

LEFT Eight of VF-2's ten F-14Ds sit on the squadron ramp at Oceana in early June 1999, days away from flying cross-country to North Island and embarking in *Constellation* for CVW-2's WestPac/NAG deployment. Heading the line-up is VF-2's colour jet, BuNo 163901, which features the names of the unit CO and XO rather than the CAG and his deputy on the starboard side of its canopy rail. *(Takashi Hashimoto)*

CVW-8's deployment in 2001 on board *Enterprise* initially saw the air wing performing OSW missions in the traditional style, but it ended with units flying myriad combat missions over Afghanistan following the start of OEF in the wake of the 11 September 2001 terrorist attacks on New York and Washington DC. This patch was created for Tomcat aircrew who completed 50 OSW missions over Iraq. *(Paul Newman collection)*

BELOW Two F-14Bs from VF-32 fly in formation with a pair of F/A-18Cs from VFA-37 during CVW-3's Air Wing Fallon deployment in summer 2000, which saw all carrier air wing units brought together to complete their pre-cruise training. For CVW-3's Hornet squadrons and VF-32, the aim of the two-week exercise period in Nevada was to prepare them for typical OSW missions. *(US Navy)*

LEFT Photographed during VF-32's Desert Shield/Desert Storm cruise in 1990–91, Dave 'Hey Joe' Parsons was a NFO for 15 years – he had previously served for five years as a Marine. He joined defence contractor Whitney, Bradley & Brown immediately after leaving the US Navy in March 1994 and was a key facilitator in the 'great LANTIRN integration caper' that turned the F-14 into a precision bomber. *(Dave Parsons)*

War on Terror

Thanks to its new-found precision-bombing capability, combined with its unrivalled range and proven worth as both a fighter and tactical reconnaissance asset, the Tomcat found itself very much at the 'tip of the spear' as US forces were committed to the global War on Terror.

The first operations conducted by the F-14 during the final phase of its operational life occurred just hours after the 'twin towers' and the Pentagon had been attacked by al-Qaeda terrorists in hijacked airliners. That morning, VF-11 and VF-143 were preparing to embark in *John F. Kennedy* as part of CVW-7's cruise work-ups off the Virginia coast. North American Aerospace Defense Command (NORAD) contacted the US Navy soon after the south tower was hit and asked for its help in securing the airspace over the eastern seaboard. Both *John F. Kennedy* and USS *George Washington* (CVN-73) were put to sea by the Second Fleet, and the vessels embarked a handful of fighter squadrons from Oceana.

VF-11 and VF-143 were sent to CV-67, and pilot Lt(jg) Joseph Greentree from the latter unit subsequently flew several missions in support of the NORAD-controlled sea shield that had been hastily established off the coast of New York:

For the first 72 hours that VF-11 and VF-143 were embarked in Kennedy, *we flew round-the-clock CAPs up and down the eastern seaboard. The skies remained eerily empty during this time, with all civilian air traffic having been grounded. After three days Second Fleet told us to abandon these CAP missions and commence our work-ups.*

With al-Qaeda directly linked to the 11 September attacks, the US government turned its attention to the terrorist group's home in Afghanistan. Less than three weeks after the atrocities in New York City and Washington DC, carrier-based aircraft would be in the vanguard of a joint operation to remove the Taliban from power and destroy the organisational infrastructure that al-Qaeda had established in Afghanistan. The carrier closest to this land-locked country was *Enterprise*, with the F-14As of VF-14 and VF-41 embarked. These units were nearing the end of their last cruise with the Tomcat, and had seen action in Iraq during five weeks of OSW patrols. Also steaming towards the Arabian Sea from the Indian Ocean was *Carl Vinson*, with the F-14Ds of VF-213 on board. These three Tomcat units would be in the vanguard of what was codenamed Operation Enduring Freedom (OEF) by Pentagon planners.

Sailing off the coast of Pakistan in the northern Arabian Sea, both carriers were in position to commence strikes on al-Qaeda and Taliban targets by late September, although the first OEF mission was not generated until 8 October 2001. Politically prevented from using nearby land bases in the NAG and India, and with the Bush administration reluctant to overcrowd front-line airfields in Pakistan, Uzbekistan and Tajikistan, aircraft carriers were the only way initially open to the US military to bring tactical air power to bear in Afghanistan. The strike fighters of CVW-8 (CVN-65) and CVW-11 (CVN-70) duly hit terrorist training camps, Taliban barracks, air bases and SAM/AAA sites in the longest carrier-launched strikes in history. Tomcat, Hornet and Prowler units routinely operated more than 700 miles from their carriers in sorties that lasted between 6 and 10 hours.

With no Coalition troops in theatre to support during the early phase of OEF, the Tomcat crews worked instead with two-man Special

BELOW Getting on the tanker expeditiously was always an issue for pilots flying the notoriously short-legged Hornet in OEF. Here, watched by F-14D 'Blacklion 107' (BuNo 164344) from VF-213, a section of F/A-18Cs from VFA-94 heading into Afghanistan take it in turns to top off their tanks from a Diego Garcia-based KC-10A assigned to the 32nd ARS/305th AMW.
(Tony Toma)

Operations Forces (SOF) teams, who sought out targets to be attacked – they would also provide crews with target 'talk-ons'. Thanks to the F-14's legendary range, the jet was also tasked with taking out targets in the far north and west of Afghanistan. US Navy strike aircraft

ABOVE The officer cadre of VF-41 pose for their end of cruise photograph during *Enterprise*'s brief three-day port call to Souda Bay, in Crete, in late October 2001. Following the 'Black Aces' 'history-making Operation Allied Force/OSW cruise in 1999, when the unit dropped more than 200,000lb of ordnance, the 2001 deployment could have been something of an anticlimax for the crews involved but OSW and OEF strikes ensured it was not. *(Brian Gawne)*

BELOW LEFT 'Blacklion 111' (BuNo 161159) armed with a single 2,000lb GBU-24A/B Paveway III LGB is marshalled towards one of *Carl Vinson*'s waist catapults. A handful of these weapons were expended in OEF. VF-41 made two GBU-24 attacks, with one being delivered by Lt Peter Gendreau and his RIO, Lt Cdr Scott Butler who flew a daylight strike on a weapons storage facility on the outskirts of Kabul. *(US Navy)*

BELOW Cdr Chip King (CO of VF-213, left) and Lt Cdr Kevin Claffy compare notes on the flight deck at the end of an OEF mission in early November 2001. Behind them, one of the 'Black Lions" hard-working armourer teams has already started uploading GBU-12s on to BuNo 163899's BRU-32 bomb racks. *(Tony Toma)*

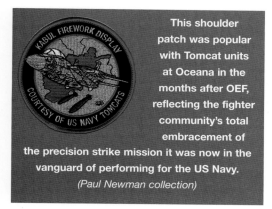

This shoulder patch was popular with Tomcat units at Oceana in the months after OEF, reflecting the fighter community's total embracement of the precision strike mission it was now in the vanguard of performing for the US Navy.

(Paul Newman collection)

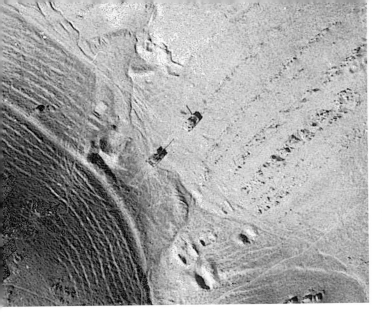

ABOVE AND ABOVE RIGHT 'Before' and 'after' shots of two Taliban T-62M Main Battle Tanks caught out in the open by a TARPS-equipped VF-213 jet on 11 November 2001. These photographs were taken by the pod's KS-153B long-range camera, the tanks having been struck by GBU-12s. *(VF-213)*

relied heavily on 'big wing' tanker support throughout OEF, with crews refuelling at least three times from USAF KC-10s and KC-135s, as well as RAF VC10Ks and Tristars, during the course of these marathon missions.

Exclusively employing LGBs, VF-14 and VF-41 expended some 380,000lb of ordnance between 8 and 23 October, when CVN-65 was relieved by CVN-71 (with the F-14Bs of VF-102 embarked). 'VF-41 achieved an 82% hit rate, which was a level of accuracy that had never previously been achieved by the US Navy,' recalled unit CO, Cdr Brian Gawne. Both Tomcat squadrons in CVW-8 also buddy-lased Maverick missiles and LGBs for Hornet units.

VF-213 was in the thick of the action during this period as well, with the unit being heavily involved in supporting the Northern Alliance's ground offensive against the Taliban in November. On the 5th of that month, the squadron's CO, Cdr Chip King, and his RIO, Lt Cdr Michael Peterson, made history when they became the first US Navy crew to use the F-14's 20mm cannon in action. King recalled, 'I remember thinking to myself at the time what a disparity in technology. It was like "Buck Rogers" meeting the "Arabian Nights", as the Taliban fighters that we were strafing were on horseback.'

Both VF-213 and VF-102 flew some of the most challenging missions of OEF as Taliban and al-Qaeda fighters fled east towards the Tora Bora cave complex and the Pakistani border. CVN-70 was eventually relieved by USS *John C. Stennis* (CVN-74) on 15 December

LEFT Armed with a pair of 1,000lb GBU-16 LGBs, VF-213's 'Blacklion 101' (BuNo 164603) closes on a KC-10 for 'front side gas' during an early OEF mission. The 'Black Lions' expended 157 GBU-16s during the OEF campaign, primarily against fixed targets. Bomb loadouts were constantly altered as the war progressed due to the changing nature of the targets on the ground. *(USAF)*

LEFT The pilots and RIOs of VF-213 get together with 'Blacklion 101' and a selection of LGBs (from left to right – GBU-16, GBU-24 and GBU-10) towards the end of the unit's OEF cruise. Boasting a 99.6% sortie completion rate during its ten-week spell in the northern Arabian Sea, VF-213 expended 452 bombs and 470 20mm cannon rounds on cruise. *(VF-213)*

2001, by which time VF-213 had expended 452 LGBs and 470 20mm cannon rounds. The F-14As of VF-211 were embarked in CVN-74, and four days after the unit's arrival in theatre the Tora Bora offensive ended and the fighting in Afghanistan drastically reduced in its intensity. Things did not flare up again until early March 2002, when the US Army's Task Force Mountain launched Operation Anaconda in the mountains of eastern Afghanistan. Targeting more than 1,000 hardcore al-Qaeda fighters entrenched in ridgelines and caves throughout the Shar-i-Kot Valley, the offensive got badly bogged down to the point where the survival of US troops in contact with the enemy was only

ensured through the overwhelming employment of tactical air power.

During the final stages of Anaconda, CVN-71 was relieved by CV-67, whose CVW-7 (including VF-11 and VF-143) flew its first missions on 11 March. An F-14B from VF-11 made history on this date when its crew dropped the first Joint Direct Attack Munition (JDAM) expended in combat by a Tomcat. This GPS-guided weapon would subsequently see widespread use with F-14B/D-equipped units (the A-model lacked the software to employ JDAM) in OIF.

In the autumn of 2002, the focus of the War on Terror switched to Iraq. By then, the Tomcat had proven itself to be a true multi-

LEFT VF-102's colour jet (BuNo 163225) cruises over inhospitable terrain heading north towards Afghanistan soon after the unit's arrival in the northern Arabian Sea on 15 October 2001. Like all of the 'Diamondbacks'' ten-strong fleet of F-14Bs, this aircraft was worked hard during the unit's 159-day unbroken stretch on the line in OEF. *(US Navy)*

ABOVE LEFT Four storeless VF-211 jets join up in close formation for their run in and break over *John C. Stennis* in late March 2002. Both 'Nickel 101' (BuNo 161603) and '102' (BuNo 162612) boast barely discernible bomb tallies beneath their cockpits. The canopy rails of each VF-211 Tomcat bore the names of New York Police and Fire Department personnel killed on 11 September 2001. *(Mitch McAllister)*

ABOVE The large 8 x 8-inch Programmable Tactical Information Display screen in the rear cockpit of a VF-102 F-14B reveals the rugged Afghan landscape near Tarin Kowt on 17 November 2001. No other TACAIR platform in OEF – Navy or Air Force – had a tactical display of this size, and when combined with the LANTIRN pod, the Tomcat became the precision bomber and SCAR/FAC(A) platform of choice in-theatre. *(VF-102)*

LEFT VF-11's Lt Cdr Chris Chope and his pilot take on mid-mission fuel from a KC-10 during an OEF patrol in May 2002. Chope recalled, 'If you were a little short on fuel you could ask the pilot of the tanker to roll out on to a certain heading so as to drag you closer to your objective while you were still plugged in replenishing your tanks.' *(Chris Chope)*

LEFT Armed with a single 2,000lb GBU-31 JDAM, VF-11 CO Cdr John Aquilino and RIO Lt Cdr Kevin Protzman prepare to launch from *John F. Kennedy* on an OEF mission. This crew made Tomcat history by dropping the first JDAM in anger from 'Ripper 201' (BuNo 162912) on the night of 11/12 March 2002. *(US Navy)*

role combat platform capable of precision bombing, buddy-laser target designation through use of the LTS pod, FAC(A), Strike Co-ordinating Armed Reconnaissance (SCAR), photo and digital reconnaissance and, of course, fighter interception.

One of the primary weapons that would be employed by the Tomcat in OIF was the GBU-31 2,000lb JDAM. Initially cleared for use by the F-14B only, the JDAM was hastily made compatible with the F-14D through the installation of the DO4 weapons computer upgrade in the weeks leading up to OIF. VF-2, embarked with CVW-2 in *Constellation*, was

the first D-model unit to get the upgrade. On 28 February 2003, VF-2 dropped the first GBU-31s expended by an F-14D in anger during an OSW mission over southern Iraq. The D-model Tomcats of VF-31, embarked in USS *Abraham Lincoln* (CVN-72), were reconfigured with DO4 straight after VF-2. Assigned to CVW-14, VF-31 had been on deployment with the air wing since 20 July 2002. The final Tomcat unit to receive the DO4 mission tape upgrade was VF-213, operating from *Theodore Roosevelt* in the Mediterranean Sea.

Of the two remaining Tomcat squadrons committed to the conflict, VF-32, again in the

LEFT One of the primary weapons employed by the Tomcat during OIF I in 2003 was the 2,000lb GBU-31 JDAM, which had made its combat debut with the aircraft over Afghanistan during OEF in March the previous year. These GBU-31s are seen on CVN-75's flight deck on 21 March 2003 waiting to be attached to the under-fuselage racks of the F-14Bs (from VF-32) chained down behind them. *(US Navy)*

Mediterranean aboard *Harry S. Truman*, had had its F-14Bs made JDAM-compatible prior to deployment, but VF-154's baseline A-models,

flying from *Kitty Hawk* in the NAG, remained restricted to LGBs.

VF-2 was at the forefront of OIF from the word go, participating in the 'Shock and Awe' strikes on the night of 21/22 March 2003. Indeed, F-14Ds from VF-2 led the first non-stealth strike package (consisting exclusively of jets from CVW-2) to venture into Baghdad's 'Super Missile Engagement Zone' to hit targets in the Iraqi capital, its Tomcats dropping JDAM as well as performing DCA and reconnaissance

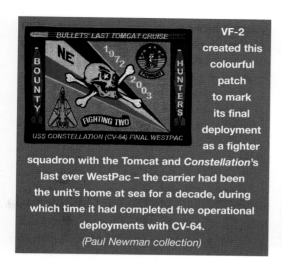

ABOVE Proudly displaying its bomb tally, VF-2's 'Bullet 106' (BuNo 164342) taxis towards one of *Constellation*'s bow catapults on 15 April 2003. VF-2's hardworking maintenance personnel applied ordnance tallies to their jets after OIF I had come to an end, as there had been little time available to mark the aircraft up between missions during the campaign itself. *(US Navy)*

BELOW Sandwiched between two S-3Bs from VS-35, F-14D BuNo 163898 of VF-31 has its windscreen polished by its brown-shirted plane captain on board *Abraham Lincoln* on 5 April 2003. As is clearly visible on 'Bandwagon 104', VF-31 used a generic 'Felix and bomb' silhouette to denote each weapon dropped by its aircraft in OIF I. *(US Navy)*

missions. They were engaged by at least 12 unguided SAMs and non-stop AAA while over Baghdad.

Operating from Fifth Fleet's designated OIF night carrier, VF-2 proceeded to fly the bulk of its missions masked by the cover of darkness. It initially used JDAM to hit fixed targets such as command and control nodes, SAM and radar sites, airfields and Republican Guard barracks, as well as presidential palaces and Ba'ath party buildings. VF-2 then switched to CAS strikes as the ground push towards Baghdad gained momentum. The Tomcat's ability to perform the demanding FAC(A) and SCAR roles for other strike fighter assets was also greatly appreciated as Coalition forces engaged the Republican Guard around cities such as Karbala and An Nasiriyah.

During the 28 days of OIF, VF-2 successfully completed 195 combat sorties totalling 887.5 hours. Its ten aircraft dropped 221 LGBs (217 GBU-12s and 4 GBU-16s) and 61 GBU-31 JDAM. Some 1,704 20mm cannon rounds were also fired in strafing passes and no fewer than 125 targets were photographed using TARPS.

The other Tomcat squadrons in the NAG also flew a broad mix of missions ranging from precision strikes to CAS and FAC(A). VF-31 was flying from CVN-72, which was the designated day carrier. The unit operated closely with VFA-115, which was conducting the very first cruise with the F/A-18E Super Hornet as part of CVW-14. With the latter jet boasting Tomcat-like endurance, VF-31 often flew mixed section strike missions with VFA-115. By the time CVN-72 and CVW-14 were relieved in theatre

RIGHT A division of four Qatar det F-14As prepare to taxi out for a dusk mission from Al Udeid in late March 2003. Behind them can be seen F-16CJs from the USAF's 389th FS, as well as RAAF F/A-18As from No 75 Squadron and RAF Tornado GR 4s. The shore-based VF-154 crews got to work closely with all three types, as well as the co-located F-15Es of the 4th FW. *(VF-154)*

by *Nimitz* and CVW-11 (which was the first air wing to deploy with Super Hornets rather than Tomcats) on 14 April, VF-31 had flown an astounding 585 combat sorties totalling 1,744 combat hours during its marathon ten-month OEF/OSW/OIF deployment. The unit had expended 56 JDAM, 165 GBU-12s, 5 GBU-16s and 13 Mk 82 'dumb' bombs and fired 1,355 20mm cannon rounds.

BELOW A pilot from VF-154 checks the guidance vanes on a 2,000lb GBU-24 Paveway III LGB attached to his F-14, which is chained down to the flight deck of *Kitty Hawk*. The weapon's larger stabilisation package allowed it to travel further in flight. The 'Black Knights' expended 358 LGBs between 21 March and 14 April 2003, flying primarily FAC(A) and SCAR missions. *(US Navy)*

Unable to employ JDAM with its F-14As, VF-154's war was undoubtedly the most unusual of any of the Tomcat units committed to OIF. Deployed on its final cruise with the F-14 as part of CVW-5, the squadron ventured into the NAG aboard *Kitty Hawk* in mid-February 2003. While conducting combat missions alongside USAF assets in theatre, VF-154 was asked by the latter to detach four aircraft and four crews to provide dedicated FAC(A) and SCAR support for Coalition fast jets flying out of Al Udeid air base in Qatar. Aside from performing these missions, the VF-154 Tomcat crews were also given the responsibility of instructing their F-15E brethren from the 336th FS/4th FW on how to conduct effective FAC(A) and SCAR.

According to VF-154's post-cruise summary of its contribution to OIF:

Never in recent history had a carrier-based strike fighter squadron been tasked to fight a war from ashore and at sea at the same time. FAC(A) specialist crews on the beach amassed more than 300 combat hours and delivered more than 50,000lb of ordnance in 21 days of flying with their four crews and four jets.

The unit did not escape from its shore-based foray unscathed, however, for on the night of 1 April the crew of a VF-154 jet was forced to eject over southern Iraq when its Tomcat

suffered a single (port) engine and fuel transfer system failure. The latter caused the remaining 'good' engine to run dry, so the crew were forced to 'bang out' over hostile territory. Fortunately they were quickly retrieved by a Combat Search and Rescue team from Kuwait. The shore detachment returned to CV-63 in the second week of April, and by the end of the aerial campaign on the 14th of the month, VF-154 had dropped 358 LGBs during the course of 286 combat sorties.

The war waged by the two Mediterranean-based carriers contrasted markedly with that fought by the vessels sailing in the NAG. With Turkey having denied the US Army's 4th Infantry Division use of its territory as a jumping-off point, northern front activities centred on the support of SOF teams operating behind enemy lines. These teams relied heavily on close-air support (CAS) from CVW-3 and CVW-8, the latter embarked in CVN-71, which was also positioned in the eastern Mediterranean. F-14s from both air wings flew CAS missions in support of SOF units, often putting ordnance dangerously close to friendly forces. The support these aircraft provided undoubtedly saved the lives of Coalition forces on the ground, and eventually led to the capitulation of 100,000 Iraqi soldiers.

Prior to immersing itself in CAS missions with SOF, both VF-32 and VF-213 had completed a number of conventional strikes with JDAM and LGBs against fixed targets in Iraq. These missions, flown at the start of

ABOVE Carrying a mixed load of GBU-12s and JDAM, three F-14Bs from VF-32 prepare to be directed out to *Harry S. Truman*'s catapults on 7 April 2003. All three aircraft feature VF-32's duelling swordsmen stencil on their radomes, while 'Gypsy 107' also has the silhouette of a Space Shuttle beneath its nose modex to honour the Shuttle *Columbia's crew* who perished on 1 February 2003. *(US Navy)*

RIGHT This amazing photograph of a GBU-12 heading for its target (an SA-2 SAM site, some 20,000ft below) was taken by a TARPS-equipped VF-32 jet during OIF I. The aircraft's RIO was Lt Cdr David Dorn, who recalled, 'We got some great TARPS footage of the LGB coming off our jet and heading down to impact the SA-2 site.' *(VF-32)*

LEFT VF-32 and VF-213 regularly carried mixed weapon loads in OIF I, this 'Black Lions' jet being armed with a 500lb GBU-12 LGB and a 2,000lb GBU-31(V)2/B JDAM. VF-213 pilot Lt Cdr Marc Hudson explained the thinking behind such a loadout. 'With the Tomcat capable of employing both JDAM and LGBs, we could service two different targets during the course of one CAS mission.' *(VF-213)*

CENTRE 'Blacklion 106' (BuNo 163893) participated in CVW-8's first OIF I strike. VF-213's aircrew, having summed up their OIF I experiences with the phrase 'living after midnight, bombing 'til the dawn' following their myriad nocturnal 'Vampire' missions, tallied 198 sorties totalling 907 flight hours during the conflict. Achieving a 100% sortie completion rate, VF-213 delivered 102 LGBs and 94 JDAM in OIF I. *(US Navy)*

BELOW The old meets the new in May 2003 overhead Virginia. VF-2's CAG jet (BuNo 163894) was intercepted by one of the first two F/A-18F Super Hornets issued to newly redesignated VFA-2 when the 'Bounty Hunters' performed their fly-in to Oceana at the end of their OIF I cruise in June 2003. By month-end the last of the unit's F-14s had gone. *(VF-2)*

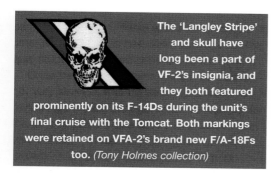

the conflict, were some of the longest of the war, covering distances of up to 800 miles each way. As the Tomcat had proven in OEF, it was more than capable of handling such sorties, and the mission lead for these more conventional strikes was often an F-14 crew. Further strikes on fixed targets followed, with mission times being reduced slightly once Turkey permitted overflights. CVW-3 was designated as the day carrier throughout OIF, while CVW-8 handled much of the night work. VF-213 soon dubbed its nocturnal missions 'Vampire' sorties, with jets regularly launching from the pitch-black deck of CVN-71 into poor weather conditions. The constant night operations eventually inspired the aircrew to coin the phrase 'living after midnight, bombing 'til the dawn'!

One of the more unusual missions flown

ABOVE VF-211's 'Nickel 115' (BuNo 161297) is launched from one of *Enterprise*'s waist catapults in December 2003. The unit spent much of its time on station in OIF II performing Intelligence, Surveillance and Reconnaissance (ISR) patrols over southern Iraq, often in partnership with F/A-18A+s from VMFA-312, this squadron also being part of CVW-1. *(US Navy)*

BELOW Replacing *Enterprise* on station in the NAG in spring 2004 was *George Washington*, with CVW-7 embarked. The latter boasted two F-14B units, VF-11 (whose 'Ripper 201' and '202' are seen here) and VF-143, making their last deployment with the jet prior to transitioning to Super Hornets. Unlike VF-211, both squadrons got to deliver ordnance in combat during their time in the NAG following a dramatic increase in insurgent activity across Iraq. *(US Navy)*

Most F-14 crews were reluctant to switch from the Tomcat to the Super Hornet, and this was one of several patches produced by units at Oceana that summed up the emotions surrounding the transition. *(Tony Holmes collection)*

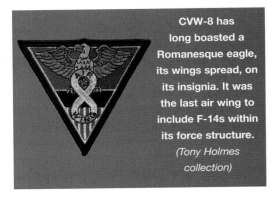

CVW-8 has long boasted a Romanesque eagle, its wings spread, on its insignia. It was the last air wing to include F-14s within its force structure. *(Tony Holmes collection)*

CENTRE From late 2004 the Tomcat presence in OIF III was assumed by VF-32, which was part of CVW-3 embarked in *Harry S. Truman*. As with other Tomcat units in-theatre post-OIF I, the 'Swordsmen' flew mixed formations – dubbed 'Covey' flights – with the air wing's trio of Hornet units, and F/A-18A+-equipped VMFA-115 in particular. *(Erik Hildebrandt)*

WWLEFT VF-32's 'Gypsy 101' (BuNo 161860), flown by staff officers from CVW-3, circles over the Swords of Qādisīyah and the Monument to the Unknown Soldier in central Baghdad during the Iraqi elections on 30 January 2005. The F-14B's front-line service with the US Navy came to an end with the completion of CVW-3's combat cruise on 18 April 2005. *(Erik Hildebrandt)*

ABOVE Capt Bill Sizemore, CAG of CVW-8, pops a flare from VF-213's 'Blacklion 207' (BuNo 161166) as he breaks away from the C-2A of VRC-40 Det 1 over the NAG during a mission on 2 February 2006. Capt Sizemore had joined the exclusive 'Grand Club' when he made his 1,000th carrier landing in 'Blacklion 213' on 16 December 2005. *(Richard Cooper)*

by VF-213 saw the unit providing CAP for the airborne assault on Irbil air base carried out by 1,000 paratroopers of the US Army's 173rd Airborne Brigade. Conducting the largest parachute drop since the Second World War, the soldiers jumped from a fleet of C-17s into Kurdish-controlled northern Iraq. The Globemaster transporters were escorted by three waves of strike aircraft from CVN-71, with the US Navy jets also bombing Iraqi command and control bunkers and troop and artillery positions close to nearby Bashur airfield. As the war progressed, CAS for SOF teams became the staple mission for both VF-32 and VF-213, and their success in this role was related by the commander of CVW-8, Capt David Newland:

Dropping precision-guided ordnance for a SOF team was a mission that gave aircrew immediate gratification. They were told where to aim the munitions, and they got direct feedback from the troops after they had expended their bombs.

By the time VF-213 ceased combat operations in OIF on 15 April, its crews had flown 198 combat sorties totalling 907.6 combat flight hours, with a 100% sortie completion rate. No fewer than 196 precision-guided munitions weighing 250,000lb had been expended, with 102 of these being LGBs and the remaining 94 JDAM. VF-32 completed an impressive 268 sorties and 1,135.2 hours in combat, dropping 247 LGBs and 118 JDAM (totalling 402,600lb).

Its crews also expended 1,128 rounds of 20mm high-explosive incendiary in strafing passes.

The F-14 remained an important asset for the US Navy in its post-OIF I operations over Iraq, the aircraft supporting Coalition forces as they struggled to keep the rising insurgency in check. VF-211 (2003–04), VF-11 (2004), VF-143 (2004), VF-103 (2004) and VF-32 (2005) all completed their final tours with the Tomcat during this period, performing missions similar to those flown during the invasion in 2003. By the autumn of 2005, just two Tomcat units remained in service with the US Navy, with all other fighter squadrons having by then re-equipped with either the E- or F-model Super Hornet. Upon their transition to the new Boeing aircraft, the squadrons were redesignated as strike fighter units. The Tomcat's final deployment commenced in September 2005 when F-14D-equipped VF-31 and VF-213 teamed up with CVW-8 aboard CVN-71. Both units would see considerable action over Iraq during the cruise, which lasted until early March 2006 – the final combat trap for the F-14 was made by a VF-213 jet on 8 February 2006. By the time the squadrons returned to Oceana, they had logged 1,163

sorties, 6,876 flight hours and dropped 9,500lb of ordnance in anger.

After 36 years of fleet service, the Tomcat was officially retired on 22 September 2006. The last flight performed by a US Navy F-14 came on 4 October when VF-31's 'Tomcatter 101' made the short trip from Oceana to Farmingdale, New York, where it was subsequently placed on static display in front of the Northrop Grumman headquarters at nearby Bethpage.

This colourful patch was created for the Tomcat Sunset retirement event held at Oceana between 20 and 23 September 2006, which saw the aircraft bow out in style. *(Tony Holmes collection)*

RIGHT Three well-weathered F-14Ds from VF-31 head north over the NAG towards Iraq in early January 2006. Each aircraft is equipped with a LANTIRN pod (there were enough available for all 22 jets embarked in CVN-71), and the closest two aeroplanes are armed with GBU-38s – 'Bandwagon 112' (BuNo 163417) is also carrying at least one LGB. *(Erik Hildebrandt)*

RIGHT Carrying a GBU-38 and a GBU-12, an F-14D from VF-213 heads north into Iraq at sunset on 23 October 2006. *(Scott Timmester)*

BELOW A sight to gladden the hearts of Tomcat proponents the world over. VF-31 and VF-213 get ready for a mass launch of 22 F-14Ds from *Theodore Roosevelt* off the Virginia coast to mark the end of the jet's final operational cruise on 10 March 2006. CVW-8's Tomcats racked up a total of 9,856.2 flying hours during the Mediterranean/NAG deployment. *(US Navy)*

BELOW Four Tomcats from VF-31 perform a tight formation flypast with F/A-18Cs of VFA-34 and VFA-87 and F/A-18Fs from VFA-11 during the Oceana airshow on 10 September 2006. By month-end the 'Tomcatters' had retired the last of their beloved F-14Ds and commenced their conversion to the Super Hornet. *(US Navy)*

Chapter Four

Training Tomcat pilots and RIOs

The Tomcat was built from the start as a two-person aircraft, with its powerful radar and long-range missile capability requiring the full attention of a specially trained NFO in the back seat. In the early pre-digital days of the AN/AWG-9 in particular, radar operation was seen as being as much an 'art form' as a science, with the RIO's full attention being required to 'make the radar talk'. Doug 'Boog' Denneny instructed both new pilots and RIOs in between fleet tours, and in this chapter he details exactly how he went about this.

OPPOSITE VF-101's final colour jet, F-14D BuNo 163414, was heavily involved in the last CQ periods for Tomcat students in March–April 2005 on board *Theodore Roosevelt*. Only the third production D-model completed by Grumman, this aircraft was supplied direct from the Calverton factory to VX-4 at Point Mugu in June 1990. A CAT I pilot converting on to the Tomcat would have completed around 50 flights in the jet before going to CQ. *(Gert Kromhout)*

The Navy had two FRSs whose primary mission was to train Naval Aviators and RIOs to be qualified to fly the F-14A, B and D Tomcats. VF-101 'Grim Reapers' was stationed at NAS Oceana, in Virginia Beach, Virginia, and VF-124 'Gunfighters' was at NAS Miramar, in San Diego, California. I was one of the fortunate people who was a student and instructor in both of these squadrons during times of great change in the Tomcat community.

A quick background on me. On the east coast, I was a student NFO in VF-101 from October 1985 through to July 1986, and I was an instructor in VF-101 when I was the Chief Staff Officer (CSO) for the Commander, Fighter Wing Atlantic in 2000–01 at Oceana. I didn't

instruct a lot of students back then, but as CSO, I did a bit of easy instructing after going through a Category (CAT) III student syllabus in the F-14D en route to my tour as XO and then CO of VF-2 'Bounty Hunters'. Being the CSO at Oceana, which by then was home to the US Navy's only Fighter Wing, was a fun job, and a great way to get my feet back into the fighter community after a three-year hiatus in two Washington DC jobs.

After my first fleet tour with VF-14 'Tophatters', embarked in *John F. Kennedy*, from 1986 to 1989, I received a great set of orders to become an instructor with VF-124 at Miramar from August 1989 until August 1992. I was an instructor in the F-14A and then a student in the F-14D prior to becoming qualified to instruct and transition other aircrew, including personnel from VF-11, VF-2 and VF-31, on to the 'Super Tomcat'. It was a lot of fun to be one of the first 100 people to fly that version of the fighter, knowing that more than 450 were going to be built. Unfortunately, due to budget cuts, less than 60 F-14Ds were completed, and we saw the number of fleet Tomcat squadrons halved in the early 1990s and then go away completely in 2006. It was a real shame because the D-model was an exceptional strike fighter.

By the time I transitioned from the Tomcat to the Super Hornet in the summer of 2003, I had more than 3,100 hours in the F-14A, B and D models. Aside from my time with VF-14, and tours with the FRSs, I was fortunate enough to have been a Topgun instructor, completed two fleet tours with VF-213 'Blacklions' and be selected to serve as the XO and CO of VF-2 in peacetime and combat. Although my time in the D-model was extensive, the clear majority of those 3,100 hours were in the F-14A, with only a handful of hours in the B. As a RIO who

served on both the east and west coasts before the F-14s all moved back to Oceana, I got to know great officers, aviators, maintainers and sailors in the Tomcat community.

I was not happy when the jet was picked to retire early, and saddened with the decision to destroy virtually all of the jets in storage at Davis-Monthan AFB [so as to prevent Iran from securing valuable spare parts for its F-14s]. I was pleased, however, to see the fighter spirit live on in the F/A-18E/F community, where I commanded VFA-2 and flew Lot 25 Super Hornets. But the Super Hornet story is another chapter in another book at another time.

To set the stage, we need to talk about numbers, production and scale. If you were the CO, OPS O (Operations Officer), MO (Maintenance Officer), Training Officer or Phase Leader at VF-124 or VF-101 in the 1980s, you were worried about taking the resources the Navy had given you – people, planes, parts and flying dollars (a budget) – and producing trained Tomcat pilots and RIOs at the end of a ten-month to one-year process. Sometimes, the latter would stretch to an 18-month syllabus for new students if you didn't have enough 'up' jets available to train folks in a year or less. Occasionally, the FRS struggled to get them through in two years.

It was hard on students who had to endure stops and starts in their training. Flying is not like driving a car – you must keep at it all the time so as to get better. You couldn't just take a few months off between phases and come back with the same skills you had before. You needed warm-up flights for all the right safety reasons. These warm-up flights, and other friction caused by delays, made the entire process less productive.

The primary mission of both VF-101 and VF-124 was to train (or re-train) NFOs and Naval Aviators in how to fly and fight the F-14. During the heyday of training, and I consider that the 1980s and early 1990s, each FRS supplied aviators for approximately 12 squadrons per coast. With a new class starting approximately once a month, and composed of at least six new Category (CAT) I pilots [newly winged] and six new CAT I RIOs, this meant both VF-101 and VF-124 had more than 70 CAT Is on the books at one time. They were

joined by about 30 CAT IIs (folks who had flown Phantom IIs during their previous tours and needed a shortened syllabus) and CAT IIIs (lieutenant commanders and above who had a lot of experience in the Tomcat, but who had been in non-flying posts for some time).

The FRSs needed to have about 50 qualified instructors (25 pilots and 25 RIOs), more than 50 aircraft and in excess of 500 maintainers. At times these numbers swelled to more than 1,000 people and 70+ jets in different phases of maintenance. Those totals varied wildly based on the timeframe and the missions of both FRSs.

So, it makes sense to start with some good flying stories. However, I won't do that. Instead, I'm going to start with what made it all possible for an instructor RIO to do his job. And that is the massive team of maintenance professionals in both FRSs who made the 'up' jets happen and allowed us to fly and produce training 'Xs' or checks in the block. Some may think I'm pandering here by starting with maintenance. However, if you've never been in the fighter community, let me tell you that no jets means no MiG kills. No parts, no flights. No people, no traps (carrier arrested landings). No quality Airframers (maintenance technicians), and you've got a lot of flap slat lockouts because nobody knows how to rig the flaps and slats properly. It all starts with maintenance.

Maintenance

As a RIO or pilot instructor, you would probably be in charge of one of the divisions or branches of the maintenance department during your three-year tour at either VF-101 or VF-124. A branch or division is composed of anywhere from 15 to more than 100 enlisted maintenance professionals. An instructor during a normal flow of responsibility in his ground jobs would generally be a branch or division officer in maintenance, then a training phase leader (more on that later) and, possibly near the end of his tour, a schedules officer, once he had figured out how every piece comes together.

As a senior lieutenant commander coming back as an instructor, there was a chance you would be an OPS O at either FRS, or the MO in VF-101 in the 1980s or 1990s. In VF-101, the MO was an experienced Tomcat pilot or RIO who had finished a fleet tour as a MO and

excelled in that role in their fleet squadron. If tagged for the MO or OPS O jobs, you were a community leader who would unquestionably get command of an F-14 squadron. Once made the MO in VF-101, the CO soon informed you that although you were an instructor first and foremost, your primary job in the unit was to manage the massive FRS maintenance department. Your goal was to produce 'up' jets to support the OPS O and the flight schedule. It was a massive rock pile that you were constantly shovelling. It was unrelenting, with no breaks, ever.

You had very talented people to help with this task, however. The fleet squadrons cherry-picked your chiefs and petty officers for their fleet squadrons, and you needed to protect them, motivate them and retain them. They were the people who knew how to fix jets, and fix them quickly and competently. The master chiefs and senior chiefs were running the show, and dealing with the 24-hour maintenance activities needed to not only support day and night flying, but manage the entire process in real time from the maintenance desk. It was a massive production effort, requiring constant prioritisation and reprioritisation, as well as exceptional decision-making ability by both senior and junior enlisted personnel, all of which was conducted in a very dangerous and demanding environment.

The jet that landed at 0200hrs may have needed to be turned around overnight so that it was a 'go bird' for the first event of the day that took off at 0600hrs. To further complicate matters, this event was a guns hop, which meant that its 20mm weapon needed to be tested and then loaded. To ensure that such a sortie could be flown precisely when it was scheduled, the maintenance department at VF-124 or VF-101 worked 24 hours a day, seven days a week. Even on holidays, there was somebody there, either working on a jet or doing a hangar watch to make sure those 80 or so aircraft were safe, secure and not leaking.

Unlike VF-101, where the MO was always a pilot or RIO, the VF-124 MO was a senior maintenance officer, or 'Limited Duty Officer' (LDO), and not an aviator. You had probably been promoted through the enlisted ranks to chief or petty officer first class, and were

then selected for the LDO community. You then worked your way up to be the MO for a carrier air wing [also dubbed a CAG, after the air wing's previous incarnation as a Carrier Air Group]. You'd just finished a sea tour as a 'CAGMO', and now got the tough job of managing a massive maintenance department.

One of the first challenges was looking at the make-up and composition of your fighter force. At different times, the FRS maintenance department was composed of the following;

- Brand new F-14As that were your jets. You were flying them so much that you had to keep deferring routine maintenance as much as possible, for you needed them to make your flight schedule every day. Therefore, you were doing everything you could to keep them on your flight schedule. They required very little in the way of corrosion control (a problem with your older jets), and helped you get a lot of training accomplished for the OPS O. You knew you could run them through your mandatory phase maintenance cycles really quickly and get them back in the air.
- Your old and tired F-14As. Some of these aircraft were gems that seemed to never break down, while others were problem jets that required an inordinate number of man-hours to fix nagging and repeated problems. There were different versions of the A, some with different radios, modifications, others that were TARPS-compatible, LANTIRN (FLIR) configured, etc.
- Brand new F-14Bs or F-14Ds with new and different engines and improved avionics, but assigned to you by CNAF (Commander, Naval Air Forces) or CNAL (Commander, Naval Air Forces, Atlantic Fleet) as your permanent jets. The differences between these aircraft and the A-models was a management challenge because some maintainers were only qualified to work on one type, and you had to constantly work through training people to be qualified safely on multiple versions of the Tomcat.
- Other new jets destined for a fleet squadron but in your stable as temporarily assigned aircraft because the new fleet squadron wasn't certified 'Safe for Flight' and they couldn't maintain them. You tried to assign

the transitioning squadron's aircrew to those jets exclusively, but that got difficult to manage very quickly. You flew the heck out of those 'loaner' jets though because they were usually new and in great shape.

Among your other challenges was the fact that the FRS was always seen a resource by the carrier air wings or the Fighter Wing from which to 'steal' jets and personnel for front-line units. A fleet squadron before going on deployment might be in very bad shape, and the CAG could strike a deal with the Fighter Wing CO (the RAG's CO's boss) to allow the unit to steal three of your best jets to ensure that the squadron could go to sea in two weeks with its full complement of F-14s. Basically, you were constantly helping make the fleet functional at the expense of your FRS birds, and your best people. You were the bank full of talent and resources, and if there was a mishap in the fleet, you would end up probably giving up one of your best jets to 'support the warfighter'. This constant change and unpredictability made it difficult to manage your fleet of fighters.

During the airshow season, you had to ring fence out of the production flight schedule at least two of your best jets as a primary and backup to support weekend displays across the country. And during a CQ detachment, or other dets, you had to fence those jets as well. You also had constant little nagging activities, including your hangar space being encroached on by contractors doing long-term modifications, the Wing using your people, resources and time for some VIP event or special project.

Aside from overseeing operations from Oceana or Miramar, you were also running detachments with your own jets in far-away places. Many times you had concurrently an ACM det at NAS Key West, Florida, or NAS El Centro, California, a CQ det on a carrier off either the east or west coasts and, finally, a Guns det or a Strike det in different locations. You would assign your best jets and your best folks to run separate, smaller maintenance functions when they were required for these dets. If you were sending jets on the road every weekend to conduct training flights, invariably some would break down, and you might have

ABOVE VF-124 always maintained a small cadre of Tomcats in high-visibility colours during its 22-year association with the F-14, these jets being routinely called on to perform Demonstration Team flights at airshows on the US west coast. Here, 'Gunslinger 451' (BuNo 162589) flies in close formation with 'Gunslinger 453' (BuNo 162591) over San Diego Bay in 1989. Both of these aircraft were delivered new to VF-124 in November 1985. *(VF-124)*

some of your best mechanics on 'rescue detachments' to far-flung locations.

Moreover, there were also the previously mentioned Phase inspections (daily, 7-day, 14-, 28-, 56-, 112- and 224-day, etc.). There

LEFT A student pilot prepares to taxi out from the VF-124 ramp in 'Gunslinger 400' (BuNo 161620) at the start of a training flight in March 1992. Clearly visible from this angle is the yaw string forward of the cockpit, used by the pilot to determine his trim settings to provide zero side-slip. When the string was straight back towards the windscreen and a proper angle of bank had been achieved, the jet had zero slide-slip. *(US Navy)*

were also major maintenance inspections, administrative inspections, corrosion inspections, quality assurance issues, safety issues and 'Red Stripe' bulletins that could throw a wrench in any good maintenance plan. There were bulkhead cracks, tough wing improvements, mishaps, personnel issues and borderline unrealistic plans and flight schedules that you had to sign off on or, conversely, push back. But it was all about production, and you and the OPS O worked hard together to get it done, all in support of the syllabus and generating 'Xs'.

The OPS O, the training officer and schedules officer were in charge of making sure the students worked their way through the syllabus as expeditiously as possible. They had a massive job creating 'Xs' by juggling the resources given to them by the maintenance department and the flying hours budgets provided by AIRLANT [Naval Air Force Atlantic] or AIRPAC [Naval Air Force Pacific].

The syllabus

As an instructor, you were eventually trained to help generate 'Xs' in all the different phases of instruction. The more phases you were checked out in, the more 'Xs' you could get for the schedules officer and the more flight time you could get. Generally, the hard-charging pilots and RIO instructors were motivated to fly, and everything else was administrative and a

burden. To fly more, you needed to be qualified asap in as many phases as possible.

The phase leads were fellow instructors, who shepherded their classes through the following phases of the FRS course – Familiarisation (FAM); Basic Weapons Employment Phase (BWEPS or BFAS, depending on your coast), shooting the 20mm gun in both air-to-air against a towed banner and strafing (Guns); Advanced Fighter Air Superiority (ADFAS); TARPS; dropping bombs (Strike); ACM and Advanced Radar Intercept work (Tactics); aerial refuelling (Tanking); and CQ.

As a new arrival, you first checked in with an office called student control and they would have a copy of your orders and would assign you to a class with a start date. Prior to the class commencing, it was student control's job to make sure that all your final training qualifications had been completed. This included ensuring you had a medical up-chit, swim qualification, physiology training, ejection seat training and firefighting training had all been completed, and later, when it became mandatory, your centrifuge (G tolerance training) was scheduled and that you were scheduled for, and duly passed, SERE school. On the east coast, SERE training occurred in the remote forests in Maine, while in California it was undertaken in the high desert near Warner Springs. Once all of this training had been successfully completed, students were allowed to begin the FAM phase.

Due to jet availability, the time between checking into the squadron, completing that training and starting the FAM phase could take anywhere from three weeks to more than a year. The disparity was due to how many classes were stacked up ahead of you, and how well each FRS was managing the process. In the glory days, a class could get through the FRS in less than a year. In the bad days, new class start dates were seriously backed up. Some of the worse delays affected the new VF-124 F-14D initial CAT I classes, a number of which were delayed for more than a year. Several of the more enterprising young men assigned to these classes took jobs as bartenders off base, while others were 'stashed as ensigns in offices around Miramar and tasked with carrying out administrative support jobs while waiting for their class start dates.

Carrier Landing Pattern diagram.

WING SWEEP 20°
LANDING GEAR DOWN
BELOW 280 KNOTS

BREAK INTERVAL—15 TO 17 SECONDS:
BREAK AT 45° TO 60° BANK,
SPEED BRAKE—EXTENDED,
THROTTLES—IDLE
LEVEL TURN AT 800 FEET

SLATS/FLAPS
EXTENDED
BELOW 225 KNOTS

WING SWEEP 68°
300 TO 350 KNOTS
800 FEET ALTITUDE,
HOOK DOWN, AND
SAS ON

DLC SELECTED

BOLTER OR WAVE-OFF
MILITARY POWER-CLIMB
STRAIGHT AHEAD, TURN
TO PARALLEL BRC

"ON-SPEED" APPROACH
INDEXER INDICATION
(15 UNITS), AUTO THROTTLE
ENGAGED (IF DESIRED).

LANDING CHECKLIST
600 FEET ALTITUDE

CROSS CHECK—GROSS WEIGHT
AIRSPEED ANGLE-OF-ATTACK

ABEAM
POSITION
COMMENCE
TURN
1 TO 1.2 nmi

CALL,
"SIDE NUMBER,
TOMCAT
BALL/CLARA,
STATE
" AUTO "
(IF APC ENGAGED)"

INTERCEPT GLIDE SLOPE
AT APPROXIMATELY 3/4 MILE 360 FEET
"ON-SPEED" APPROACH
INDEXER INDICATION

90° POSITION
INDEXER "DONUT"
450 FEET

VF-124's CO in 1991, then Cdr Mike 'Wizzard' McCabe, was a 'stash' ensign with the CVW-11 staff in early 1972 while waiting to start the F-4 Phantom II FRS at Miramar. He was offered the opportunity to deploy with the air wing when it embarked in *Kitty Hawk*, and this allowed him to learn how to be a RIO from the other pilots and NFOs in the F-4 squadrons within CVW-11. McCabe got very good very quickly, and when they started flying combat missions in North Vietnam from March 1972, he became part of the team fighting the war during a time of heightened MiG activity. Indeed, McCabe helped shoot down a MiG-21 with his pilot, Pete 'Viper' Pettigrew. When he returned home, the smart people decided that Ens McCabe didn't need to go to the RAG anymore. His Silver Star, and the fact he survived that cruise when many didn't come home in 1972 was good enough. He would jokingly say the FRS was important, but the first time he really went to the FRS was when he was the CO of VF-124 – a position that earned its incumbent the title of 'Mutha', since he was the 'Mutha' CO of all fighter squadrons at Miramar.

RIGHT VF-124's quartet of colour jets were usually kept in immaculate condition owing to their dual assignment to the unit's Demonstration Team, but the remaining 40-plus Tomcats assigned to the 'Gunfighters' usually looked like this anonymous jet photographed on a training flight from Miramar in December 1992. Aircraft such as this well-weathered machine formed the backbone of VF-124's training effort. *(US Navy)*

ABOVE VF-124 received its first four F-14Ds in October 1990. The 'Gunfighters' had sole responsibility for training air- and groundcrew for front-line units receiving the D-model Tomcat, with sister-FRS VF-101 at Oceana specialising in the instruction of personnel for F-14B-equipped units. Both squadrons also operated A-model jets. With the disestablishment of VF-124 in September 1994, 'Gunslinger 134' was reassigned to VF-101 Det A at Miramar. *(US Navy)*

Fast-forward to the early 1990s when the F-14D students showed up at Miramar before their new jets showed up. Thanks to 'Wizzard', who wanted to ensure the initial D cadre was the best of Naval Aviation, all the students were hand-picked for their very high grades in the training command. They had an entirely new flight simulator almost to themselves, and

clockwise for the other, which meant that they both put eyes on the key components and gauges independently. Rarely was anything found out of place, and if so, most discrepancies were fixed quickly. After the pre-flight was complete, both would man up their cockpits, and the RIO had the responsibility for pulling not only his ejection seat pins, but also those that armed the canopy for explosive removal in the case of an ejection or the need to blow it off for a ground egress in an emergency.

The RIO, after strapping in, would quickly push in about 30 important circuit breakers spread out on panels to the left, right and behind his shoulders. After both engines were on line, all it took to prepare an F-14A backseat to go flying was six steps. You needed to turn the AN/AWG-9 radar to standby and switch on its cooling system, put the INS to Ground Align (and ensure the right latitude and longitude were entered for your ramp position), turn on the radio and put the IFF (Interrogator Friend or Foe) system in standby mode. Once the system powered up, the RIO needed to run the Onboard Checkout, which was selected on the Computer Address Panel. This ran the all-important ramps on the F-14A intakes.

The instructor RIO paid a lot of attention to what his student pilot was doing both on the ground and, most importantly, in the air. The RIO (both instructor and student) ran the radios and got a clearance if they were the lead or single aircraft, and talked to the ground controllers and all airborne controllers if they were the lead jet. If the instructor RIO was the wingman (the usual scenario), they just followed along and listened to the lead's radio calls made by the student RIO, paying attention to what was being said.

With the canopy shut and the engines running, the cockpit of the F-14 quickly became extremely loud due to the jet's powerful Environmental Control System (ECS) that forced air into the cockpit through very narrow openings in the piccolo tubes along the edges of the canopy. Casual conversation between the pilot and RIO was impossible with the ECS on, and the only way to communicate when wearing a helmet in such an environment was via an intercom system, called the ICS. The instructor RIO spent almost all of his time watching, looking where the pilot was looking,

watching the flight lead's jet and looking out and paying a lot of attention to what the student pilot was doing. The ICS switch was his lifeline to the pilot, who may be needed to be told something very quickly. There was a foot pedal that also turned on the ICS, but it was best not to use it because it turned on both the pilot's and RIO's oxygen mask microphones, not just the RIO's, and that was rather bothersome.

In the BWEPS phase, because you were operating as a section, the take-offs were done together, in a lead-trail formation called a flight leader separation take-off. Section or simultaneous take-offs were done in the fleet, never in the FRS with a student pilot. Although some argue that section take-offs were actually safer than flight leader separations, particularly if the lead aircraft had to abort its take-off, a section go took a fair amount of airmanship to conduct safely.

In the BWEPS phase, new student pilots were still working hard to improve their formation flying skills, and it always made sense to push the learning curve, but to not push too hard to force new pilots and RIOs into dangerous situations that they didn't have the experience to handle properly. It was a fine line. Also, because the instructor RIO was writing the grade sheet on student pilots, many of the latter didn't ask as many questions as they should, and that could be very dangerous if the RIO was thinking or expecting one thing and the pilot didn't understand his flight lead, or RIO, or vice-versa. In the FRS, instructors spent a lot of time in the flight phase stressing there were no dumb questions, and to ask if you were confused.

Night form, Night tanking, Night CQ

The three FRS phases or flights that were the most demanding for instructor RIOs were what we jokingly called the 'triple crown' – the night FAM flight that included night formation flying, night tanking off an A-6 or S-3 and night CQ. Obviously, the common attribute was night-time, but even during the hours of daylight, teaching someone formation flying, tanking and day CQ, when they've never done it before in that airplane, was very sporty.

Of the three, the thing that historically banged up the jets the most was day and night tanking. The reason why was that the student pilots had never done it before, in any aircraft, and it involved putting a large piece of metal right next to another large piece of metal at close to 300mph. Both pieces of metal, the F-14, and the tanker basket, and more specifically its metal 'knuckle', which connected the basket to the hose, would become damaged rather quickly if they banged into each other due to a poorly controlled closure rate, or a last second 'stab' at the basket with the Tomcat probe.

In all three missions, formation, tanking and CQ, the smooth pilot was rewarded with success. The not-so-smooth pilot was generally not rewarded, and sometimes banged up the jets badly in the tanking phase. As an instructor, you did everything you could, as a co-pilot, amateur psychologist, motivator and safety officer to help your pilot successfully complete these missions.

The tactics phase of the FRS course was a blast. As an instructor RIO, it was the most fun because it was challenging, the student pilots were close to graduating and you could trust them more – they were becoming very experienced. Flying ACM hops, whether in the visual or radar arena, was the best. They challenged you like no other flights, and made you try to think way ahead of the airplane. As an instructor, it challenged you to help your pilot put the aircraft in the right piece of sky to be successful. If your pilot did well, you felt a lot of pride in helping him make that happen. You were actively working in those flights to put the new pilots in the position to see an opportunity, and learn how to take advantage of that opportunity, and if you were defensive, how to neutralise that attack and live another day against a simulated enemy.

In the tactics phase you flew primarily against adversary aircraft, provided by VF-43 or VFC-12 at Oceana, or VF-126 or VFC-13 at Miramar. Additionally, these adversary squadrons would go on detachment with you to Key West or El Centro – both places with direct access to instrumented ranges with ACMI (Air Combat Maneuvering Instrumentation) or TACTS (Tactical Aircrew Combat Training System) that were either overwater or overland, and blessed with exceptional weather. For VF-101 in the winter months, Key West dets

were almost mandatory to get their students through the syllabus. At VF-124, although you could do your entire syllabus out of Miramar, we just found that by doing a detachment out of El Centro you could focus your maintenance and operational teams together and knock out sorties very quickly and efficiently.

As an FRS instructor RIO, you were very close to your fellow pilot instructors and the adversary pilots that really worked hard to help you train your student pilots. After a tactics flight, you'd compare notes and listen intently to your buddies in the other cockpits,

LEFT Pre- and post-flight briefings/ debriefings were carried out using white boards and marker pens – computers were in their infancy for much of the Tomcat's front-line career. This board lists details for a one-v-one CAT I ACM training hop that marked the final flight of Lt Doug 'Boog' Denneny as an FRS instructor with VF-124 in August 1992, his pilot for the sortie being Cdr Chris 'Grits' Gratas. Their opponent was an A-4F from VFC-13 'Saints'.
(Doug Denneny)

BELOW In the ten seconds (less than a mile) prior to landing, the pilot's scan was focused on 'meatball, line-up and angle of attack', and listening keenly to any calls from the LSO, who was grading his pass and acting as a safety observer. The F-14A HUD was of no help in the final seconds, and older Tomcats did not have flight-path markers or digital flight controls.
(Dave Parsons)

who were flying F-16s, F-5s, A-4s, Kfirs or Tomcats. Collectively, the FRS instructors and their counterparts in the adversary units were working hard to train your new student pilot, ensuring that he knew what he did right or wrong so he could get better. It was a very collaborative approach, and a fighter community coming together to make each other better.

And, finally, the CQ phase. By the time they reached this point the student pilots were now the most experienced in the FRS, being the senior class, and they knew the instructor RIOs very well. The pilots got to pick which instructor RIO they wanted to go to the boat with. It was their choice, and they would pick a RIO who they felt could help them the most behind the boat.

Being an instructor RIO in the boat class was a big commitment, as you had to be available to undertake around 15 late-night FCLP flights with the student, and this was tough if you were recently married. Having worked all day, you then had to fly late at night for three weeks prior to the boat det.

Although some of the FCLPs were done at Miramar or Oceana, most were performed at Fentress, just south of Virginia Beach, for the VF-101 aircrew, or on San Clemente island, or sometimes at El Centro for VF-124. San Clemente, which was referred to as 'the Rock', is about 70 miles due west of La Jolla. An LSO

and his writer (a young FRS student pilot who wanted to be an LSO one day) would brief the CQ event and then jump in a jet and fly to San Clemente, land and head out to the LSO shack at the end of the runway. They'd wave about ten jets for at least six to eight passes each at 'the Rock', before jumping back in the jet and 'hauling the chili' back to Miramar in time to get on deck prior to quiet hours or the field closing.

'The Rock' was fantastic training due to the practice Carrier Controlled Approaches (CCAs) run by enlisted controllers and the natural 'burble' or airflow disturbances caused at the end of the runway that kind of simulated the power correction in close that carrier pilots had to encounter, and correct for, at the back of the boat when landing. 'The Rock' was exceptional training. We used to jokingly say the boat was good training for 'the Rock'.

At Oceana, Fentress airfield in Chesapeake, Virginia, was also a very good carrier landing training facility. In the 1980s, it was very dark out there in the woods and swamps of southern Virginia. Once developers built on parcels they had acquired near the field, the noise complaints increased exponentially, and Fentress became a challenging place to fly from following the introduction of new mandatory noise abatement procedures. With a spotty F-14A INS and a full pattern, both finding Fentress and your interval in the landing pattern and safely entering the downwind leg for a recovery was a varsity sport. The pilot and the RIO were eyeballs out all the time at Fentress, and there are many stories of Tomcat crews scaring the heck out of each other late at night by turning in front of jets already in the landing pattern.

The other challenge associated with FCLPs was that at the end of the day, if the jets broke from the other flights that started at 0600hrs, you might find that six pilots needed to launch for an FCLP session and there were only three 'up' jets. So then you'd have to 'hot' switch (crew swap on deck in a running jet), making it a very, very long night for you, your pilot and the LSOs, who went from a full pattern of six jets to two sessions, each with just the same three jets, staggered over 3 hours. There was a lot of flexibility and patience needed in the CQ phase, and instructor RIOs got very close with their instructor LSO pilot counterparts during this

BELOW Field Carrier Landing Practice diagram published in NAVAIR 01-F14AAA-1 publication *NATOPS Flight Manual Navy Model F-14A Aircraft*, dated 15 May 2003. *(US Navy)*

part of the syllabus. There was a lot of shared time, and respect as both were working hard to qual student pilots and get them to the fleet.

Once the boat det commenced, the hours got very strange, and the stress and workload of helping a young pilot get qualified was not for the faint of heart. There were many times when you realised you were in a pretty dangerous profession when you took a young Tomcat pilot to the boat at night for the first time. Many things were waiverable, including crew rest – there were times we pushed ourselves hard to complete the mission. It was also a matter of personal pride among the instructors to go on every boat period you could, mainly because your reputation was being judged by the entire fighter community. Most of the time, you went with CAT Is. Every once in a while an incoming XO needed to go to the boat, or a Deputy CAG or an LSO getting cross-trained in the Tomcat. Those were the most fun CQ dets. Going to the boat, particularly during the day, was fun even with a new pilot because the challenge allowed Naval Aviators to employ the unique skill set that marked them out as different to pilots from other air forces.

Night-time was always a challenge, and sometimes it was a real bear, or, as we called it, 'a varsity night'. The Atlantic in the winter could get very sporty, and there was the added joy

LEFT A student pilot slightly overshoots his approach to runway 8/26 at Naval Air Facility El Centro so that RIO instructor Lt Doug Denneny could take a quick photograph. Being very close to some of the best ranges in the country, El Centro, in Imperial County, California, was frequently used by both VF-124 and VF-101 throughout their time with the Tomcat.
(Doug Denneny)

of wearing bulky anti-exposure suits to turn a 6-hour long CQ evolution (sitting on the flight deck getting more gas while the carrier created operating space in the warning areas) into a test of human endurance in a 'poopie suit'.

Instructor RIOs, along with the LSOs, really considered themselves to be the front-line

BELOW By the time this photograph was taken on the Oceana ramp in September 2004, VF-101's once varied fleet of Tomcats (numbering as many as 130 aircraft in the early 1990s) had been pared down to just 12 F-14Ds following the gradual retirement of the surviving A- and B-models. Seen here devoid of its refuelling probe fairing, 'Gunfighter 155' (BuNo 163900) was initially assigned to VF-124 in March 1991. *(Gert Kromhout)*

safety officers for the CQ evolution. Every pilot and RIO wanted to be a 'can-do' person, but when the weather closed in, or there were confusing instructions, or something just didn't look right, many times the instructor RIO or LSO stepped in and kept folks from doing something unsafe around the boat. We had a saying that the 'boat' was always trying to kill you. That's because there were just two of you in the jet making decisions, but hundreds of people on that boat that were making decisions, and with human error at play, the chances of someone making a mistake on the carrier, or in another plane around you, were pretty high. We were always on high alert in the carrier environment.

Off San Diego at night, there was an ever-present marine cloud layer at 1,200ft, meaning that regardless of the moonlight above, it was generally pitch black underneath. Add to that deck movement due to an ever-present Pacific swell, sometimes right up to, if not beyond, CQ minimums, and many times a calm night on the beach became beyond a 'varsity night' for a young pilot's first night traps. With a poor HUD that was little help to the pilot, and no auto-throttles allowed for the CQ phase, night landings were a handful in the F-14A. I have great stories of pilots, after their first night trap telling me something like, '"Boog", I have no idea how you do what you do, or that you would even do it. This is crazy!' Or comments like, 'I had no idea I was going to catch that wire, and I was flying the plane!' There were a few nights as an FRS CQ instructor when my legs would be shaking uncontrollably in the landing area on the boat after a 'varsity night' and colourful pass. But that was the exception.

The skill shown by the pilots I flew with at the boat at night can't be overstated. Before modified DLC, and with a spotty Automatic Carrier Landing System (ACLS), you were

working your tail off backing up your pilot, doing everything you could to ensure they got qualified safely with a quality start to the recovery – at the ¾-mile mark behind the boat – so they could take over visually. We'd always run a backup CCA to make sure your pilot was on glideslope at night, thus ensuring that the ACLS and ILS were providing him with good information as he was heads down shooting the approach on the Vertical Display Indicator (VDI). Back in the old days, there were folks who had flown their 'needles' [cockpit gauges and instruments] right into the water, and we wanted to make sure that never happened again.

The pilot would of course peek out at times to look at the boat, because a peek is worth a thousand scans, but many pilots were glued to the VDI flying fantastic Instrument Flight Rules approaches to ensure that they got an outstanding beginning, or 'start', to their pass at the carrier.

At ¾ of a mile and about 360ft over the water with the Fresnel lens, or meatball, and datums in sight, the pilot would 'call the "Ball"' over the ICS. The RIO would then call it on the radio for every CQ pass, '"165" [the jet's nose number, called the modex] Tomcat ball, 9.8' to inform all that the pilot had spotted the 'ball', was flying visually and that we had 9,800lb of gas. Every pass, the gas would obviously decrease, and the amount would let the ship know when you had to stop on deck and get refuelled, so you always had enough gas to bingo [return] to the beach. Some pilots wanted you to call out airspeed deviations in the groove, others needed your help by methodically calling out Vertical Speed Indicator readings.

Instructor RIOs worked very hard to help our pilots get qualified. It was a huge team effort, and I felt an immense sense of accomplishment when, after the last night trap, the LSO (call-sign 'Paddles') called up my pilot, flying 'Gunslinger 101' and said, '101 Paddles' (pause). 'Go Ahead Paddles' (pause). 'Hitch, you are a qual. You'll be a pump, and a shot to the beach.'

A day in the life of an instructor

For a fully qualified F-14 RIO instructor, you could find yourself doing five or more training events in a 12+ hour day of work. The first event would be a simulator at 0900hrs. That would finish at 1015hrs, and you then would hustle over to the squadron to give a lecture from 1100hrs to 1300hrs. After wolfing down a sandwich for lunch out of the 'Roach Coach' by the side gate, you would have a 1330hrs brief for a day FAM form flight that would end at 1700hrs. At 1730hrs you had brief for a night BWEPS flight that got you airborne at 1930hrs and back on deck at 2100hrs. The debrief was complete at 2200hrs. You'd be home by 2300hrs and back at it the next day, and the next.

There was very little time to do your 'ground' job. Fortunately, with no cell phones, except those seen in the movies, you just went from event to event, an integral part of the production effort. There were few distractions in those days, and the only way to be contacted was if someone called the ready room and left you a message on a yellow government message

BELOW When photographed from the ramp of a C-130J in June 2004, storeless F-14D BuNo 164601 was being flown by the Tomcat Demonstration Team crew (pilot Lt Jon Tangredi and RIO Lt Joe Ruzicka). Initially assigned to VF-124 in April 1992, this aircraft served with VF-101 Det Miramar, VF-31 and, finally, VF-101 again. It was delivered to Castle Air Museum, in California, in September 2005.
(Erik Hildebrandt)

form. If your spouse called the ready room, which was totally normal since she had no idea that you were stuck on the boat overnight, or that your jet had broken down in Alameda (almost 500 miles north of San Diego) and you weren't coming home that night, that would usually cost you $5 on the 'hit board'. My how times have changed.

During your last year or so as an instructor, there were some good deals to be had. Most related to who you were flying with and the general fun of flying with your fellow instructors, whether it was getting trained yourself in the F-14D or flying Post Maintenance Check Flights

or Confidence hops to support maintenance, or going on cross-country flights for training 'Xs'. Another good deal was to be one of the two RIOs every summer who were members of the FRS airshow Demonstration Team. This slot was usually requested by pilots that wanted to become Blue Angels and the instructor RIOs who didn't mind working every weekend in the summer. Other good deals were an opportunity (at Miramar) of going through Topgun as a student, going to the boat with a friend who was a CAT III getting requalified or flying a lot of Instructor Under Training flights. Anytime you could fly with a pilot who was a peer, or in other

words good and competent, made flying a lot more fun. It was less stressful and you didn't have to spend as much time making sure the other guy was doing his job correctly.

Fighter spirit

Every year both the east and the west coast FRS hosted their annual 'Fighter Fling' (east coast) or 'Tomcat Ball' (west coast) activities. The FRSs had the manpower, in both students and instructors, to pull off the festivities. There were athletic competitions, including a 5-kilometre run, volleyball, softball, tennis, a triathlon at Miramar, including both aviators and spouses, and a golf tournament that generated stories for several years. There was also a formal ball, where the entire community got together in a hotel downtown. There was an annual happy hour where awards were passed out, a top-notch video and great revelry throughout the week.

On the west coast, the culmination of the event was the FRS CO's announcement of his decision on who was the fleet fighter squadron with the most spirit. This resulted in the presentation of the 'Mutha' trophy. Squadrons worked hard to win this award by winning over 'Mutha's' heart, and those of the FRS instructors who met secretly to help their CO decide through metrics and other unscientific methods who was the best-spirited squadron

on base. The recipients of the trophy then had to defend the little statue against repeated, and creative, attempts to steal it. If a theft was successful, and credit was given for cunning instead of brute force, then the normal ransom payment for 'Mutha's' return was a case of beer. Winning the 'Mutha' was both an honour and then a bit of a burden.

During the 1980s and 1990s, the Officer's Clubs at Miramar and Oceana were fun, and a great place for officers from the fighter, attack and early warning squadrons to get together. It was an amazing time to be in those clubs after June 1986, when the movie *Top Gun* came out. There are many husbands and wives that met at those O'Clubs. Unfortunately, the clubs have never returned to their heyday, and only a few survive throughout the Navy, mainly the Fallon O'Club in Nevada and at a few other naval air stations.

In conclusion, the life of an FRS RIO instructor was about as good as it could get. You worked incredibly hard, but it was a business that rewarded you for your hard work, and the folks that surrounded you, both officers and enlisted, were some of the best people I've ever served with and for. Being a Tomcat RIO was a great way to spend a good part of my twenties, all of my thirties and part of my forties, and I only wish today's pilots and NFOs had the opportunity to live through that era of when the F-14 was the king of naval aviation.

LEFT 'Gunfighter 163' is milliseconds away from engaging one of CVN-71's four arrestor wires during the March 2005 CQ period. VF-101's last Tomcat CO, Cdr Paul Haas, said the F-14 was a fairly difficult aircraft to land aboard a carrier. 'It is large and heavy so you have to fly precisely in order not to damage the plane.' *(Gert Kromhout)*

Chapter Five

Back-seat magic

Having completed the FRS course, the 'nugget' RIO experienced a steep learning curve once in a fleet squadron, as veteran NFO Bill 'Libby' Lind recalls in this chapter. Indeed, he provides a rare insight into how the various systems controlled by a Tomcat NFO worked – and were employed – in a 'real-world' environment.

OPPOSITE **Having completed his deck-level and overwing pre-flight inspection of 'Bandwagon 102' (BuNo 163904), the RIO prepares to climb into the back seat of the VF-31 F-14D on the flight deck of** *John C. Stennis* **during the vessel's Joint Task Force Exercise in the southern California operating area in April 2004. To gain access to his lofty perch the NFO has climbed the integrally stored three-part ladder and boarding step.** *(US Navy)*

I commenced my long association with the F-14 in mid-1992 when selected, after Intermediate NFO training with VT-10 at NAS Pensacola, Florida, as a RIO 'under training'. Those of us destined for jets after Primary Training now subdivided into platform-specific 'tracks' at VT-86, also based at Pensacola. A-6E Bombardier/Navigators (B/Ns) and EA-6B Electronic Countermeasures guys did the Tactical Navigator syllabus, S-3B folks did a Tactical Coordinator syllabus and we F-14 guys did the RIO course. It's important to consider RIO training when considering F-14 systems.

The RIO and, to some degree, BN courses were seen as the roughest for NFOs. A lot of this was to do with the 'eat your young' mentality of the instructors at VT-86 – no one wanted to be the guy who sent a weak student to an FRS. We were taught basic radar theory and intercept geometry in T-39N Saberliners fitted with 'watered-down' F-16 APG-66 radar, running intercepts with a basic pulse ('radar blip') display. There was no processing or computer track files, just old-school 'figure out what the bogey is doing' based on the 'blip's' drift rates and geometry, and innumerable 'rules of thumb' to move your jet into proper intercept and/or rendezvous position. We also did rudimentary low-level visual navigation and culminated with Basic Fighter Manoeuvre training in the T-2C Buckeye.

Having graduated from VF-86, it was off to either VF-101 or VF-124, where the would-be RIO was introduced to the F-14 and, more specifically, its legendary AN/AWG-9 radar.

The RIO and AN/AWG-9 basics

The F-14A/B of 1993–98 were functionally similar in respect to their avionics and weapons systems. The AN/AWG-9 and associated displays had not radically changed from when the Tomcat entered service in October 1972. Minor upgrades to software (the AN/AWG-9 was analogue, with about 128K of processing power) improved things a bit, but the radar always had 1960s technology at its core. This is why the 'basics' taught to students at VT-86 were critical.

Unlike the T-39N's 'watered-down' F-16 APG-66 radar, the AN/AWG-9 had computer processing and generated a track file (the computerised symbol representing a bogey, with somewhat accurate speed, heading and altitude), which meant that the RIO needed to understand basic theory, particularly as the target manoeuvred. The AN/AWG-9, like most early pulse-Doppler (PD) systems, could not keep up with a target manoeuvring to the 'beam' – *ie* moving on a parallel course towards or away from the F-14. AN/AWG-9 also had issues with 'look down' over land, although it was far better than most systems of the era.

The real beauty of the AN/AWG-9 was 'power out'. Generating more than 5,000W of microwave energy, it could see a 'hot' target flying towards the F-14 at altitude out to 120 miles or greater. This power also allowed it to 'burn through' many types of rudimentary jamming. Designed to take on Soviet cruise-missile firing bombers, the AN/AWG-9 could identify and account for many types of barrage and deceptive jamming, and adjust for each. When paired with AIM-54 missiles, with their own countermeasures capability to include home-on-jam, the AN/AWG-9 was extremely lethal in what was expected to be a chaotic electronic environment.

The AN/AWG-9 was married to an early mechanical gyroscope-driven INS, which was relatively reliable. It did, however, have a propensity for failure during dynamic flight. When this happened, AN/AWG-9 processing (which relied on the INS to determine the F-14's dynamics and radar tracking to determine the bogey's dynamics) suffered. Following an INS failure, the RIO would rapidly switch the

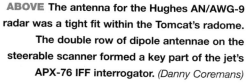

ABOVE The antenna for the Hughes AN/AWG-9 radar was a tight fit within the Tomcat's radome. The double row of dipole antennae on the steerable scanner formed a key part of the jet's APX-76 IFF interrogator. *(Danny Coremans)*

ABOVE VF-31 CO Cdr James 'Puck' Howe and CVW-8 staff officer, and veteran RIO, Lt Cdr Bill 'Libby' Lind pose on the Oceana ramp before the latter made his 'fini flight' in F-14D BuNo 164603 on 4 October 2006. The following day this aircraft ('Bandwagon 101') made its final flight from Oceana to Republic Airport at Farmingdale, Long Island, for display at the Northrop Grumman facility in nearby Bethpage. *(Bill Lind)*

AN/AWG-9 into pulse mode (the old-school 'blip') and use basic geometry and 'mental gymnastics' to keep track of the radar picture.

RIO's workspace – more *Mad Men* than Xbox

The RIO's cockpit in the F-14A/B cockpit did not benefit from later ergonomic design or technology that allowed for the creation of integrated controls. In these early Tomcat models, separate systems had separate control boxes with unique switches, knobs and dials. Furthermore, these were spread throughout the cockpit, often in non-intuitive locations or combinations. The F-14A/B showed only a modicum of the system integration and coordinated aircrew interface common in more modern fighters. Understanding cockpit systems and layout is critically important when analysing how the RIO employed the Tomcat as a weapon system.

The cockpit was dominated by a large, 9in-diameter monochromatic Tactical Information Display (TID) in the centre of the instrument panel. For 1960s technology, it displayed a surprising variety of information.

Across its centreline, 'three' to 'nine o'clock' was a horizon line, giving rudimentary aircraft attitude. When in 'tactical' mode, the aircraft's symbology was displayed at the 'six o'clock' position and a V-shaped 'whisker' display indicated selected radar volume in azimuth (how wide the radar was looking, left to right). The jet's heading and speed were at the top ('12 o'clock') until a track was detected and selected. The display would then swap to target range and speed. Radar elevation volume (bottom and top of the altitude block the radar was covering) was displayed at 'nine o'clock' and further target information was shown at 'three o'clock'.

The RIO could also select a 'ground-stabilised' display, placing his aircraft at the TID's centre and giving him a sort of 'bird's eye' view of things. This was a must in a busy exercise or dynamic, scaled-up combat environment, as the RIO could then visualise generalised 'broadcast' situational calls from the E-2, AWACS or other fighter controller. When data links were used, these would display contact data everywhere. Having a 360-degree display was very useful, therefore, although it required some getting used to.

As the AN/AWG-9 'saw' targets over multiple radar sweeps in its various automated PD modes, it built and displayed these computer-derived composite symbols, which were called track files. On the TID, these appeared as 'staples' – boxes with no bottoms. These

'staples' had a velocity vector extending downward, giving a rough idea of target heading and speed, based on the length of the velocity vector. AN/AWG-9 could track and display up to 24 targets, which was impressive for a 128K analogue computer. The TID also showed rudimentary jamming symbology, as well as the radar's various modes and, if selected, special 'war' modes utilising a primitive frequency and mode-hopping capability. Weapon select/ weapon status was displayed at 'five o'clock' and a cycling system fault analysis (three-letter codes) at 'seven o'clock'.

Most TID functionality and radar elevation was controlled by the Hand Control Unit (HCU), mounted on a pedestal between the RIO's knees. It was essentially a 7in joystick that worked somewhat like a mouse on a modern computer. Press the trigger halfway and a faint cursor appeared on the TID. Full depression 'clicked' on a track updated its 'staple' display to a more detailed track and made it brighter. A similar full trigger squeeze over various menu items on the TID's edge could select different modes of operation on the display. The HCU also controlled radar antenna elevation scan via a thumbwheel. Keeping track of the up-and-down 'slice' that the radar was scanning was critical, as junior RIOs routinely allowed a closing bogey to 'fly out' of the top or bottom of their radar's vertical volume as range decreased.

Controls for adjusting the TID display, and its range scale, were also mounted to the HCU pedestal. On the TID console itself were control knobs for INS alignment, set up and mode, as well as 'steering' for manually entered waypoints (the F-14A/B baseline's AN/AWG-9/INS could generate eight wind-corrected steering waypoints for the jet to head towards – think of these as

RIGHT The RIO's cockpit shared little in common with the space occupied by the pilot – it was also less cluttered. The central console was dominated by the 9in-diameter TID, with its dedicated hand control unit mounted on a pedestal immediately in front of it. The rectangular panel above the TID was the Detailed Data Display console and at its centre was a small CRT display. *(Danny Coremans)*

'addresses' in Google Maps). These waypoints were displayed on both the TID and the pilot's displays, and RIOs could get very creative by using them to visually display anything from 'do not go here' locations (things like Iranian-controlled islands in the northern Arabian Gulf), to threat sites ('we know there is a SAM site here') to points on a navigation route. Another common mistake made by junior RIOs was forgetting to switch to the 'next' waypoint on a route. This usually resulted in the pilot having to ask why his steering cues were pointing behind the aircraft, as neither he nor the AN/AWG-9 could manually switch to the subsequent turn or landmark the RIO had entered.

Working above the TID was the Detailed Data Display (DDD) console. At its centre was a small cathode ray tube display. Its primary use was in pulse (the old-school 'blip-only' raw radar return mode), this basic display being quite useful

when PD modes failed as targets manoeuvred to the beam. It also came into its own if the RIO suspected multiple targets were in close formation and the AN/AWG-9 was unable to discriminate multiple bogeys (*ie* only indicating a single track file when there were actually multiple targets). RIOs would often quickly swap to pulse when 'sorting' targets in formation to later employ weapons. Sort contracts [target division] between wingmen was, at a minimum, called out by the lead RIO, and was usually

LEFT The left console in this F-14B has a hand control joystick fitted in place of the TARPS control panel. Sourced from the cancelled A-12 programme, the joystick was used by the RIO to steer the seeker head of the AN/AAQ-25 LANTIRN pod. To the left of the joystick are just some of the myriad push/pull circuit breakers. *(Danny Coremans)*

left unspoken as they were pre-briefed, if not outright standard doctrine. A hallmark of modern BVR employment is a well-thought-out 'divvying up' of who shoots whom. The DDD also displayed target azimuth (left/right of the nose) and range rate (the target's rate of closure to the F-14, roughly) when in a PD mode.

To the right of the DDD were the radar mode pushtiles. The AN/AWG-9 boasted several PD 'scan' multiple target track modes, namely the old-school 'blip' pulse and single-target track in both PD and pulse ('radar lock'). RIOs became

very adept at punching the proper radar mode pushtile without looking. Other controls on the DDD were radar fine-tuning and ECM controls, as well as mechanical wheels to manipulate radar frequency channels.

The vertical console near the RIO's right knee housed another monochrome display that could show radar warning receiver (RWR) information from the ALR-45/50, or a compass rose/radio navigation aid display. The ALR-45/50 was more 1960s vintage gear, and by the 1990s it was very limited in capability. The F-14B included a stand-alone display for the new ALR-67 on the right instrument vertical panel.

The left knee vertical console housed the AWG-15 weapons controls. Each armament station had mechanical controls, allowing the RIO to individually select which weapons were to be employed (the pilot physically released the ordnance by depressing – 'pickling' – the bomb release button on the top right of the control column, however) or jettisoned. The RIO also controlled bomb quantity (the number of bombs dropped each time the pilot 'pickled') and their interval. The RIO also had a large 'Fire' button on the HCU that allowed him to shoot AIM-7 and AIM-54 missiles, provided the pilot selected the master arm switch 'hot' and had the proper missile type selected.

By the late 1990s, after years of back and forth in the Tomcat community, doctrine finally dictated that only the pilot fire missiles. The possibility of each aircrew firing a weapon, and consequently releasing two missiles when intending to fire only one, was too great. Most RIOs took no offence, as we were more interested in saving weapons for the next target. Cockpit teamwork was critical, as there was little redundant weapons system function in

both cockpits. RIOs had their gear and tasks, pilots theirs. Working in coordination was a must, otherwise the Tomcat was little more than a big, fast jet you saw in the movies.

The horizontal consoles outboard of the RIO's legs housed ancillary equipment. On the left was the computer address panel (CAP), which was a mechanical interface through which you could programme the AN/AWG-9. Typically, the RIO would use it for running built-in tests, entering navigational waypoint data and for selecting training simulations that would display ersatz contacts and ECM, although the latter feature was rarely used. The sensor control panel was outboard of the CAP, and it featured mechanical knobs moving radar azimuth (where the radar looked left to right) and Television Camera System (TCS) functions. This console also housed the RIO's radio panel, controlling either an ARC-182 UHF/VHF/FM set or an ARC-210, the latter including frequency-agile modes ('Have Quick'). TACAN radio navigation aid, KY-58 radio encryption and intercom controls rounded out this panel. TARPS-equipped F-14s also had the reconnaissance panel on the left console.

The right horizontal console housed IFF, the APX-76 interrogator, RWR (ALE-45/50 or ALR-67), the ALE-39 chaff/flare dispenser set-up and other radio antenna, and ECM and radar beacon (used to assist in ground-controlled approaches) controls. The Link 4A data link control was also on the right console.

Surrounding the TID on the instrument panel were standard 'steam gauge' aircraft instruments such as airspeed, altitude and compass. The RIO had no engine or flight system instrumentation, save a fuel totaliser of dubious accuracy. The Tomcat had a monumentally complex fuel system, and it was contingent on the RIO as one of his many co-pilot duties to coordinate with the pilot as he regularly checked the various fuel tank quantities and transfer throughout a flight.

The walls of the RIO's cockpit were lined with more than 180 push/pull circuit breakers. Savvy RIOs could find by feel critical flight control and weapon systems breakers. Often, the archaic nature of Tomcat systems needed a 'kick' to reset or renew their functionality. The best RIOs developed or learned the tricks not in the books

to regenerate failing systems, and a 'breaker drill' cycling seemingly unrelated systems in particular orders could often regenerate the INS and associated computers, the AN/AWG-9 power supply, radar antenna function (albeit briefly – had to pick your spot!) and even the outboard spoilers on each wing. Although strictly forbidden, breakers controlling flaps could also be articulated, temporarily giving the Tomcat outsized lift in a visual engagement but with great risk to flight control mechanical gear if not done properly. Woe betide the crew who came home after such a stunt went poorly.

I have mentioned a few of the key systems, and their location and integration in the RIO cockpit. To expand, the following were mounted on the baseline F-14A/B:

Television Camera System (TCS) – A long-range camera under the nose that could be 'slaved' to the radar within 20 or so degrees of the nose and at varying levels of look-down/up. An 'aftermarket' add-on in the early 1980s, TCS came from Navy and Air Force experiences in Vietnam. Often, fighters could not employ weapons without visual confirmation that their radar targets were indeed hostile. TCS was an attempt to extend this range past normal sight. In non-dynamic flight and good lighting/weather, TCS could 'see' a fighter-sized target well enough to ID out to around 20 miles – further if a larger aircraft. If either the Tomcat or target manoeuvred, performance degraded quickly. TCS would attempt to lock itself (independent of the AN/AWG-9) based on

RIGHT The shape of the Tomcat's distinctive 'beaver tail' between its twin fins varied during its fleet service, with there being at least four different versions for the A-model alone. This underside view is of the fourth production type, which was found on late production F-14As and on virtually all B- and D-models. At the very end of the tail is an antenna for the AN/ALR-67(V) mid- and high-band radar-warning receiver, which was installed on the later Tomcat variants – this is a photograph on an F-14D. The tagged pin in the centre of the red square secured the tailhook in its stowed position while the jet was on the ground, the hook itself obscuring the fuel dump pipe to the right of the antenna. To the left of the hook are two 30-cartridge BAE Systems (formerly Tracor) AN/ALE-47 Airborne Countermeasures Dispenser System chaff/flare dispensers, which were retroactively fitted to surviving F-14s from 1998. *(Danny Coremans)*

target-to-background contrast. 'Seeing' a bogey well enough to identify his aircraft type was usually enough confirmation to take a shot, but taped confirmation was always required in large exercises.

APX-76 IFF interrogator – This device was part of the AN/AWG-9 antenna, and, based on RIO input, could interrogate a specific IFF 'code' or simply 'see' who was emitting ('squawking', again based on RIO set up) particular IFF modes. APX-76 was also encrypted with US/NATO Mode IV each day, so it could further determine if a bogey was 'squawking' wartime 'friendly' codes. Lack of APX-76 identifying a bogey as 'friendly' (and therefore apparently hostile) was never included in any RoE – such a lack of ID was passive vice positive confirmation, and weapons release always depended on someone (the fighter, controller or higher control agency) positively determining a contact was hostile.

APX-76 returns were displayed on the DDD, and it was mostly used to build general SA. In particular, when headed to large-force exercises

or combat areas where multiple tankers may be orbiting, RIOs would note their assigned tanker's IFF code pre-flight, and use APX-76 to pick out the right guy from a mass of radar contacts at range. We would also use it to find the ship if the carrier's radio aids to navigation (or our normal systems on the Tomcat) were inoperative. We would simply look for the mass of returns created on the DDD by the rest of the air wing's IFF hits as we neared recovery time and head that way, and chances were an aircraft carrier was nearby.

Link 4A/Fighter to Fighter Data Link (FFDL) – As the Tomcat's primary mission circa 1970 was defence at great range (and likely in heavy ECM) defending the battle group, it was anticipated voice communication would not be possible for a multitude of reasons. Furthermore, the battle group and its defenders needed a consolidated view of the battlespace (what modern military leaders call a 'common operating picture'), and a way to transmit information. The first synthesised attempt at a tactical data link resulted in Link 4A, and the F-14 was so equipped. Link 4A was a UHF broadcast system, and by the late 1970s, every US warship and most F-14s and E-2s carried the system.

As an adjunct, and unique to the F-14 in the Link 4A construct, was FFDL. Facilitated by an extra circuit board in its existing Link 4A box, FFDL allowed up to four F-14s to create their own link network that was capable of displaying each friendly aircraft, and if so designated by the RIO, transmit what he was seeing on radar. Other useful features included auto transmission of fuel and missiles remaining. F-14 aircrew used FFDL not just tactically, but also to effect rendezvous and a host of other administrative functions involving multiple aircraft. In large-scale exercises, single F-14s in each element of a strike would 'represent' the element to the lead Tomcat, allowing the lead some awareness of where up to three other portions of the package were, and what they were doing. FFDL was a somewhat limited precursor to the capability F-14D and F/A-18 aircrew would enjoy from the late 1990s as Link-16/Joint Tactical Information Distribution System entered wide use.

ALR-67 – While F-14As carried the archaic ALR-45/50, by the 1990s aircrew would only turn these on if they knew specific threats may be nearby – the false alarm rate for the ALR-45/50 was simply too high to make the system an effective tool. ALR-67 gave F-14B aircrew a somewhat modern RWR, and with further refinements over the last eight years the Navy flew Tomcats, aircrew sometimes made tactical decisions based on empirical data gleaned from RWR returns, as opposed to always assuming the bandit had superior radar SA. The net of this meant Tomcat crews could sometimes continue 'pointing' at bandits BVR, consequently not destroying our own radar picture while manoeuvring to defeat theoretical enemy radar coverage and missiles.

Employment – from 'Gouge' to science

My review of the F-14A/B's AN/AWG-9 systems and cockpit layout reveals just how busy the RIO was in the Tomcat. As I mentioned earlier, the pilot only controlled short-range ACM radar modes that were designed to achieve radar lock of a 'seen' bandit, ultimately allowing a radar missile shot. While the AIM-54 could indeed be launched 'Mad Dog' – fully active/unsupported by the AN/AWG-9 off the rail – this was not advisable for a number of reasons. It did, however, cause the bandit to react to his own RWR indications after we locked on to him, and this gave the Tomcat crew increased SA in a fight. The RIO was responsible for all sensor and display management at range, as well as communication.

Let's now turn to see how an effective air-to-air mission brief was conceptualised, and how Navy tactical crews raised this critical skill to a new level.

An effective air-to-air engagement began with planning and briefing. Both pilots and RIOs were fully responsible for understanding and discussing both BVR and visual weapon employment from the perspective of each cockpit. This was a result of the Tomcat's absolute reliance upon both crewmen to effectively operate and coordinate activities both internally and with their flights, and as part of a larger force or exercise. Obviously, pilots were the true visual range 'dogfight' experts,

while RIOs specialised in BVR and radar/sensor employment. Either experienced Tomcat aircrew could discuss each other's mission responsibilities effectively, thus ensuring that junior crews they briefed and flew with were both well trained and mentored.

The 1990s saw the tactical elements of Naval Aviation raise planning and briefing to high art and science. Led by the NFWS (Topgun) and the Naval Strike Warfare Center (Strike), the employment of naval fighters went from localised, squadron-centric 'lore' to what amounted to an evidenced-based, empirical set of recommendations on how best to optimise the Tomcat's systems and crews. This 'gospel' was promulgated throughout the fleet. With it came a push for standardisation in tactics and techniques across air wings and squadrons. Such homogeneity was nothing new to Navy aircrew.

The horrendous non-combatant loss rates of the 1950s led the Navy to standardise basic safety and operational procedures, and create the RAG [a term still used today, despite such units having been officially known as Fleet Replacement Squadrons since 1958!] in which newly winged Naval Aviators and NFOs initially learn how to safely fly their fleet aircraft and are then taught basic tactics. Moving this mindset on to advanced tactics wasn't a great leap.

The tactical standardisation that Topgun and Strike (which, in 1995, merged at Fallon to form NSAWC) set in motion in the 1970s (Topgun) and 1980s (Strike) came into its own

ABOVE The Hand Control Unit on the F-14D was significantly different to that in the earlier Tomcats and it also boasted increased functionality. The F-14A/B's HCU ran only the radar display on the TID and the DDD immediately above it. Again located on a pedestal between the RIO's legs, the HCU in the D-model was essentially a 7in joystick that worked like a mouse on a modern computer. *(Danny Coremans)*

in the late 1990s with a structured programme and syllabus that squadrons could use to train, evaluate and qualify new or returning aircrew.

Combined with RAG syllabi, this new structure held even experienced, fully qualified aircrew to a high standard, and upped everyone's game. Older aircrew initially chafed at the perception of NSAWC 'dictating' tactics, but the system soon proved its value. It allowed for local variations and personal 'techniques', for while the 'programme' came from NSAWC, it was 'owned' locally by air wing and squadron commanders.

To this day, a tactical training continuum starts in the RAG, continues as junior aircrew enter their first fleet squadrons, requalifies returning senior aircrew and holds everyone to a measurable standard. The aircrew responsible for this programme are Topgun graduates in the coast-centric Weapons Schools and RAGs, and every Hornet and Super Hornet squadron boasts two or more of these highly skilled training officers responsible for facilitating local syllabus implementation.

BELOW Another key addition to the D-model Tomcat's rear cockpit was the Sensor Slaving Panel (SSP) mounted forward of the grab handle atop the instrument console. It had three windows with buttons that determined which sensor – the AAS-42 IRST, APG-71 or AAX-1 TCS – was the master and which two were slaved off. The SSP also told the RIO what mode the sensors were in.
(Danny Coremans)

Plan your brief, brief your plan – employment and preparation

Planning a mission always starts at the 'end' – what is our objective? What do we want things to look like at mission's end? From here, we next consider risk. Does the objective merit risking loss? While we never 'plan' to lose a jet, some missions require far more risk than others, based on mission success criticality. These two elements are often expressed in guidance from the air wing commander or higher in a simple 'commander's intent' statement. The fighter and attack communities of the 1980s, pivoting off hard lessons learned over Lebanon and Libya, took mission planning to high levels. When married with the previously discussed fighter 'professional planners/briefers' mindset, the Tomcat crew of the 1990s and 2000s understood the need for careful planning and preparation for every flight.

Next up was a laydown of the enemy's order of battle, and threat picture. Paper charts depicting fighter airfields, SAM sites, expected surveillance radar coverage and other elements were prepared by intelligence personnel. We then considered friendly available forces. Fighters, desired loadout, airborne (or ship) early warning/fighter direction, electronic warfare assets and the like were in the mix.

Basic air-to-air employment centred on the two- or four-ship element. Each aircraft had somewhat rigid assignments on radar 'looks' – the parts of sky they were required to sanitise. Based on the expected threat profile, the lead RIO would sometimes concentrate three radars in a particular geographic zone or altitude block, and rely on the fourth aircraft to monitor the balance. Based on the mission, threat and overall risk mindset, decisions were then made on when to 'commit' or, more simply, begin addressing enemy formations. Fighters didn't even necessarily need their own radars to 'see' bandits. Based on the 'picture' painted by the E-2 or other controllers, we could plan criteria to commit on just about any picture provided by any source, depending on scenario.

Radar techniques were part of the plan. As noted, radar looks were planned to 'sanitise' airspace, with the majority of radars (or the time these radars spent scanning a particular region of sky) focused on threat sectors or altitudes.

Once the fighters had radar contact, a planned 'meld' range was determined that married fighter element radars from their sanitised looks into the enemy formation. A 'sort' was also determined at this point, delineating who was to shoot or monitor who – this was critically important. If later decisions merited proceeding to a visual engagement, involving AIM-9s and 20mm cannon, the Tomcat crews wanted to be sure that as many bandits as possible had absorbed, or at least accounted for, a radar missile. Even if no visual engagement occurred, we wanted to maximise 'warheads on the most foreheads' – two AIM-54s against a single bandit was beyond overkill.

The F-14A/B as discussed in this chapter had several semi-automated PD modes capable of scanning varying volumes of airspace. Based on the number of radars and expected threat axis, the plan would include mode manual (usually Track While Scan [TWS]), with one of the settings defining its width in azimuth and volume in altitude. TWS would automatically 'build' track files, but it was reliant on the RIO to ensure that the radar looked in the right piece of sky at all times. Again, a lack of awareness of the location of enemy formations within your radar's scan volume could bite you. As ranges decreased, relative angles off your nose to the bandit also decreased, while the possibility that the contact would fly out of your scan volume increased. TWS included an auto setting, autonomously tracking the highest threat target (as perceived by AN/AWG-9). A spurious contact could easily pull the auto track away from your true bogeys, however, and if this occurred the RIO was required to physically revert to manual and reset his scan volumes.

Later refinement to RIO techniques saw the less-detailed, but larger scan volume-capable Range While Search (RWS) mode come to the fore. RWS could cover greater volumes in azimuth, but with less detailed track info. The idea was to locate all enemy formations at range, develop a picture then revert to TWS to focus on a targeted group.

Sort contracts were usually straight doctrine, and were common sense. In their simplest form, sort contracts directly linked to how we would employ weapons. Right fighter shoots the right guy, left fighter shoots the left guy, lead shoots the nearest bandit, wingman shoots the trail bandit. The complexity came when considering multiple bandits, or a threat that merited more than one radar missile at range. The balance between ensuring we killed as many bandits at possible at the longest, most effective range was balanced by the desire to conserve missiles, and the latter was linked directly to the overall mission mindset.

Once radar SA was gained, the fighters now really concentrated on timeline. BVR tactics were predicated on predictable timelines – we would take certain actions, shoot missiles or undertake manoeuvres based on our own aircraft and weapons capabilities, assumed enemy capability, certain pre-planned 'if/then' decision points and a host of other (hopefully) predictable factors. The key point in any timeline is the range at which the fighters decide to either continue to a visual engagement or duck out and head away to reassess or egress. Timeline and attendant considerations were big parts of pre-flight planning and briefing.

While called a 'timeline', this linear engagement/decision flow was really about range. We knew our own weapons and aircraft capabilities – how fast a missile would cover a particular distance and, most critically, at what range our fighter would be from the bandits when the missiles impacted. As expected threats of the 1990s and early 2000s did not carry viable 'active' missiles capable of autonomous tracking, destroying the enemy fighter or forcing your opponent to 'trash' his radar picture by turning away before his missile hit you effectively defeated the weapon for it could no longer track on you. While you may not have scored a kill, having defeated an enemy missile and the radar guiding it was almost as good. Your opponent was now far less effective and on the defensive. He was reacting to you and, most likely, had lost track of your precise location and range.

We also knew how fast our jet could be turned around, maximising the kinematic impact on enemy missiles in flight (while missiles are fast, if you turn away early/fast enough, they will run out of propellant before catching you). Speed also disrupted your opponent's radar picture (Soviet-built radars of the 1980s and 1990s were assessed as having minimal capability in tracking targets perpendicular to, or headed in the same direction, as the bandit – sidestep or turning away effectively rendered his radar blind; this is not the case any more), making the prospect of chasing the Tomcat a poor tactical decision for the bandit. We were very hard to catch, and had the gas to outlast just about everyone. So our timeline included manoeuvres away from directly pointing at the bandits so as to slow downrange travel, while maintaining our ability to keep radars on the bandit formation (and support our own missiles), and, if need be, turn completely away, accelerate, regain some range and potentially turn back towards the enemy. Finally, preserving your aircraft to fight another day was no dishonour if tactical situations were not in your favour.

So timeline, and the attendant cues, considerations and decisions, made up a fair portion of the plan and brief. While many of the ranges were rote, the overall mission objectives could change timeline complexion. If you were escorting or sweeping ahead of a strike package, our willingness to proceed to a visual engagement may be greater than if we were out alone, trying to neutralise threat bandits that could jeopardise future operations. While the Tomcat in able hands was lethal in the visual arena, it is to no modern fighter's advantage to accept visual combat without good reason. Kill the enemy at range, for there is too much left to chance when in close. Fuel consumption increases, tactical confusion abounds and an enemy with a lesser weapon system is now within his theoretical range.

That said, considerations on how best to conduct visual engagements remained, as they had since 1915, the core of a fighter pilot's being. The Tomcat was a large aircraft, but a capable dogfighter in the proper hands. Its energy addition/sustainment was impressive, variable-geometry wings an advantage and, when crewed properly, the second set of eyes a real plus. The F-16's turn rate and the F/A-18's ability to fight slow made these tough adversaries.

In respect to Russian-built aircraft, the Su-27/30 class were high fliers, fast and had impressive high AOA ability, while the MiG-29 was broadly comparable to the F/A-18. Both

Russian (or foreign-built/flown variants) were considered inferior in cockpit management/display capability, and particularly after the fall of the USSR, crews were thought to suffer through lack of flying time and proficiency. Nevertheless, the Russian jets had a superior visual range/infrared seeking missile in the AA-11 'Archer' (R-73/-74) family. Client states were expected to field baseline/export MiG-29s, along with familiar MiG-21 and MiG-23 fighters, as well as Sukhoi fighter-bombers. These all went into game plans and briefings on when and how to conduct a visual engagement.

The Tomcat crew, like all other US fighter crews, relied on having a better understanding of 'energy management' than their opponents. The F-14 had particular airspeed regions in which turn rate (number of degrees per second the nose could come around) and turn radius were optimised. Based on how the fight was going, crews would pick times for 'excursions' in which turn rate (and g-forces) were increased to bring the nose to bear for a shot or to improve SA. Other times called for a lessening of the turn, allowing the Tomcat to regain speed and energy. If you continually lost or 'bled' energy (a combination of speed, available thrust and, depending on the situation, altitude convertible to kinetic energy), the aircraft became far less manoeuvrable and, in an extreme situation, uncontrollable.

Based on our expected adversary, and with an intimate knowledge of our own weapons and aircraft capability, we then planned and briefed how we would conduct visual engagements. A basic tenet when engaging most modern fighters was to keep the fight close – we wanted to pressure the adversary, not allowing him turning/acceleration room, nor grant him adequate separation to employ his close-in weapons.

In any visual fight, 'first tally' was critical – see first, have an advantage. You may determine your enemy's range, nose position and formation composition and plan accordingly. You can also identify aircraft type and begin applying the 'game plan', optimising the Tomcat's capabilities while minimising his advantages. 'First to see, lives' and 'keep sight, win the fight' were worn, but apt, maxims. Gaining 'tally ho' and setting your element up for success began at range, with the radar

sort, good communication outlining the bandit formation and, frankly, knowing where to look. While the radar showing '25 degrees right of the nose, 14 degrees high, ten degrees right target aspect at eight (the angle at which the Tomcat is from the bandit's perspective) and 11 miles' may sound geometrically clean, knowing which piece of canopy to look at as you draw the contact to the nose was critical.

Once the 'merge' occurred (fighters and bandits passing each other's wing line), planning and execution worked three ways. First, the game plan. Best case, what will I do against a MiG-29? The answer was different if the bandit passing you turned out to be a MiG-21. Second, how would the element work together? A few maxims held. We would do our best to account for each bandit and, with two sets of eyes, attempt to keep track of the entire fight within each cockpit (or at least as good a portion as was able). Each fighter would look to support his wing, and good communications across the element could result in setting the wing up for an advantage as you pressed (or were pressed) by a bandit. Similarly, if there was a mismatch (say, two fighters and one bandit) we would discuss 'free' and 'engaged' fighter roles, possibly allowing the free fighter easy re-entry to the fight in a highly advantageous position. Third, we would consider how we managed our own cockpit. Generally, the RIO was responsible for the aft side of the sky – no bandit should approach to within visual weapon shot range without the RIO knowing. The RIO would also endeavour to keep track of the wing's fight, and would manage discharging expendables as required.

Furthermore, an experienced RIO could analyse F/A-18 nose aspect and range to determine if he was approaching a guns solution. It was always disconcerting to see an adversary Hornet reefing its nose to bear as your pilot fought for his own shot on another bandit, and you waited until the very last instant to call your pilot to defend, hoping he'd make his kill first.

Finally, once the engagement ended, now what? Head home, or was there a target to proceed to? Post-merge planning was a microcosm of our larger 'intent' consideration. If we had gotten into a visual scrape, chances were we were depleted somewhat on weapons and perhaps had lost (either shot down or disconnected from the formation) some of our wingmen. Was there a reason to stay in 'bad guy country'? How we would rejoin and flow back to the carrier were of paramount consideration, thus ensuring a successful end to the mission.

As I hope I have detailed in this chapter, the RIO had a key role to play in the effective employment of the Tomcat in all of its many missions, from fleet defender to tactical reconnaissance platform to precision bomber. The F-14 was conceived from the outset as a two-seat warplane, and it took a dedicated and highly trained pilot and RIO to get the most out of its myriad sensors, systems and weapons.

Chapter Six

Tomcat maintainers

The Tomcat was 'set upon' by a veritable army of maintainers between sorties when flying from a carrier deck, racing against the clock to have the 'Big Fighter' prepared for the next launch cycle. Among the sailors tasked with providing his squadron with an 'up' aircraft during blue water ops was Daniel 'Dsquare' Dixon.

OPPOSITE The last Tomcat to grace *Kitty Hawk*'s flight deck was this anonymous airframe, used by the ship's crash-and-salvage personnel for training. Usually hidden away in the hangar bay, it was brought up on to the flight deck for specific training scenarios. In this 2005 photograph, the jet has been lifted into place by the ship's A/S-32A-35A aircraft crash handling and salvage crane. *(US Navy)*

Following 20 years of service as a jet engine mechanic in the US Navy, during which time I made four WestPac cruises with the F-14, I can accurately state that there was rarely anything typical about any Tomcat operations. However, there were occasional cases of nearly perfect (textbook) turnarounds between the recovery (landing) and the launching of the aircraft for the next mission. This is an account of one of those occasions.

The first thing that needs to be noted is that there was a huge difference between shore and shipboard operations. Due to the limited parking space on an aircraft carrier's flight deck, the airplanes were backed into their parking spaces with their tail sections jutting out over the catwalk, safety nets and water. This eliminated safe access to any part of the aircraft that wasn't directly over the flight deck, so inspections in those areas were delayed until the aircraft was being taxied forward, which was typically done on its way to the catapult

for launch. On shore, all of the turnaround inspections were completed before the aircrew came out to man-up the jet because safe access wasn't restricted.

Usually, there was an hour or more between flights, but under extremely rare circumstances, the jet was hot-seated, where the returning aircrew would only shut down the port (left) engine (leaving the starboard engine running), unstrap and climb out, and another crew would climb in. In the hot-seat crew-switch scenario, the turnaround inspections weren't as thorough, and rarely went beyond an external search for leaks or damage. The following account details typical shipboard evolutions, from the arrested landing to the catapult launch for the next mission.

The second item of note is that the flight deck is an extremely chaotic, noisy and dangerous place to work and operate. It would not be prudent to list all of the dangers, but jet blast (thrust) blowing someone over the side and jet engine ingestion are two of the major ones that can prove fatal. Spectators are not allowed on the flight deck during flight operations for their safety, and the safety of others. Flight operations can be safely observed from an elevated exterior catwalk located on the island structure called Vulture's Row.

Everyone on the flight deck has a job to do, and once done, they vanish to safer territory, out of the way. An individual's job function is readily identified by the colour of the flight deck jersey, float coat (inflatable life preserver) and helmet that they wear, and the prominent markings on those garments. Examples of this colour coding are mentioned in this account, and I identify some of the job functions undertaken by the wearers of these jerseys.

Now, to set up the scenario, the recovery (landing) evolution is under way, with the returning aircraft circling the ship awaiting their turn to trap (land, using arresting gear to bring them to a stop). The pattern is stacked by the air traffic controllers, with the landing order determined by each aircraft's remaining fuel load, relative weight and other safety factors. As each airplane lands, it takes a minute or two to move the aircraft out of the landing area and to reset the arresting gear cable and machinery. The aircraft are staggered in the pattern to make this as efficient as possible.

For the purpose of this chapter, an F-14A has just landed, catching the number three arresting gear cable (wire) and earning its pilot a good landing score by the Landing Signals Officer (LSO). The arresting gear crew clear and retract the wire and the aircraft director ('Yellow Shirt') signals the pilot to raise the tailhook and taxi the aircraft out of the landing area. Another Tomcat is already on the final approach glide-slope, under the direction and control of the optical landing system and the LSO.

From the moment that the aircraft is marshalled out of the landing area, the inspection process is in play, even as the jet is being taxied. The 'Yellow Shirt' parks the Tomcat in a temporary holding area until all of the aircraft in the landing pattern have safely landed. Once stopped, and as directed by the 'Yellow Shirt', the parking brake is set, the landing gear down-lock pins are installed, the ordnance safety pins are also installed, the airplane is chained down and the wheels chocked to prevent rolling. Before the last engine is shut down, the flight deck coordinator, through hand signals, receives the general

ABOVE LEFT Corrosion control was a major job for maintenance personnel when squadrons were embarked, as they fought to protect their aircraft (this is F-14B 'Gypsy 103' (BuNo 162915) of VF-32 in November 2004) from the damaging effects of salt spray. All aircraft at sea were thoroughly hand cleaned, washed and extensively rinsed at least once a week with a special compound – not fresh, precious, water – to prevent corrosion. *(US Navy)*

ABOVE A corrosion control team from VF-11 give an F-14B a fresh-water scrub-down between missions on the flight deck of *George Washington* at the start of CVW-7's Mediterranean and Persian Gulf deployment in January 2004. The normal land-based calendar cycle for US Navy aircraft cleaning is every 14 days, with a 3-day window on either side. When these aircraft deploy to the carrier, their wash cycle is cut in half. *(US Navy)*

BELOW When the availability of fresh water becomes a problem on board a carrier, maintenance line divisions and corrosion control teams routinely perform 'scrubby bubbles' wipe-downs of aircraft whenever possible. A 'scrubby bubbles' wipe-down – which these F-14Bs from VF-32 are experiencing on board *Harry S. Truman* during its brief seven-week-long WestLant/Mediterranean deployment in July 2004 – is officially called the waterless wipe-down method. *(US Navy)*

RIGHT A ubiquitous A/S-32A-31A flight-deck tractor is used to tow a VF-31 F-14D towards the stern after the recovery cycle on board *John C. Stennis* had ended during the vessel's Comprehensive Training Unit Exercise (COMPTUEX) in November 2003. Once chained down on the ship's fantail – traditional 'fighter country' for VF units over the years – work would begin on turning the aircraft around for the next launch period. *(US Navy)*

aircraft status report from the aircrew (thumbs up or thumbs down) and the squadron troubleshooters glance over the exterior surfaces for any signs of obvious problems.

Once properly chained, the aircrew shut down the engines, open the canopy and deplane, immediately after which the plane captain climbs the boarding ladder to install the safety pins in the ejection seats. While the jet is in the temporary holding area, maintenance personnel are not allowed to open any access panels that can impact or delay its mobilisation. All preliminary external inspections are usually completed before the deck is respotted (aircraft moved) for the next launch cycle, especially in the areas aft of the Tomcat's main landing gear, as this could be inaccessible once the jet is moved. The plane captain sits in the pilot's seat while the aircraft is respotted, operating its brakes as directed during the movement.

Below decks, the aircrew debrief in the squadron's Maintenance Control office, giving their observations about the condition of all

BELOW Photographer's Mate 3rd Class Paul Taylor, assigned to VF-32, runs a system check on the LANTIRN pod attached to F-14B 'Gypsy 107' (BuNo 163224) at dusk in the NAG prior to the aircraft being declared ready to fly a night mission over Iraq from *Harry S. Truman* on 20 January 2005. *(US Navy)*

BELOW RIGHT Senior Chief Aviation Electrician's Mate Michael Wheeler updates the status of VF-31's 'Bandwagon 101' (BuNo 164603) in the squadron's Maintenance Control Center on board *John C. Stennis* in June 2004. Green arrows meant that the jet was in 'up' status, ready for flight. Red arrows indicated an unserviceable aircraft. A Tomcat unit would have aimed for six 'up' jets at the start of the day's flying when on deployment. *(US Navy)*

LEFT Red-shirted 'Ordies' from VF-2 have used a weapons hoist to lift a live AIM-54C from its trolley and on to the port wing glove multi-purpose pylon during pre-mission preparations on board *Constellation* at the very start of OIF I in March 2003. Two of the weapon's four main guidance vanes can be seen on the flight deck to the right of the 'Red Shirt' operating the hoist. *(US Navy)*

of the aircraft's flight systems. Maintenance Control communicates the jet's flight status to the Squadron Duty Officer and to Flight Deck Control. The latter uses the flight status and pending flight schedule to determine the most efficient parking locations for the jets that are slated for the next launch. Flight Deck Control formulates the parking plan and the 'Yellow Shirts' respot the deck as per its instructions. At some point during the turnaround procedure, either while the F-14 is in the temporary holding area or once respotted, the aircraft fuellers ('Purple Shirts' or 'Grapes') refuel the airplanes that are slated for the next launch. All of this is coordinated through, and directed by, Flight Deck Control.

Frequently, as the incoming aircrew are debriefing about their mission, the aircrew for the next mission are elsewhere getting briefed about the specific details of their pending mission and about the weather conditions that they may encounter. A part of that flight preparation includes reviewing the aircraft maintenance logbook for their assigned jet in Maintenance Control to familiarise themselves about any system limitations that might exist, and about any recent maintenance issues and repairs.

Once the aircraft is respotted, parked and properly secured with chocks and tie-down chains, the plane captain checks the aircraft's fluid and oxygen systems levels, and services them as needed. The maintenance personnel perform those jobs identified by Maintenance Control as needing attention in order for the jet to be declared mission ready for the next flight. The ordnance personnel ('Ordies') reconfigure the Tomcat's

LEFT The plane captain for 'Bandwagon 102' (F-14D BuNo 163904) cleans the canopy of his jet with a lint-free cloth before declaring it mission ready on board *Theodore Roosevelt* in October 2005 during VF-31's final deployment with the Tomcat. The canopy was usually polished multiple times a day during cyclic operations in an attempt to keep it free from salt spray. *(US Navy)*

ABOVE Clutching his flight bag, the RIO of 'Bandwagon 100' (BuNo 164342) climbs up into the cockpit while the pilot waits his turn to follow. Alongside the VF-31 'CAG jet' is 'Bandwagon 102' (BuNo 163904), which appears to be suffering from a last-minute technical snag judging by the frenzied activity taking place in the cockpit and the brown-shirted troubleshooter waiting to climb down from the port engine intake. *(Richard Cooper)*

BELOW The pilot of F-14D BuNo 164604 'Vandy 1' (the very last Tomcat built) of VX-9 signals to his plane captain shortly after engine start-up on the Key West ramp during Exercise Cope Snapper 2002 in October 2002. Excessive jet noise after engine start-up makes pre-briefed hand signals a must between air- and groundcrew. *(USAF)*

weaponry (missiles, bombs, etc.) if required. Usually, the mission profiles did not call for varying ordnance loads between flights, but it did happen, especially when the Tomcat was tasked with a bombing or reconnaissance mission.

The only maintenance actions allowed during the turnaround were critical issues that could be performed in short order, without negatively impacting the aircraft's mission capability, or delaying its launch schedule. The tail-over-water status of the jet also impacted which maintenance actions could take place due to safety considerations.

As the launch time approaches, the pilot and RIO show up in full flight gear to perform their pre-flight inspection of the aircraft's exterior, starting with the underside. Once this is completed, the aircrew climb the boarding ladder and inspect the top side of the aircraft, before removing the safety pins from the ejection seats and getting into the cockpit. Once both the pilot and RIO are in their seats, the plane captain climbs up to assist them with getting strapped in and stowing their gear (maps, pocket checklists, etc.). A squadron troubleshooter is standing by to assist with fixing any minor maintenance issues found, such as a loose screw or fastener.

Once strapped in, the pilot signals for electrical power and the plane captain or other maintenance person plugs in the power cord and pushes a button to supply the aircraft with external electrical power. With the latter provided, the aircrew perform their prestart checklist, testing all lights, switches and instruments. They also check the jet's avionics in preparation for engine start. Having completed this task, the aircrew establish radio communications with the Air Boss [who oversees all flight deck movements] and the control tower.

When given the clearance to start engines, the pilot signals for an external air source and the aircraft handling crew ('Blue Shirts') hook up and provide external air pressure to turn the aircraft's air turbine starter. Once one engine is running at idle speed, the Environmental Control System is operating and the aircraft generator is online to provide electrical power, the aircrew close the canopy, signal to disconnect external electrical power and start the other engine. On the ground, a troubleshooter or other maintenance person disconnects the electrical cable from the aircraft and closes the connector external power access door.

Once both engines are running, the pilot signals to disconnect the external air source. The 'Blue Shirts' shut off the air source and disconnect the hose from the aircraft, and a

BELOW VF-11's Aviation Structural Mechanic Christopher Maple, a qualified plane captain, asks the pilot to initiate trim checks in F-14B 'Ripper 200' (BuNo 163227) on board *George Washington* in the Red Sea during CVW-7's OIF II deployment in February 2004. Airwoman Christina Anderson, standing behind him, was a plane captain trainee who was shadowing Maple to learn her new job. *(US Navy)*

ABOVE A yellow-shirted plane director guides the pilot of bombed-up 'Gypsy 111' (F-14B BuNo 161428) to the right as the jet is lined up for waist catapult three on board *Harry S. Truman* at the start of another OIF III mission over Iraq in March 2005. Aircraft moving on the flight deck are handed off from one 'Yellow Shirt' to another as they progress towards their allocated catapult. *(US Navy)*

ABOVE RIGHT A diminutive Fly 2 plane director signals to the pilot of 'Blacklion 107' (BuNo 161166) to raise all eight of the jet's overwing spoilers for visual inspection by the deck checkers. They would remain open until Fly 2 lowered her palms from the wrists, signalling to the pilot to close the spoilers. *(US Navy)*

BELOW The pilot of VF-143's 'Dog 111' (F-14B BuNo 162701) is instructed by a 'Yellow Shirt' to make a very minor nose wheel steering correction to the left during the final line-up of the jet on CVN-73's bow catapult two in late January 2004. Straight alignment over the catapult track will ensure the launch bar attached to the Tomcat's nose strut is correctly aligned on top of the catapult shuttle. *(US Navy)*

troubleshooter then closes the air connection access door.

The aircrew continue with their pre-flight checklist, coordinating any flight control movements and system checks with the plane captain, to ensure proper ground and personnel clearance. The landing gear down-locks are removed, shown to the pilot and then stowed in a box located in the nose landing gear wheel well. Once ready to go, the pilot signals the 'Yellow Shirt' to this effect and then waits for further direction.

When available, a 'Yellow Shirt' would take direct control of the aircraft and signal for the 'Blue Shirts' to remove the tie-down chains and aircraft chocks, before instructing the pilot to release the parking brake. Once free, with the parking brake having been released, the pilot is directed to taxi forward. As the aircraft is positioned on the catapult, three squadron troubleshooters carefully and skilfully walk around the aircraft looking for leaks or any other abnormalities, two inspecting each side of the jet and the third walking down the centreline of the jet to check its underside. The troubleshooters complete their final check while the aircraft is being positioned on to the catapult, before clearing the immediate area.

Once the aircraft is in position, the catapult crew hook the jet to the catapult shuttle via a hold-back fitting, which is located on the backside of the aircraft's nose landing gear. The three troubleshooters position themselves where they can observe the pending engine run-up,

RIGHT Two white-shirted deck checkers take a closer look at 'Bandwagon 101' (BuNo 164600) while the Fly 2 plane director tells the pilot via clenched fists to keep the brakes firmly on. One of the deck checkers is running his bare left hand over the AN/ALQ-100 antenna beneath the chin pod, while his colleague appears to be pointing at the raised launch bar attached to the nose landing gear. *(US Navy)*

and flight surface movements, remaining close enough to see fluid leaks, but not too close to be in undue peril. They remain within line of sight of the catapult officer's position.

Once the aircraft is properly hooked up to the shuttle, the catapult crew turn the directive command over to the catapult officer, known as 'Shooter', who then signals the pilot to advance the throttles to maximum afterburner and operate all of the flight control surfaces. The troubleshooters observe the flight surface movements, looking for any abnormalities or fluid leaks. Each of them then gives a 'thumbs up' signal to the 'Shooter' if everything looks good, or a 'crossed arms' signal to suspend the launch if anything is wrong. With three thumbs up from the troubleshooters, the 'Shooter' salutes the pilot, crouches down, points toward the bow of the ship and touches the deck to signal for the catapult release. A mere fraction of a second later, the catapult 'fires' to accelerate the aircraft from 0 to approximately 150 knots in 2 seconds.

At the end of the catapult track, when the pilot feels the shuttle disconnect, he instantly pulls the flight control stick back and the jet commences its climb. The Tomcat is airborne once again.

The timing and frequency of flight operations depended greatly on the operational tempo required to meet the commitments of the battle group tasking. Under normal circumstances, launch and recovery operations were separate evolutions, but with four catapults, we had the capability of launching and recovering aircraft at a fairly rapid pace (almost simultaneously). Typically, the only time that I witnessed or participated in such high-tempo operations was during carrier qualification detachments off the California

coast, where the same crew would launch, circle and recover numerous times for training and qualifications. Every pilot and RIO had to attain a predetermined number of day and night launches and good traps in order to deck qualify, or requalify, before cruise.

This detachment took place within a short flight distance of land-based airfields, the latter acting as a safety net in the event that a jet ran low on fuel before a crew could get on board. Once on cruise, you don't have the luxury of alternate landing fields in close proximity, so landing on what seems to be little more than a bobbing cork when you arrived overhead for the first time has to be practiced to proficiency before we head out on deployment. The only other option for getting aboard can be expensive and wet, and sometimes fatal.

BELOW The pilot and RIO keep a close eye on the plane director, who is signalling brakes off as the Tomcat gently rolls forward to achieve connection with the catapult shuttle on board *Theodore Roosevelt* in January 2006. *(US Navy)*

ABOVE A deck checker from VF-31 grabs hold of the stowed tailhook attached to an F-14D as part of his under-fuselage checks prior to the jet being declared ready for launch from CVN-71 in WestLant in March 2005. He has to ensure that the locking pin securing the tailhook has been removed and that the tailhook remains secure in the stowed position even without the pin in place. *(US Navy)*

RIGHT Each squadron has a dedicated three-man team of troubleshooters, or deck checkers, assigned to the various catapults that are in use during a launch cycle. It is their job to carefully and skillfully walk around the aircraft looking for leaks or any other abnormalities, two inspecting each side of the jet and the third walking down the centreline of the aircraft to check its underside. *(US Navy)*

RIGHT A weight board is held up as 'Dog 111' (BuNo 162701) of VF-143 comes under tension on bow catapult one of CVN-73 in January 2004. The board shows the pilot the estimated weight of his aircraft, and he has to visually confirm this with the catapult crew before the jet is cleared for launching. Each catapult shot is adjusted for the aircraft based on its total weight. *(US Navy)*

RIGHT The 'Shooter' for *Enterprise*'s waist catapult three sends VF-103's 'Victory 112' (F-14B BuNo 161422) on its way in May 2003 during CVW-17's brief embark on the carrier during its sea trials in the WestLant following CVN-65's 16-month-long $250-million dry-dock overhaul in the Norfolk Naval Shipyard. A second 'Shooter' is crouching alongside the catapult centredeck operator, whose job is to ensure communication with the catapult deck edge operator. *(US Navy)*

CENTRE Aviation Boatswain's Mate Third Class Neri Umila, a deck edge operator on *Kitty Hawk's* bow catapult one, turns his head away from the jet blast of a VF-154 F-14A launching in afterburner in late March 2003 during OIF I. The 'hands' of the launch safety officer on the flight deck, the deck edge operator is in constant radio communication with the catapult stations below the flight deck to ensure the launch proceeds safely. *(US Navy)*

BELOW F-14B 'Gypsy 104' (BuNo 161428) powers away from CVN-75's waist catapult four on 20 July 2005, thus marking an end to VF-32's eight-day CQ and sustainment training period during JTFEX 05-2 in the WestLant. Already flying at around 160kts by the time this photograph was taken just 2½ seconds after the 'cat shot' had commenced, the jet was bound for Oceana. *(US Navy)*

Chapter Seven

Tomcats and Topgun

Forever inextricably linked, thanks to the box office hit *Top Gun*, released in the summer of 1986, the Tomcat and the Navy Fighter Weapons School – Topgun's official title – came to symbolise the very best of US naval fighter aviation throughout the jet's three decades of fleet service. Dave 'Bio' Baranek was a graduate of the Topgun course when serving as a RIO with VF-24 in the early 1980s – he later returned as an instructor.

OPPOSITE Tomcat units were heavily involved in ACM training from the start of the jet's fleet service in the early 1970s. Initially, much of the dissimilar aerial threat was provided by the T-38A Talon, two examples of which from Oceana-based VF-43 'Challengers' are seen here in formation with F-14As from co-located VF-142 in January 1977. These aircraft were photographed heading for the R-2301W range near MCAS Yuma. *(US Navy)*

LEFT VFC-12 of the Atlantic Fleet unit flew A-4s for 21 years from its establishment in September 1973 through to 1994 (when they were replaced by F/A-18s). The 'Fighting Omars' flew F-model Skyhawks from the early 1980s, with this aircraft being photographed at the merge with an F-14 from VF-101 in 1989. 'Mongoose' BuNo 154996 features the glossy overall 'engine grey' scheme that was favoured by VFC-12. *(US Navy)*

BELOW VF-143's 'Dog 112' (BuNo 159612) sticks to the tail of a T-38A from VF-43 during an ACM hop over Yuma's R-2301W range in 1980, the Tomcat pilot having selected two-thirds wing sweep so as not to overtake the much lighter Talon when diving after his opponent. 'You could fly the snot out of the F-14, if you bent some rules', recalled pilot Hank 'Butch' Thompson. *(US Navy)*

The Navy Fighter Weapons School started in 1969, a result of the Ault Report that examined the worse-than-expected air combat performance of US Navy fighter aircraft in the skies over Vietnam. The investigation [conducted by veteran Naval Aviator Capt Frank Ault and formally known as the Air-to-Air Missile System Capability Review] uncovered a range of problems from technical to training, and the school was one of the outcomes. It was quickly christened 'Topgun'.

Topgun's philosophy was to train the trainers, providing exceptional knowledge and experience to Navy and Marine Corps fighter aircrews in five intense weeks of classes and flights. Graduates were expected to return to their squadrons and pass along their training. Each squadron received one or two slots in a Topgun class roughly every 18 months, ensuring a steady flow of graduates into the fleet.

I was an F-14 RIO, and after about 20 months in Pensacola and the F-14 RAG I joined the 'Fighting Renegades' of VF-24 as an ensign in 1981. By this time Topgun was known to provide some of the best flying an aircrew would experience in their career, and I think everyone wanted to attend. Once in the fleet I flew a lot and completed a seven-and-a-half-month deployment, so when VF-24's next Topgun allotment started I'd accumulated 650 flying hours in the F-14. This was just below the minimum recommended, but I was selected and approved to attend.

In September 1982 I reported to Topgun spaces in Hangar 1 at NAS Miramar. My excitement grew as I walked up the stairwell, adorned with dozens of silhouettes of enemy aircraft shot down by Navy and Marine Corps pilots and RIOs over Vietnam – the most recent war at the time. The upstairs hallway

was adorned with imaginative photos and clever plaques donated by previous students who went through the class in F-4s, F-8s and F-14s. One plaque displayed an actual F-4 panel deformed by the air loads of a high-speed flight during the class. Worn blue carpet, simple furniture and wall-mounted air conditioners characterised the classrooms, which could best be described as adequate.

My class consisted of four Navy F-14s and four F-4s from Marine Corps Reserve squadrons. The 16 pilots and RIOs were joined by other aviators and intelligence officers who listened to the lectures but didn't participate in the flying syllabus. The first day was all academics, and I was immediately amazed at the Topgun instructors' wealth of knowledge and the polished delivery of their lectures. It started when the commanding officer, Cdr Ernie 'Ratchet' Christensen, welcomed us and gave a concise overview of the history of aerial combat, emphasising lessons that applied to the present day. In addition to having thousands of flight hours in fighters and light attack aircraft, many of them clocked up during 360 combat missions over Vietnam, 'Ratchet' had been a Blue Angel. It was obvious that he relished his job as Topgun CO, and the professionalism of his introduction set a high standard. In fact, all of the instructors did their part to uphold Topgun's reputation through roughly two-dozen classes over the next five weeks. Impressive, but we were there to fly.

The flying begins

During the class I would fly with Lt Sandy 'Jaws' Winnefeld, who had been posted to VF-24 at around the same time as me. Typical for a new pilot, 'Jaws' had flown mostly with experienced RIOs since joining the unit, while I had flown with experienced pilots. We both looked forward to flying with another junior Naval Aviator. 'Jaws' brought great pilot skills and equal amounts of intelligence and aggressiveness to Topgun. I had decent radar skills. We both wanted to do well, and were confident in our abilities.

Our first flight came on the second day, when we faced Marine Corps Capt Dan 'Spartan' Driscoll, a former F-4 pilot, in the F-5E Tiger II. The sortie began with a scripted performance demonstration above the Pacific about 60 miles south-west of San Diego. 'Spartan's' detailed briefing, expert management of the flight and exceptional piloting skills would set our expectations for the course. In just a few minutes he taught us a handful of new things about our jet. Then it was time for an unrestricted 1-v-1 engagement.

Spartan said, '"Jaws", let's steady up on a heading of 270 degrees at 18,000ft and 350 knots. Let me know when you're ready.' We flew a steady heading while 'Spartan' moved out to 1½ miles separation and matched our speed and altitude. In a few seconds we called, '"Jaws" ready on the left.'

'"Spartan's" ready, fight's on', came his reply.

The consistent pacing of his communication allowed 'Jaws' to anticipate the final words, so our jet started moving the instant the fight started. 'Jaws' aggressively and precisely whipped our big jet through the sky. He rolled sharply to the right, then pulled hard to the 6.5g limit. Although my g-suit inflated, my peripheral vision became grey as I strained to keep the small F-5 in sight. After about 90 degrees of turn, 'Jaws' eased the g, snap-rolled left and pulled again. He tried to get a short-range Sidewinder missile shot on the first pass but it didn't happen, and we began a series of hard manoeuvres until we could get into position for another shot.

With hundreds of hours dogfighting against F-14s, 'Spartan' knew where he would lose the least and where he might intimidate us into making a mistake. Even though, on paper, the F-5 was inferior to the Tomcat, in almost every category a smart pilot using the right tactics could stay alive, and even take valid (simulated) missile or gun shots at the F-14. If the Tomcat crew made a mistake, the result could be a win for the F-5.

'Jaws' and 'Spartan' both mentally analysed dozens of bits of information that changed each fraction of a second in this dynamic environment. Each second they made dozens of decisions and adjustments – a small tweak of the trim button on top of the stick, a large deflection of the stick, rudders, or throttles, or a change of flap position, weapon selector, or some other control. As in all tight 1-v-1 engagements, g-forces varied every few seconds, airspeed swept from less than 200 knots to more than 400 knots and altitude ranged thousands of feet as we shifted from horizontal turns to climbing or diving, depending on the situation.

The known 1-v-1 environment was not realistic for combat, but of course was a valuable step toward expertise. While 'Jaws' was flying, I checked the F-5's position to back him up, and anticipate when to activate one of the radar 'dogfight modes'. I twisted in my seat to practice looking behind and around us for threatening aircraft, and I checked things that could kill us or cost us the airplane, such as our altitude, fuel and airspeed. I also checked our position to make sure we had not spilled out of our assigned area. I ran through this cycle every few seconds, frequently telling 'Jaws' that I still had sight of the bandit, or reporting airspeed or fuel state – looking for a way to contribute.

After a few more turns 'Spartan' was above us, but he was running out of airspeed. This meant he would have to descend, leaving him with limited ability to manoeuvre. 'Jaws' had maintained our airspeed and could use it to get into position for a Sidewinder shot, so we had the advantage. Then 'Spartan' used one of the tricks in the F-5's repertoire. Shoving the

stick hard over and stomping a rudder pedal, he pivoted the aircraft and came nose-on faster than expected. He called a shot, '"Atoll", F-14 at 12,000ft', using the unclassified code-name for a threat IR missile. 'Jaws' had to discard his game plan to make a sharp defensive move known as a break turn, simultaneously calling 'Flares!' over the radio to simulate dispensing countermeasures. If properly executed, a combination of manoeuvres and countermeasures could defeat many missiles.

'Good break, continue,' 'Spartan' replied, having evaluated our response as effective. Although we had survived to continue the fight, we had lost some airspeed and would now have to work hard to regain an advantage and get into launch position. The fight continued through more hard turns before reaching a point of relative stagnation, from where it would take a lot of time and fuel for either aircraft to develop an advantage. At this point 'Spartan' called 'Knock it off'. We completed one more engagement, then joined up and flew back to Miramar for the debrief, where 'Spartan' showed yet another example of the precision and authority that were 'ops normal' for Topgun instructors. His emphasis was not on who won or lost, but on the learning points.

'Jaws' and I flew five more dedicated 1-v-1 hops, giving us more than a dozen all-out engagements. Most of the remaining 1-v-1s took place above a desert range east of Yuma, Arizona, where we could use the Tactical Aircrew Combat Training System (TACTS) instrumentation to enhance the debriefs. We then moved on to more complex scenarios.

2-v-unknown

The Topgun syllabus progressed rapidly after 1-v-1. We flew one 1-v-2 flight, one 2-v-1 and a 2-v-2, before settling into a series of 2-v-unknown flights – we all called them 'two-vee-unk'. By the way, the friendly aircraft are always mentioned first, so 'two-vee-unk' means two fighters versus an unknown number of bandits. 'Two-vee-unk' is a realistic and valuable training scenario because in combat over enemy territory you rarely know for sure how many aircraft you're really facing, and more could arrive at almost any time. For simplicity I'll refer to the adversaries as bandits, although bandit means a known enemy aircraft, and positive identification was becoming more important.

For flights with two fighters, 'Jaws' and I were joined by an F-14A from the 'Fighting Checkmates' of VF-211, which was the other fighter squadron assigned to our air wing [CVW-9]. Its pilot was Lt John 'Boomer' Stufflebeem, with Lt Steve 'Jake' Jacobsmeyer as RIO. We took turns as flight lead and wingman, and once an intercept developed we could switch roles based on factors such as who had a better radar picture. Thanks to shared commitment to do well and some frank tactical discussions, we soon became a well-sorted team.

Multi-aircraft scenarios gave us a real sense of the value of the TACTS system. All participating aircraft carried a pod the size of an AIM-9 Sidewinder, which transmitted the necessary data to support the system, including airspeed, altitude, g-forces and much more. When we flew over the ocean (without TACTS instrumentation) we still experienced demanding engagements and superb Topgun debriefs, but TACTS added detail to the debrief. Besides, flying over land increased the realism of our training, considering the likely scenarios in which we would be engaging enemy fighters. When we used the Yuma TACTS range, we recovered and debriefed at MCAS Yuma, then launched from there for the short hop back to the range.

Typical starting distance for Topgun 'two-vee-unk' runs was around 35 nautical miles, whether over land or water. The fighters usually started at an altitude of between 20,000 to 25,000ft, and accelerated from an airspeed of 350 knots as they left their station. The bandits' initial situation was more variable, starting from one or more stations at the opposite side of the airspace and at almost any altitude from 5,000 to 40,000ft. Bandits also ran a variety of formations and routes, including large-formation direct approaches and multiple formations, flying deceptive tactics. In my class the Topgun aircraft most often simulated the MiG-17, MiG-21 and MiG-23, with a variety of realistic missile loadouts, but sometimes presented other fighters that were flown by unfriendly nations.

To further increase realism, Topgun had the option to present a 'Wild Card' – a bandit that could jump the fighters during their intercept, before the merge. Even when we weren't

actually jumped, the threat of a Wild Card added to RIO workload during the intercept. The multi-aircraft events reinforced what we learned during the first few days of Topgun class. The F-14 was superior in most respects to both the A-4 and F-5, as it was with the MiG-17 and MiG-21. But real-world experience teaches smart pilots to never underestimate an enemy, regardless of his machine, and Topgun instructors proved this regularly. Yes, Topgun pilots had an unusually high level of experience, but surely there were also talented and committed enemy fighter pilots willing to defend their airspace?

One of the F-14's advantages was our powerful and sophisticated AN/AWG-9 radar. It was the best among the world's fighters when it was introduced, and far better than MiG-17 or MiG-21 radars. Over rough terrain the AN/AWG-9 required a skilled RIO to sort out false returns from real bandits and adeptly use the available radar modes.

Our world-beater would have been the AIM-54 Phoenix missile, but during the Cold War the Navy planned to 'save' Phoenix missiles for use against Soviet bombers, should they attack an aircraft carrier, and we always kept this possibility in mind, so we did not plan to shoot Phoenix missiles at enemy fighters. This left us with the radar-guided AIM-7 Sparrow, heat-seeking AIM-9 Sidewinder and our gun. AIM-7s and AIM-9s were vastly improved compared to the versions used ten years before in Vietnam (thanks to the Ault Report), but in

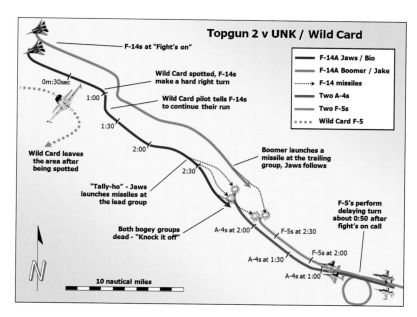

Topgun 2 v UNK / Wild Card

F-14s at "Fight's on"

Wild Card spotted, F-14s make a hard right turn

Wild Card pilot tells F-14s to continue their run

0m:30sec

1:00

1:30

2:00

2:30

Wild Card leaves the area after being spotted

"Tally-ho" - Jaws launches missiles at the lead group

Both bogey groups dead - "Knock it off"

Boomer launches a missile at the trailing group, Jaws follows

F-5's perform delaying turn about 0:50 after fight's on call

A-4s at 2:00

F-5s at 2:30

A-4s at 1:30

F-5s at 2:00

A-4s at 1:00

N

10 nautical miles

F-14A Jaws / Bio
F-14A Boomer / Jake
F-14 missiles
Two A-4s
Two F-5s
Wild Card F-5

ABOVE This diagram details the simple intercept and engagement flight undertaken by Lts Baranek and Winnefeld during their Topgun course in 1982. Things became little more complicated when a 'Wild Card' F-5 tried to intercept to F-14 section as it ran in for a head-on interception against pairs of A-4s and F-5s. *(Dave Baranek)*

some respects they were only a little better than analogous adversary missiles. But this was what I expected to use if it came to real combat during one of my deployments.

The Navy's MiG-ace pilot from Vietnam, Randy 'Duke' Cunningham, often said, 'The more you sweat in peace, the less you bleed in war.' I 'sweated in peace' a lot during the Topgun class.

A 'two-vee-unk' that I recall began on a Wednesday morning, and 'Jaws' and I had the lead, with 'Boomer' and 'Jake' as wingman. We were in loose formation at 22,000ft, flying about 220 knots indicated – 'max conserve' in the F-14A – waiting for another section of fighters to finish so we could take our turn on the range. We had launched a few minutes early, but rather than just kill time waiting, we switched the front-seat radios in both jets to listen to the other section. It helped us get our heads in the game. When they knocked off their last engagement, we switched radios to our assigned frequencies and checked in.

'Topgun 3 and 4 at Telegraph Pass, ready for weapons checks.'

Telegraph Pass was a visual landmark at the north-west corner of the range where the fighters usually started. We completed the checks promptly, and our controller said, 'Bandits on station, ready.' Having done this about two-dozen times in Topgun, our section was ready, so I replied, 'Fighters are ready.' The controller said, 'Recorders on, fight's on.

Bandits 108 degrees at 36 miles, angels 22, headed north-west.'

As we completed our left turn, 'Jake' and I both slewed our radars to the limit of their scan volumes to point toward the threat. I was searching medium-to-high altitude and he was searching medium-to-low. For initial detection I used Track-While-Scan Auto (TWS/A), and almost immediately saw initial radar contacts. '"Jaws", contact that call. Fighters steady one-zero-zero.' The hits on my radar were off a few degrees from the controller's call, but it was close enough for the start of the intercept. My directive call to the pilots – fly a heading of 100 degrees – was more important than the target's exact location at this point. During the intercept, the lead RIO has to drive the fighters. The radar placed a small symbol on the TID [Tactical Information Display], and 'Jaws' had a repeat of the picture, but he wasn't looking at it. At this point he was looking outside the cockpit.

I took 2 seconds to look high over my left shoulder and then threw my head in the opposite direction to look high over my right, scanning for a Wild Card. Nothing up there. 'Jake' was doing the same in his jet. I returned to my radar. My left hand reached up to select pulse search and my right thumb set antenna elevation using the antenna control stick on the centre console. My left hand then adjusted radar gain and video to optimise the radar picture. These actions were essentially subconscious. I leaned forward to squint at the DDD [Detailed Data Display]. On its glowing green screen I saw black blobs representing mountains, and I also discerned several well-defined black dots. '"Jaws", single group, 108 at 32', I estimated over the radio. I reached up and switched back to TWS/A. I told 'Jaws' about my radar mode switches.

'Jake' said, '"Boomer" same.'

We were flying at about 350 knots and accelerating, with the bandits at about the same speed. Every second that passed we came almost 1,200ft closer to each other. This was the slow part of the intercept. I continued to monitor the radar, which occasionally showed additional symbols but I couldn't yet distinguish all targets. I didn't need to give direction for a few seconds. We were headed 100 degrees, with 'Boomer' and 'Jake' on our left side about 1½ miles away.

BELOW Armed with a solitary, live, AIM-7M Sparrow missile, F-14A 'Rage 206' (BuNo 159625) of VF-24 accelerates in Zone Five afterburner for the benefit of Lt(jg) Dave Baranek and his camera at dusk over the central Pacific during the unit's 1981–82 WestPac/Indian Ocean deployment on board *Constellation*. Baranek and 'Jaws' Winnefeld would fly a similarly marked Tomcat during the Class 05-82 Topgun course almost a year later. *(Dave Baranek)*

Every few seconds I looked for a Wild Card. I looked up and left again, then right, and said over the UHF radio, '"Jaws", hard right, tally, right five high!' I'd spotted a bandit about 10,000ft above us, just beginning his attack – a Wild Card. 'Jaws' added power and pulled our jet into a level 4g turn to the right, abandoning the intercept to deal with the immediate threat. 'Boomer' started to go nose-low so both fighters were not in the same piece of sky. Four sets of eyeballs looked high and to the right. After 30 to 40 degrees of turn we heard over the radios, 'Fighters continue'. Yes! We had seen him early enough to meet the training objective, so now we could turn our attention back to the intercept.

Over the radio I immediately said, '"Jaws" left, steady 110.' Estimating we were about 25 miles from the bandits, I wanted to get them on radar and reassess. The AN/AWG-9 lost the target in the turn but displayed an estimated location. In just a few seconds the target reappeared, and now my radar broke out additional targets. '"Jaws", single group, 115 at 22 miles, come left 090. They're at angels 18, let's go down.' 'Jake' answered, '"Boomer", second group in 8-mile trail.' We immediately recognised this tactic from our classes. While we were dealing with the Wild Card, one or two bandits performed a tight delaying turn that put them a few miles behind the lead, which would complicate our decision-making. The AIM-54 would have come in handy about now. As briefed, 'Jake' focused his radar on the second group.

We were now inside 20 miles to the lead group. 'Jaws' descended to 16,000ft and levelled off. I switched again to pulse search and got an accurate look at the bandit formation as we approached each other at 1 mile every 4 seconds. On the radio I said, '"Jaws", lead group is lined-out right, 18 miles, angels 18.' 'Jake' radioed, '"Boomer", trailers at 25 miles.' It sounds like a long distance, but things would happen fast in the next minute. We were completely prepared for this.

I switched back to TWS/A and adjusted the scale of my display. The radar took a few sweeps to process information. Now we were about 13 miles to the lead group. On the ICS [Intercommunications] I said, '"Jaws", look at the TID.' For most of the intercept up to this point

'Jaws' had been looking outside the aircraft, but we briefed that at 15 miles to the merge I would set up a picture on the display that he could see. This was his cue to say, '"Boomer" is at left 8 low', using the common clock code. 'Jaws' looked into the cockpit to get the tactical picture and I looked out to locate our wingman. He said, 'Got it', and I said, 'Visual', so we both accomplished what we intended.

I looked at the radar again and took a radar lock on the lead bandit. In a second or two I saw the two small green lights above the DDD indicating a good lock. Over the radio I said, '"Jaws", locked lead, 10 miles, lined-out right.' 'Jake' said, '"Boomer", trailers at 16 miles, angels 15, line-abreast.' 'Jaws' turned our fighter to the right to put the targets on the nose, then looked through the HUD, where a green diamond showed target location based on our radar lock. He called, 'Speck in the diamond', to let everyone know that he could see something where the bandits were supposed to be, which was good.

ABOVE Although from the outside Hangar One looked just like the other buildings that housed the Pacific Fleet's fighter units at Miramar, 'inside, it was different, starting with the stairwell adorned with dozens of silhouettes of enemy aircraft shot down by Navy and Marine Corps pilots over Vietnam', recalled Dave Baranek. *(US Navy)*

LEFT Dave Baranek's pilot during Class 05-82 was then Lt James 'Jaws' Winnefeld, also from VF-24. Seen here almost 30 years later in 2011 as a four-star admiral, Winnefeld enjoyed a long association with the F-14 – including a tour as an instructor at the NFWS – that finally culminated in 2005–06 when he was Commander, Carrier Strike Group Two/USS *Theodore Roosevelt* Carrier Strike Group during the Tomcat's final operational deployment. *(USAF)*

ABOVE NFWS's instructor cadre – including Dave Baranek, standing, fifth from left – pose for a group photograph in their blue flightsuits in front of one of their F-5E Tiger IIs at Miramar in 1985. That summer most of these instructors were involved in flying A-4s and F-5s for the memorable action scenes that headlined Paramount Pictures' movie *Top Gun*. *(via Dave Baranek)*

I divided my attention between ensuring the radar lock stayed good, checking 'Boomer's' position, checking fuel and actually making notes for the debrief. I didn't write a lot of notes during intercepts, but the Topgun debrief was always in the back of my mind.

BELOW Lt Dave Baranek conducts a flight briefing in Hangar One's Classroom 2 at Miramar. 'A few months after becoming an instructor [in the summer of 1984], I started briefing students for flights in the Topgun class,' 'Bio' recalled. 'It was demanding because you had to cover everything from flying safety to tactics. Every instructor gave at least one tactics lecture to students during the five-week Topgun course.' *(Dave Baranek)*

'Fox One, lead A-4, 20,000ft.' 'Jaws' squeezed the trigger on his stick and a tone indicated that the simulated AIM-7 Sparrow shot registered on the TACTS instrumentation. He had identified the aircraft type to show he was not just taking a wild shot.

For the next 30 seconds things happened fast, and there was a lot of information to process. 'Boomer' made a radio call that he saw both bandits in the lead group. 'Jake' made a radio call about the trail group – he had a radar lock. I updated 'Jaws' on 'Boomer's' position (left 'nine o'clock low', 1 mile). The bandit we shot was called dead by the TACTS controller. 'Jaws' selected a Sidewinder (training round), got a tone and called a shot on the second bandit in the lead group. That one was also a kill. The lead group was gone. 'Jaws' gave 'Boomer' the lead to get us to the trailers, 8 miles away now. I'd been looking out and forward to acquire the bandits, but went back to the radar and took a lock on the second bandit of the trail group.

'Fox One, northern F-5, 15,000ft.' 'Boomer' identified and shot one of the trailing bandits. On his call the entire formation was considered hostile, so 'Jaws' also launched a missile. 'Fox One, southern bandit that group.' The TACTS controller announced both bandits killed, and then, 'Knock it off, knock it off.' I echoed, '"Jaws" knock it off.' 'Jake' said, '"Boomer" knock it off, state 10.8.''Damn, that was cool!' I thought. Over the ICS 'Jaws' said, 'Nice work, "Bio!"'

We flew back to Telegraph Pass and set up for the next run. On the second run we did not have a Wild Card. Instead, that aircraft flew with the other bandits, so we had a 2-v-5. We also did not kill all the bandits before the merge, so we had some great engaged time! We then flew a third engagement – a short set-up of about 20 miles – before landing at Yuma to debrief, turn the jets around and brief for an afternoon go.

'Four-vee-unk'

The challenges steadily increased throughout the class, and we soon became intimately familiar with the principles that Topgun recommended. These were not simple learning exercises or things to trip us up in debriefs. This was exactly how they recommended we operate in combat. The principles were

validated in flight and constantly scrutinised. One of those principles was that if you leave an engagement, you should not go back in. There were examples from combat (and other Topgun classes) of fighters becoming engaged and 'bugging-out', and then re-engaging with bad results, such as being shot down.

On a 'four-vee-unk' hop in Week Five, flying over the Pacific, we were in a large 'furball'. There must have been nine or ten aircraft within about 5 miles – a sphere of airspace in which they could influence each other. Some bandits had already been killed. After 'Jaws' and I took several shots, we decided we should leave, so we coordinated with 'Boomer' and then called, '"Jaws" bugging north.' The answer we received was, '"Boomer" bugging west.' Good.

'Jaws' pushed the stick forward to descend and went to Zone 5 – maximum afterburner in the F-14A. My job was now defensive lookout, so I focused my attention behind us, watching the swirling black dots recede as we rapidly accelerated through Mach 1. I told 'Jaws' it looked like a clean 'bug', and when I looked forward I saw the amazing spectacle of a shockwave sliding backwards on the Plexiglas canopy. It looked like a plate of glass that conformed to the shape of the canopy and moved aft as our speed increased. We easily hit Mach 1.3 (about 940mph) and were still accelerating. When I said it was a clean 'bug' 'Jaws' pulled the throttles back from Zone 5 and the shockwave rapidly slid forward and disappeared as we slowed below Mach 1.

He then said, 'Feel like poking our nose back in?' I replied, 'Sure!'

ABOVE From the mid-1980s the NFWS course went from being a virtually all-Tomcat affair to including a growing number of F/A-18s. Mixed formation training missions such as this one, including two F-14As from VF-24 (BuNo 160889) and VF-211 (BuNo 159631) and a pair of F/A-18As from recently established VFA-136, seen near the Salton Sea, would be generated towards the end of the Topgun syllabus. *(Dave Baranek)*

'Jaws' executed a max-performance left turn while I slewed the radar to its limits and selected pulse search. The small black dots on my scope were A-4s or F-5s, while the larger dots were the two F-14s still engaged. On the ICS I told 'Jaws' I had contacts at 9 miles and said, 'Steady 190.' Squeezing the trigger on my hand controller, I took a lock. The symbology on 'Jaws" HUD changed and the diamond showed the radar target. Although I tried to be selective, he said, 'That's an F-14', so I went back to pulse search, looked for a smaller blip and took another lock. The second lock led 'Jaws' to make a radio call of, 'Belly Fox One, A-4 chasing the F-14 at 13,000ft.' The A-4 immediately performed a roll to acknowledge that he was dead. We had attacked from his belly side, so he had no way to see the shot and no chance to defeat it. Over the ICS 'Jaws' said, 'Let's not press our luck.' We rolled into another max-performance turn, once again away from the 'furball'. Over the radio I said, '"Jaws" bugging north.' We joined up with 'Boomer' and returned to Miramar.

Since we were not on TACTS, the debrief relied on reconstructing the intercepts and engagements from memory, notes and cockpit tape recorders. Our decision to return after bugging out was

The highly prized cloth Topgun patch, which was presented to students who successfully completed the demanding five-week-long NFWS course. It was traditionally worn on the right shoulder of graduates' flightsuits. *(Tony Holmes collection)*

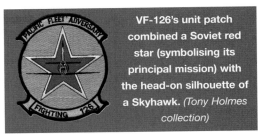

ABOVE During the late 1980s some Pacific Fleet fighter units occasionally experimented with temporary water-based schemes that were applied to F-14s participating in Air Wing Fallon or FFARP/Fighter Derby courses – they were never seen on operationally deployed jets, however. VF-2 was particularly active in this respect, with the latter unit's 'Bullet 200' (BuNo 162594) being crudely camouflaged in two shades of grey while flying ACM missions over Yuma's R-2301W TACTS range. *(Dave Baranek)*

BELOW By the mid-1980s the US Navy was keen to acquire a fighter type to better represent fourth generation threats for its adversary training to complement its A-4s and F-5s that it had operated for a number of years. The US Navy eventually acquired 26 'customised' F-16Ns (22 single-seaters and 4 two-seaters) from 1987, these aircraft being based on the F-16C/D block 30 powered by the F110-GE-100. *(Dave Baranek)*

mentioned by one of the bandits who had been killed early and zoomed high above the fight to watch it all. However, because we didn't press our return, and succeeded in getting another kill, we weren't chastised. The mission had gone well for the fighters. With only a couple of flights remaining, I'm sure the instructors took some pride in seeing the performance of our class after all of their hard work.

Soon our Topgun class was over, and 'Jaws' and I returned to VF-24. We eventually became the pilot and RIO training officers, respectively, according to the plan. We both eventually returned to Topgun as instructors, but that's another story.

Changes to Topgun

Several years after my time at Topgun, the unit traded its F-5s for F-16Ns, which finally provided a radar-equipped aircraft capable of simulating the latest threats. The A-4 continued to provide challenging training for a few more years, however. Topgun instructors then shifted to flying F/A-18s and F-14s – the same aircraft flown by students – in both the Red Air opposing role and as Blue Air, flying alongside students. Today, Topgun flies a mix of F-16s and F/A-18 Hornets and Super Hornets, and is supported by F-5-equipped, Reserve-manned VFC-13.

LEFT VF-126's 'Bort 05' (BuNo 163567) was photographed with 'Bullet 202' (BuNo 162598) over southern California in early 1989 before VF-2 left on its WestPac/Indian Ocean deployment on board *Ranger*. Both aircraft are equipped with AIM-9L acquisition rounds, and the Tomcat's wing glove vanes are also extended. The F-16Ns only managed ten years of service as adversaries before they were permanently grounded due to cracked bulkheads caused by high-g manoeuvring. *(Dave Baranek)*

The course has grown from five weeks in the 1980s to nine weeks today, with the addition of an air-to-ground curriculum and the increased complexity associated with air warfare weapons and tactics.

In the late 1980s Topgun moved to a brand new facility on Miramar, but it was a relatively brief stay, for in 1996 the school moved to NAS Fallon, Nevada, and became part of the Naval Strike and Air Warfare Center (NSAWC), which is now the Naval Aviation Warfighting Development Center. Through it all, Navy Fighter Weapons School instructors have upheld the highest standards of flight skill and discipline, combined with outstanding classroom instruction, to ensure Navy and Marine Corps aircrews are ready when called upon.

Comparing the A-4 and F-5 to the F-14A

In its first two decades Topgun primarily used the A-4 Skyhawk and F-5 Tiger II to simulate enemy fighters. The A-4 was designed as a light attack jet, had no afterburner and could not exceed the speed of sound, but the basic design was very manoeuvrable. Topgun A-4s were lighter than those flown by regular squadrons and had the most powerful engines possible, which improved their dogfighting performance. The A-4 usually simulated the MiG-17, which in the early 1980s was still used by dozens of unfriendly nations.

The F-5 was created from the start as a fighter, but it was a simple design intended for export to American allies, rather than the complex aircraft type normally operated by US forces. Small, light and manoeuvrable, and easily supersonic, the F-5 usually stood in for

The NAS Miramar patch, adorned with the base motto – 'Home of the Pacific Fleet Fighters'. Situated just ten miles north of downtown San Diego, it became a US Navy Master Jet Base in the 1950s and expanded significantly during the Vietnam War period. It officially became MCAS Miramar in October 1997. *(Tony Holmes collection)*

COMPARING THE A-4 AND F-5 WITH THE F-14

	A-4F	F-5E	F-14A
Length	40ft 3in	47ft 5in*	62ft 8in
Wingspan	26ft 6in	26ft 8in	64ft spread, 38ft swept
Internal fuel capacity	5,500lb	4,500lb	16,200lb
Typical take-off weight	18,000lb	16,000lb	62,000lb
Maximum thrust	11,200lb	10,000lb	41,800lb**
Maximum speed	670mph	1,060mph	1,553mph
Service ceiling	42,000ft	52,000ft	56,000ft

* This is the length of an F-5E as used at Topgun, with the 'shark-nose' modification, and differs from information shown in some published sources.

** Based on published figures. Actual thrust was less because F-14A engines were detuned (thrust reduced) to reduce tendency to stall and increase engine life.

BELOW Selected F-14 crews were given the opportunity to fly familiarisation/ACM sorties with MiG-21s (mainly Chinese F-7 copies) operated by the USAF's top secret 4477th Test and Evaluation Squadron based at Tonopah, Nevada, from the early 1980s. Graphically illustrating the disparity in size between the Tomcat and the 'Fishbed', a pair of F-14Bs from VF-103 are led over Pula airport by a Croatian air force MiG-21bisD during Exercise Joint Wings 2002. *(US Navy)*

the MiG-21 and its Chinese-built clone, the F-7. Both types were also used by dozens of air forces in the 1980s, and hundreds of the aircraft – particularly in F-7 form – remain in service today. Topgun used the single-seat F-5E and two-seat F-5F. The squadron had also used similar T-38 Talon trainers for several years until the F-5s became available.

The MiG-17 and MiG-21 were the most common opponents when I went through the Topgun class, but the A-4 and F-5 sometimes simulated other aircraft based on the training scenario, including the MiG-23 and other types flown by unfriendly air forces.

ABOVE The NFWS acquired its first Tomcats in August 1991 when four veteran jets were assigned to the school after completing their fleet service. One of the aircraft was BuNo 159855, which received this Su-27 'Flanker'-inspired scheme within weeks of its arrival at Topgun. This aircraft had shed its TPS greys for a scheme inspired by the camouflage worn on Soviet Air Force Su-27s at the time. *(US Navy)*

BELOW An anonymous F-14 from the NFWS prepares to land at Fallon in April 1994 following a training mission over one of the base's live ranges. It is carrying not only a TACTS pod and a Sidewinder acquisition round but also an empty BRU-42 Improved Triple Ejector Rack on its port under-fuselage weapons pallet. *(Takashi Hashimoto)*

Flying with the 'enemy'

For almost 20 years, NFWS instructors saw the Tomcat exclusively as the 'enemy', as they strove to train fleet pilots and RIOs in the best ways to defeat their potential opponents across the globe. However, from the early 1990s, with the reduction in the size of the F-14 community post-Operation Desert Storm (as detailed in Chapter 3), there was a surplus of Tomcat airframes available that in turn meant a handful of jets – never more than six – were supplied to the NFWS. These initially served as backup aircraft for students (primarily from Atlantic Fleet units) should their now-ageing F-14s suffer mechanical problems during their time with Topgun. The NFWS Tomcats also undertook instructor proficiency check flights, allowing both pilots and RIOs to remain proficient in the workings of the jet during their three-year assignments out of the front line with the NFWS.

Only high-time F-14As were ever supplied to Topgun, which steadily worked its way through more than 20 airframes as the original jets were retired to the 'boneyard' at Davis-Monthan AFB, Arizona, and replaced by other fleet-surplus Tomcats. Aside from being flown as backup aircraft by students and for instructor check flights, the aircraft were also progressively used as teaching aids thanks to their ability to simulate the BVR multi-sensor threat posed by MiG-29s, MiG-31s and Su-27s, as well as potentially hostile Western types. Adversary units had traditionally opted not to use aircraft types already in fleet use, since the value of fighting a dissimilar type was greatly appreciated. However, an F-14 could provide an accurate representation of a potential threat, and that made it useful to the NFWS.

As noted by Dave Baranek, Topgun moved to Fallon in mid-1996 as the US Navy consolidated its tactical air warfare training at the Nevada naval air station. Here, the NFWS became part of NSAWC, the unit flying 12 F/A-18As and six F-14As in from Miramar on 30 May. Although the unit's designation and location had changed, the mission remained the same. Camouflaged in a variety of colour schemes loosely based on those worn by potential real-world adversaries, the Tomcats would remain active with NSAWC until the last examples were retired in October 2003.

RIO Ted 'Chick' Ricciardella was one of the last NFOs to fly in the F-14 in the adversary role with NSAWC, having been posted to Fallon following a tour with VF-11:

I initially went through the Topgun course in the Tomcat during the summer of 2002. There were two F-14 crews and six F/A-18 pilots on the course, as well as adversary and AIC [Air Intercept Controller] students [NFOs, destined for the E-2C]. At that time, the Topgun course was still really focused on air-to-air training – this is still the case today, although now much more air-to-ground training is flowed throughout the syllabus.

We flew F-14A/Bs during the course, which were fitted with the once-mighty AN/ AWG-9. A pulse Doppler radar with analogue electronics, the AN/AWG-9 was cutting-edge technology when it was developed in the 1960s and introduced in the 1970s, but by 2002 it had been surpassed in technology

ABOVE By 2002, all six of NSAWC's F-14As were painted in standard TPS greys. Despite hardly being in the flush of youth, these venerable fighters were used as teaching aids thanks to their ability to simulate the BVR multi-sensor threat posed by MiG-29s, MiG-31s and Su-27s, as well as potentially hostile Western types. *(Ted Carlson)*

BELOW ACM training over, an NSAWC crew lead VF-32 F-14B 'Gypsy 112' (BuNo 161608) back to Fallon. Both jets are carrying TACTS pods (BuNo 162591's is on its port shoulder pylon, out of shot) that will have sent real-time flight data to Fallon for post-mission analysis in the various debriefing classrooms on base. The VF-32 jet is also equipped with a LANTIRN pod. *(Ted Carlson)*

LEFT For less than a year NSAWC operated its 6 F-14s alongside 14 F-16A/Bs and 12 F/A-18A/Bs from Fallon, the Fighting Falcons having spent more than a decade in storage at AMARC after their delivery to Pakistan was embargoed by the US government. F-16B 92-0460, here leading F/A-18A BuNo 162894 and F-14A BuNo 162591 over Lake Tahoe south-west of Fallon, was one of the first examples delivered to the unit in December 2002. *(Ted Carlson)*

BELOW Three of NSAWC's final six Tomcats sit on the Fallon flightline during the spring of 2003. Each jet has tell-tale damp patches underneath it where hydraulic fluid and fuel have leaked between flights – the aircraft was notoriously porous. The two jets closest to the camera (BuNos 162591 and 160913) have been manned up and will soon taxi out on another Topgun sortie. The third Tomcat (BuNo 160669) is under repair. *(Ted Carlson)*

by most air-to-air radars fielded by most US fighters. This in turn meant that it took a good operator to get the most out of the AN/AWG-9, ensuring that the Tomcat remained both lethal and viable in the fight. As a RIO, I took pride in working the scope to its maximum potential, being able to troubleshoot on the fly and bring in every other sensor available to run an intercept successfully.

After successfully completing the nine-week Topgun course, I stayed with NSAWC as an instructor. Fallon is about 80 miles east of Reno. There isn't too much surrounding the air station, and that's what makes the flying so great here. As a Topgun instructor, you would fly on average four times a week when working with students on the course. Although the flight itself could take only 1.5 hours to complete, the event would last all day long. Some Topgun debriefs lasted 5 or 6 hours by the time all the tapes had been reviewed, we had listened to the communications from the event and then played the flight back on the TACTS. No learning point was left unevaluated, and one had to develop a thick skin because the debriefs could be brutal.

I remember one class hop I did as a student that was prematurely curtailed due

LEFT Lts Ted Ricciardella and Charlie Brown walk away from F-14A BuNo 160913 after completing a Topgun class event in the spring of 2003. Both men had graduated from the nine-week Topgun course the previous year and then been posted to NSAWC. Ricciardella flew the F-14 as an NSAWC staff NFO for a year prior to transitioning to the F/A-18F when the Tomcat was retired by Topgun in October 2003. *(Ted Carlson)*

to weather – we only got a chance to do one run before we had to return to base. On the way back, I said to my pilot, Lt Rob 'Shooter' Simone, something to the effect of, 'At least the debrief is going to be quick.' It lasted 5 hours, for one run – and the flight went pretty well! That's why the training is so good, and that same mindset has permeated both into the fleet and the SFTI [Strike Fighter Tactics Instructor] syllabus that all Strike Fighter aircrew go through today. Naval aviation is better for it.

Often, Fallon-based Tomcats would fly in Red Air missions, playing the adversary role, where they would augment the F-5s and F-16s (and, occasionally the NSAWC F/A-18s as well) that were normally used as adversary airplanes. The Tomcat would often be used as the high/fast flyer simulation – think MiG-25 'Foxbat' or MiG-31 'Foxhound'. It was always so much fun to fly in a Red Air hop, launching out of Fallon about halfway through the event and well after 'fight's on'. We'd head north to the B-20 restricted area, where we'd climb to the upper 30s [35,000+ft] in altitude and time it such that you were going Mach 1 when you reached the supersonic corridor – a specific area in the Fallon Range Training Complex – and chase down the fighters as they egressed the target area. We'd reach 1.4 or 1.5 IMN [Indicated Mach Number], and I was always amazed at how fast we closed on the egressing fighters if it all worked out. Often, the Blue Air fighters thought they could outrun us, but if they didn't turn back in a timely fashion, they wouldn't survive the fight.

I flew the Tomcat for a year on staff at NSAWC before transitioning to the F/A-18F Super Hornet. I love the Super Hornet, its APG-73 and APG-79 AESA [Active Electronically Scanned Array] radar, AMRAAM missile, MIDS [Multifunctional Information Distribution System] and the host of other 'Gucci' toys the airplane has compared to the Tomcat. But there's just something about the 'Big Fighter' that makes it special. I liked the effort that both the pilot and RIO had to put into not only making all the 'bells and whistles' work, but just getting the darn thing to fly sometimes. I once looked out the

ABOVE VF-213's 'Blacklion 103' (BuNo 163899) pulls away sharply after carrying out a simulated bombing run over the Bravo 17 Range at Fallon in May 2000, the F-14D's LANTIRN pod being visible it its familiar position on the starboard shoulder pylon. During the final decade of the Tomcat's fleet service, undertaking strike training missions grew in importance for fighter units sent to Nevada on Air Wing Fallon detachments. *(Takashi Hashimoto)*

canopy while starting up a Tomcat on the Fallon flightline to see an airframer pounding on one of the spoilers on the left wing with a hammer to beat it back into shape. We were flying that airplane about 30 minutes later. Try doing that to an F/A-18 or F-35!

BELOW Trailing wingtip vortices and with overwing vapour building above the fully extended flying surfaces, VF-31's 'Bandwagon 101' (BuNo 164603) is put through its paces during CVW-8's final Air Wing Fallon deployment in the spring of 2005. The Tomcat's agility was legendary thanks to its variable-sweep wings and, with the F-14B/D, the engine power to match. *(US Navy)*

Appendix 1

Specifications

	F-14A Tomcat	F-14B/D Tomcat
Crew	Pilot and Radar Intercept Officer	Pilot and Radar Intercept Officer
Length	62ft 8in (19.10m)	62ft 8in (19.10m)
Wingspan	64ft 1.5in (19.55m) wings spread, 38ft 2.4in (11.65m) wings at full sweep, and 33ft 3.5in (10.15m) wings overswept for stowage	64ft 1.5in (19.55m) wings spread, 38ft 2.4in (11.65m) wings at full sweep, and 33ft 3.5in (10.15m) wings overswept for stowage
Wing Area	565sq ft (52.49m^2)	565sq ft (52.49m^2)
Height	16ft 0in (4.88m)	16ft 0in (4.88m)
Weights	39,921lb (18,108kg) empty and 74,349lb (33,724kg) maximum take-off weight	41,780lb (18,950kg) empty and 74,349lb (33,724kg) maximum take-off weight
Service ceiling	56,000ft (17,070m)	53,000ft (16,154m)
Maximum range	1,740 nautical miles (3,220km)	1,600 nautical miles (2,965km)
Maximum speed	1,553mph (2,485km/h)	1,248mph (1,997km/h)
Cruising speed	463–636mph (741–1,019km/h)	477mph (764km/h)
Engines	2 × 20,900lb st (93 kN) Pratt & Whitney TF30-P-414A afterburning turbofans	2 × 23,100lb st (103 kN) General Electric F110-GE-400 afterburning turbofans
Armament	1 × M61A1 Vulcan 20mm cannon with 675 rounds of ammunition, up to 8 × air-to-air missiles (AIM-54A/C Phoenix, AIM-9L/M Sidewinder and AIM-7F/M Sparrow) on four wing glove and four fuselage stores pylons and up to 14,500lb (6,577kg) of conventional bombs	1 × M61A1 Vulcan 20mm cannon with 675 rounds of ammunition, up to 8 × air-to-air missiles (AIM-54A/C Phoenix, AIM-9L/M Sidewinder and AIM-7F/M Sparrow) on four wing glove and four fuselage stores pylons and up to 14,500lb (6,577kg) of conventional bombs

Appendix 2

Persian Cats

Despite the Tomcat evoking interest from a number of potential customers, its expense and complexity meant that it was never going to enjoy the same kind of success that its predecessor, the F-4 Phantom II, had achieved in the export market. In fact the only country to buy the F-14 was also an operator of the McDonnell Douglas fighter.

Iran had long been one of the few allies of the US government in the Middle East. Its military was equipped with modern American hardware, and when Mohammad Reza Pahlavi, the Shah of Iran, expressed an interest in buying the Tomcat to President Richard Nixon during a trip to America in the summer 1972, the deal was as good as done. Nevertheless, this controversial purchase, which also involved the acquisition of AIM-54A Phoenix missiles, was not approved by the US government until November 1973 due to concerns in the State Department that there was discontent among the Iranian populace over the Shah's excessive spending on weaponry.

During the evaluation phase of the F-14, the Imperial Iranian Air Force (IIAF) also tested McDonnell Douglas's rival F-15 Eagle, but found that the Tomcat's AN/AWG-9 and AIM-54 pairing were unmatched when it came to long-range detection and interception of incoming hostile aircraft. The latter, in Iran's case, were Soviet air force MiG-25R 'Foxbat' reconnaissance aircraft that had been overflying the country, safe in the knowledge that they were immune from interception. The high-flying MiG-25Rs had, in turn, been responding to numerous overflights by USAF and IIAF RF-4s. The Iranians quickly realised that the only way to stop these 'Foxbat' missions was through the acquisition of an effective AWACS aircraft (E-3 Sentries were ordered in 1977 as part of a record-breaking $5.7 billion arms package, although the country's Islamic Revolution in 1979 prevented their delivery)

and a long-range interceptor equipped with a powerful radar and long-range air-to-air missiles.

Having received US approval for the purchase of the Tomcat, which was code-named Project Persian King, the Iranians ordered 30 A-models, spare parts, replacement engines and a complete armament package (including 424 AIM-54As) on

BELOW The F-14As destined for Iran received their distinctive 'Asia Minor' camouflage scheme once they had been assembled on the Calverton production line. They also had a two-digit serial, prefixed by an 'H', stencilled on to their twin fins, with H29 (BuNo 160327) in the foreground of this photograph being the 29th F-14 built for the IIAF – it received the serial 3-6029 once in Iran. *(Grumman via David F. Brown)*

ABOVE F-14A BuNo 160299 (initially 3-863, as seen here, and later 3-6001) was the first of 80 Tomcats built for the IIAF, the aircraft making its maiden flight on 5 December 1975. Painted in the IIAF's 'Asia Minor' scheme, this aircraft was photographed during flight-testing from Grumman's Calverton plant during the last week of 1975. (Grumman History Center via Tom Cooper)

save both the Tomcat and Grumman itself, for in August 1974 US Congress halted the supply of funds to the company due to spiralling cost overruns on the jets being built for the US Navy. Desperate to get his F-14s, the Shah instructed the Iranian Melli Bank to lend Grumman the money necessary for it to complete the IIAF order. He also encouraged other investors to underwrite loans to the company, allowing Grumman to weather the financial storm and keep the Tomcat production line open until 1992.

The F-14s supplied to Iran were virtually identical to the aircraft being delivered by Grumman to the US Navy at that time, and their Phoenix missiles were also very similar to those in the fleet. Indeed, with the latter, only their ECCM suites were downgraded so as to make the missiles less effective in combat against US-built aircraft and their ECM systems.

The first IIAF aircraft made its maiden flight on 5 December 1975, and late the following month the first three Tomcats to reach Iran arrived at Tehran (Mehrabad) air base. Most F-14s would be operated by the 8th TFW from the new facility in the desert near Esfahan known as Khatami. The aircraft were flown by IIAF aircrew (all with F-4 experience) who had received training at VF-124 in 1974–75. Additional training support was supplied by US Navy instructors on secondment in Iran, while technical help was provided to IIAF groundcrews by engineers from Grumman and Hughes.

7 January 1974. It was followed six months later by a second order for a further 50 F-14As and 290 Phoenix missiles. The overall bill for Persian King totalled $2 billion, which at the time was the highest-value single foreign military equipment sale in US history. This order would ultimately

BELOW Eleven of the twelve Tomcats that had been delivered to the IIAF by May 1977 – when Iran celebrated the 50th anniversary of the Royal House – sit with their engines idling at Khatami prior to taxiing out and taking off for a formation flypast over Tehran. All of the jets have had their refuelling probe fairings removed. (Grumman via David F. Brown)

Capt Javed was one of the early converts on to the Tomcat, switching from the Phantom II when he was assigned to the 81st Tactical Fighter Squadron. 'As a former F-4 pilot, I found the F-14A light years ahead right from the start of my training. I had no problem in leaving my Phantom II squadron for a new Tomcat unit. I loved the Phantom II, but learned to love the F-14A even more.'

By July 1978, 79 of the 80 Tomcats ordered had reached Iran, with the final jet being retained in the USA by Grumman for further avionics testing. The IIAF had also received 284 of the 714 AIM-54As that it had ordered, but the rest failed to materialise following the overthrow of the Shah in early 1979 as part of Iran's Islamic Revolution. US technical support was also pulled out at around this time, and the Islamic Republic Party that now ruled Iran arrested numerous IIAF aircrew (many of whom were assigned to the Tomcat) that it claimed were 'Shah's pilots'. Many more fled the country, as did a number of F-14 groundcrew. Training of replacements also ground to halt, and the bulk of the Tomcat force remained unserviceable well into 1980.

This situation changed in September of that year when Iraq invaded Iran to signal the start of the first Gulf War. The F-14 would play an increasingly important role in this conflict, as more aircraft were returned to service. Many of the pilots who had been languishing in jails awaiting their execution were also freed and told to fight for their country. Their experience soon came to the fore, and between September 1980 and July 1988, no fewer than 159 Iraqi aircraft were claimed to have been shot down by the F-14. A further 34 claims remain unconfirmed. One of the war's earliest aerial engagements, on 13 September 1980, saw an IRIAF F-14 from the 81st Tactical Fighter Squadron shoot down an Iraqi Air Force (IrAF) MiG-23MS with an AIM-54. This encounter was the first time that two 'swing-wing' aircraft had fought each other in aerial combat. The destruction of the MiG also gave the Phoenix missile its first combat victory.

The IRIAF had used all the weapons available to the Tomcat during the eight-year conflict, with the performance of the AIM-54A being particularly noteworthy. The clandestine supply of parts from the USA and reverse engineering programmes instigated by the Iranians helped

ABOVE Iranian F-14s were rightly feared by the IrAF during the Iran–Iraq War, with Tomcat crews claiming as many as 180 enemy aircraft destroyed of which around 60 were officially confirmed by the IRIAF. As many as 16 F-14s were lost during the eight-year conflict. Aircraft 3-6056 (BuNo 160354), armed with two AIM-54As and two AIM-9Ps, is seen patrolling the northern Iranian border at the height of the war. *(via Tom Cooper)*

keep both the F-14 and its complex radar and weapons systems operable, although by the latter stages of the conflict the Tomcat force was beginning to suffer from reduced availability. It also experienced a handful of losses in 1981 to

BELOW F-14 crews from Tactical Fighter Base (TFB) 8 pose with one of their aircraft at Khatami in 1985–86. Despite severe maltreatment by the revolutionary regime, which branded these men the 'Shah's pilots', they remained determined to defend their country by fighting the IrAF whenever the opportunity arose. *(via Tom Cooper)*

LEFT F-14A 3-6060 (BuNo 160358), closest to the camera, is armed with a red-finned MIM-23 I-HAWK surface-to-air missile (SAM) as part of Project Sky Hawk. In order to turn the SAM into an effective air-to-air weapon, IRIAF engineers simply retuned its seeker head to allow the MIM-23 to interface with the AWG-9's CW-illuminator when searching for an aerial target. *(IRIAF)*

IrAF Mirage F 1EQs equipped with the very latest French air-to-air missiles that had been trained to lock on to radar emissions from the F-14's AN/AWG-9. By war's end, six Tomcats had been lost to enemy action and six in operational accidents. On a more positive note for the IRIAF, at least three F-14 pilots had claimed five or more aerial victories to give them ace status in the Tomcat during the first Gulf War.

The F-14 still remains a key weapon in the IRIAF today, with most surviving airframes having completed a complex overhaul and modification programme with Iranian Aircraft Industries (IACI) at its Mehrabad plant. New weapons (some, like the Vympel R-73E short-range air-to-air missile, of Soviet origin), data links and communication systems have all been added to the aircraft. The venerable Phoenix missile has also benefited from local upgrades that has boosted its capability to match the performance of the US Navy's AIM-54C variant. Thoroughly overhauled, the weapon has been redesignated the Fakkur-90. Furthermore, at least four F-14s have been made compatible with the MIM-23B I-HAWK surface-to-air missile (locally designated the AIM-23C Sejjil) as part of Project Sky Hawk.

More than 40 Tomcats remain in regular service with the IRIAF, with an additional 12+ airframes kept in storage. Formations totalling up to 25 jets having been periodically tracked by US AWACS aircraft operating in Iraq since 2003.

BELOW War-weary F-14A 3-6060 was photographed on display in Tehran in the early 1990s surrounded by other military hardware used in the Iran–Iraq conflict. This aircraft was one of the Tomcats that frustrated seven consecutive IrAF attempts to attack Iranian shipping convoys in the northern Persian Gulf on 9 February 1988. *(Farzin Nadimi)*

LEFT Closing on an IRIAF KC-707 with its refuelling probe and glove vanes (still painted in 'Asia Minor' colours) extended, this aircraft was photographed while on patrol over northern Iran in early 2009. The glove vanes were locked shut on most US Navy Tomcats in the mid-1980s. The fighter is armed with two elderly AIM-9P Sidewinder missiles. *(IRIAF via Tom Cooper)*

RIGHT A four-aircraft formation of overhauled F-14As from TFB 8 hold station off the starboard side of an IRIAF KC-707 during a training mission over Iran in 2012. Furthest from the camera is 3-6079 (BuNo 160377), the last F-14 delivered to the IIAF. During the Iran–Iraq War, crews flying this fighter downed a MiG-21 and a MiG-23 in 1980 and three Mirage F 1EQs on 9 February 1988. *(IRIAF)*

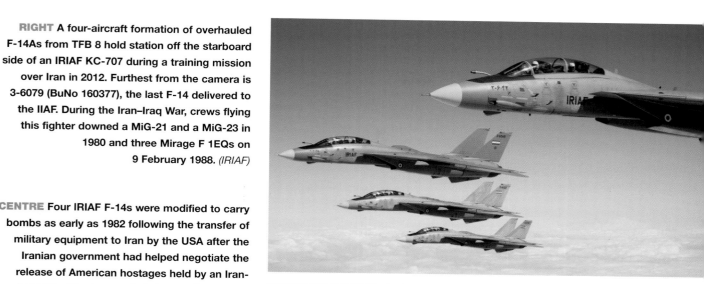

CENTRE Four IRIAF F-14s were modified to carry bombs as early as 1982 following the transfer of military equipment to Iran by the USA after the Iranian government had helped negotiate the release of American hostages held by an Iran-backed militant group in Lebanon. Among the equipment supplied to the IRIAF were Phoenix missiles and bomb racks. *(IRIAF)*

BELOW 3-6049 (BuNo 160347) became the first, and only, Tomcat upgraded to F-14AM ('Modernised') standard in 2012. Photographed landing at Tehran Mehrabad International Airport in April of that year, the aircraft's avionics and weapons were upgraded by Iranian Aircraft Industries during an extensive rebuild. Once reassembled 3-6049 received a three-tone 'Asia Minor II' camouflage pattern that resembled schemes seen on Russian fourth and fifth generation fighters and USAF aggressor types.

(Babak Taghvee)

Index